Meric Casaubon

**Of Credulity and Incredulity, in Things Natural, Civil, and Civine**

Wherein, among other things, the sadducism of these times, in denying spirits, witches, and supernatural operations, by pregnant instances, and evidences, is fully confuted

Meric Casaubon

**Of Credulity and Incredulity, in Things Natural, Civil, and Civine**
*Wherein, among other things, the sadducism of these times, in denying spirits, witches, and supernatural operations, by pregnant instances, and evidences, is fully confuted*

ISBN/EAN: 9783337393106

Printed in Europe, USA, Canada, Australia, Japan

Cover: Foto ©Suzi / pixelio.de

More available books at **www.hansebooks.com**

# OF CREDULITY AND INCREDULITY,

In things *Natural, Civil*, and *Divine*.

WHEREIN,

Among other things, the *Sadducism* of these times, in denying *Spirits, Witches*, and *Supernatural Operations*, by pregnant instances, and evidences, is fully confuted: *EPICURUS* his cause, discussed, and the *jugling* and *false dealing*, lately used, to bring Him, and *Atheism*, into credit, clearly discovered: the use and necessity of *Ancient Learning*, against *the Innovating humour*, all along proved, and asserted.

By *Meric Casaubon*, D.D.

LONDON,
Printed for *T. Garthwait*, in St. *Bartholomews*-Hospital, near *Smithfield*, 1668.

# TO THE
# READER.

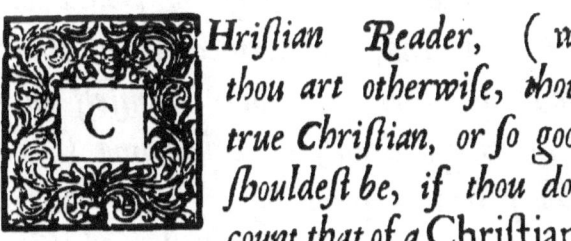

Hriſtian Reader, ( what ever thou art otherwiſe, thou art not a true Chriſtian, or ſo good, as thou ſhouldeſt be, if thou doeſt not account that of a Chriſtian, thy beſt title ) though it doth concern thee, no further, perchance, than I ſhall tell thee by and by; yet it doth me very much, in thankfulneß to God, and to acquit my ſelf of wilful negligence in ſome particulars of this enſuing Treatiſe, to acquaint thee with the occaſion, and in what condition I was, when I wrote it. I will not go back ſo far, as to tell thee, what I have ſuffered, ſince I have been in the world, by ſickneſſes, and ſome other accidents, the

## To the Reader.

*relation whereof though very true, yet I am sure, would be* incredible *unto many. There may be a time for that, if God please. It shall now suffice to tell thee, that about three years ago and somewhat better, being in* London, *I was seized upon with a cold, and shortness of breath, which was so troublesome, that I went to an intimate friend, and learned* Physician, *for help, who made no question, but in few days he would cure me, and to that end, prescribed some things. But before many days were over, himself ended his life; in whose death, good learning ( ancient, I mean ) had a great loss. But the comfort is, which I can witness, he died a* Christian. *After him, the cause still continuing, I had recourse unto another, of the same profession, whom though I knew not before, yet I found him very friendly, and so far as I could judge, very rational in his prescriptions. But notwithstanding such help, the disease increasing, rather than abating; I at last, resolved, with Gods help, for* Canterbury *again, which I did think many times, I should never see more. Where, for eight or nine moneths, I continued much in the same case ; till*

*at*

## To the Reader.

*at laſt, that diſeaſe ended in ſome* nephritical *fits, which I did not expect to out-live. But I did; till* April 1666. *when I was freſhly aſſaulted with new fits; which, more remiſly, or ſharply, continued ſome moneths; till at laſt, divers other evil ſymptomes concurring, I loſt ſleep; and ſo loſt it, that for the ſpace of four moneths, and upwards, I may truly, to the beſt of my knowledge, ſay, I had not one hour of natural ſleep, but ſuch as was, by the advice of my* Phyſicians, *procured by Drugs, the ſtrongeſt that are, to that end: which ſleep, ſo procured, left me always in ſuch a hatred, and deteſtation of life, that nothing but obligation of conſcience could have prevailed with me, or any body elſe, I think, in my caſe, to preſerve life at ſo dear a rate. What I was unto others, I know not: I was unto my ſelf, I am ſure, a wonder; (nay* τέρας, prodigium: *a* monſter; *our old tranſlation) that I did hold out ſo long. And yet, when I did moſt deſpair of life; or rather, comfort my ſelf, that the time of my deliverance was now ſurely come; ſo it pleaſed God, I began to recover ſleep, and not long after, amended to ſuch a degree of chearfulneſs,*

## To the Reader.

*that for many weeks after, I did ever anon
doubt, whether I was not in a dream. But
finding the continuance of my chearfulnefs, though
in much other weaknefs; I think any Chriftian
Reader, if he do not think me worfe than an ordinary Heathen, or Infidel; will eafily believe,
that I had fome thoughts, how I might employ a
life, ( fo much of it, as was yet to come ) fo
ftrangely prolonged, to do Him fome fervice, whom
I looked upon, as the only Author. Firft, I re-
folved ( my moft immediate profeßion ) to preach,
as often as I could. And for the firft time, ( being an* Eafter-day, *a very proper day, after
fuch a reviving ) I thought, as to bodily ftrength,
I came off well enough. But when I attempted
it a fecond time, though till the Evening before, I
thought my felf in very good cafe; yet I found my
felf fuddenly fo difabled, and brought fo low again,
( which continued for three days ) that fince that
time, my opinion hath been, I fhould but tempt
God, to think of any fuch thing any more. After this, my chearfulnefs, and vigour of spirits
ftill continuing, I began to think of* writing; *a
trade which I began very young, and of which, I*

*thank*

# To the Reader.

thank God for it, I have had comfort at home, and abroad, as much, and more than I did ever promise my self. I did pitch upon a subject, which I did think most convenient for me, as having more immediate relation to devotion, and not unseasonable, in these ungodly times. It was not long, before I had all my materials, out of several papers, and Note-books; together and ready. But when I thought to put them into a form, by coherence of matter and stile; I found my self so unable, that I did absolutely conclude, I had no other business in this world, and to no other end God had prolonged my life, than by continued earnest repentance ( a greater work, I doubt, than many imagine ) to fit my self for a better. How I have acquitted my self, I must leave to God. But time passing, moneth after moneth, and I still continuing in as good vigour of mind, I thought, as when at the best; it troubled me not a little, that I should live profitable unto my self only. At last, this subject, once before thought upon, but since forgotten, came into my mind again. I will not be so bold, without better warrant, with God Almighty, to say, that he put it into my head,

*either*

## To the Reader.

either before, when it firſt offered it ſelf; or now, when I remembred it. But this I may truly ſay, ſince I have been a writer, I never proceeded in any ſubject, (for the time that was beſtowed upon it) with more expedition and alacrity. For it hath been my caſe, ever ſince I came out of that languiſhing extremity, which affected my Spirits moſt; that my body hath continued very weak, ever ſince; ſo that it is but ſome part of the day, when at beſt, that I can converſe with books; ſeldom ſo well, that I can walk, or ſtand upon my legs: and when once ſet in my Study to write, or to meditate; it is irkſome to me, to riſe upon any occaſion; and therefore I avoid it, without there be ſome great neceſſity: much more tedious and irkſome, and not without danger, to reach books, which I cannot reach (a great part of my books) without climbing; nor always find, very readily, though ranged and ordered with care; when I ſeek them. This is the cauſe, that my quotations are not always ſo full, or ſo punctual, as otherwiſe, they might have been. But for the truth of them, which I think is the main buſineſs, I durſt undertake. For though I have many

## To the Reader.

ny things out of my private Papers, and Note-books, or Adverſaria, which for the reaſons before alledged, I could not now reviſe in the Authors themſelves, out of which I had them: yet out of the originals I had them I am ſure, and not out of other mens quotations; which I never truſted ſo far, as to enter them without examination. If, for want of the Originals, I have taken any thing upon truſt, I have acquainted the Reader, and ſo diſcharged my ſelf. So far, I can undertake; but that in peruſing the Original Authors, either formerly, or now again, I have miſtaken in none; this I dare not undertake, who confeſs, that in the reading of one paſſage, ſometimes, once, or twice; when I made no queſtion of the ſenſe; yet in a third reading, I have found (ſometimes I ſay; not very often, perchance) that I was in an error. And if I might adviſe, I would not have any man take upon him the name of a Scholar, that will truſt any quotations, if he may go to the Originals; nor truſt any tranſlation, if he can underſtand the Authors in their own tongue: which if more practiſed, good books would be in more requeſt.

That

## To the Reader.

*That I had such a subject in my thoughts, many years ago, may appear by somewhat I did write in the* Preface *to Doctor* Dee's *book; and then, indeed, I was big with it, had time, and opportunity served. But after that I was once fixed upon other things, or cares, occasioned by that miraculous revolution of affairs in this Kingdom, which soon after hapned; I may sincerely protest, that I never thought of it any more, except some chance brought it into my mind; but never as thinking I should ever meddle with it, further than I had done. Not that I ever promised any thing, which I had not then, when promised, some probable hopes, I should; and always since, a willingness to perform; but because I have been always taken up, so far as my health, and other necessary occasions would give me leave, with somewhat, that I thought more seasonable or necessary.*

*And so I thought now of this subject, as I have handled it. For* Credulity, *and* Incredulity, *in general, being my Theme, which left me to a liberty of chusing fit instances, where I would,*

*so*

## To the Reader.

*ſo that upon them* I *might but ground ſuch rules and directions for either, as might be proper to my undertaking;* I *have endeavoured to pitch upon ſuch, as might afford ſomewhat againſt the crying evils of theſe times,* contempt of good learning, *and* Atheiſm.

*And whereas* I *mention ſometimes* three Parts, *as intended; two only being here exhibited: true it is, that* three *were intended, in caſe my health had afforded it. But it did not. And indeed,* I *wonder it hath done ſo much, the little time conſidered, that hath been beſtowed upon it. Yet, is not the work* imperfect, *therefore; which might have been finiſhed in the* Firſt, *but that, as the* Second *hath afforded more* inſtances, *( and of another kind ) than are in the* Firſt Part; *ſo might the* Third *alſo, than in either* Firſt, *or* Second, *if* I *live to do that alſo. It cannot be very ſoon,* I *am ſure, becauſe what ſpare time* I *have from ſickneſs, till this Summer be over, is otherwiſe deſtinated. And though* I *am much weaker already, than* I *was, when* I *began; yet whileſt* I *live,* I *ſhall deſpair of nothing, who have had*

*ſo*

## To the Reader.

*So much experience, what God can do, beyond all expectation; or, ( in mans judgement ) cre-dibility. Farewel.*

CANTERBURY,
1. June, 1668.

*ERRATA,* with some Additions, *at the end of the Book, which they that read the Book, are desired to be mindful of.* To which, let *this be* added.

Page 275. *line* 16. I believe, allow it but a hundred thousand spectators, a very small proportion for *Universus Populus Rom.* which we know hath been *censed* ( Citizens, inhabitants of *Rome* ) at one time, four millions, and above: at another time, six millions, and above: could not therefore, I believe, ( yet with submission to better judgments ) inclose, or cover less, than fourscore, or a hundred Acres of ground: a thing, nevertheless, scarce *credible,* I doubt, to best *Ingineers,* or *Architects,* later ages have afforded. However, though we may be mistaken, in the casting of particulars: yet that *Pliny* could mistake in his report, or the account he doth give us, of a thing so publick, and yet of fresh memory, when he wrote; no rational man can believe. A man would think, this could not, *&c.*

# OF CREDULITY AND INCREDULITY,

In things *Natural,* and *Civil.*

## The *First* Part.

MONG other errors of our Life, to which that *Caligo mentium;* or, *darkness of our understanding;* by some Ancient wise Heathens, who knew not the true cause, so much wondred at; doth expose us; there's scarce any thing, wherein men either more frequently erre, or with more danger, than in *unadvised belief,* or *unbelief.*

## Of Credulity and Incredulity,

IN Civil affairs as rash belief hath been, and daily is, the undoing of many; so obstinate *unbelief*, of as many, if not of more. *Credere, & non Credere* ( *to believe, and not to believe*; ) that Elegant *fabulator*, who lived in *Augustus* his time, and was a Servant of his, ( well deserving to be better known unto good Schools, than he is commonly ) hath made it the argument of one of his *morals*, shewing by pregnant instances the danger of each; as πίστις, and ἀπιστία, ( *belief, and unbelief* ) is the argument of two Orations in *Dio Chrysostomus*; whose very sirname, *Chrysostome*, doth testifie, what account the age he lived in, made of his wit, and language.

BUT again; easie *belief* hath contaminated, and obscured the *History of Nature*, with many ridiculous fables and fictions: but *unbelief*, with no less prejudice to *truth*, ( which according to *Plato*, most *properly*; nay, *only*, he saith; doth belong unto such *things* ) and withal, to mans nature, hath bereav'd it of its more noble function, the contemplation of *things spiritual, and eternal*; not discernable with bodily eyes, but by the light of *faith*, upon *Divine revelation* chiefly: but upon *sound reason* and certain *experience* also. A little *portion* of which knowledge, and contemplation, though but *little*, is even by *Aristotle*, that incomparable *Naturalist*, preferr'd before the most perfect knowledge of nature, that man is capable of: *De part. anim. lib.* 1. *cap.* 5.

FROM ungrounded belief, gross *superstition*, by which true Religion is not a little infected and adulterated, hath proceeded: but, from the contrary, right down *Atheism* ( whether openly professed, or palliated, as the fashion is: ) by which, all sense of piety, all sense of immortality, being taken away, and nothing left to man, but what is common unto bruits, ( since that *reason*, confined to things sensible and perishable, is little better than *sense*; and *sense*, in bruits, is by many deemed, ed, and called *reason*:) man may truly be said, to be metamorphosed into another creature.

LASTLY, if we appeal unto the Judgments of men; on the one side stands the credit and authority of so many ages, which commend that of *Epicharmus* unto us, ( Νᾶφε, καὶ μέμνασ' ἀπιστεῖν· ἄρθρα ταῦτα τῶν φρενῶν· translated by *Cicero*;) *Nervi, atque artus sapientiæ, non temere credere*; that is, *Not easily to trust*, ( or, *to believe* ) *are the very nerves and sinews of wisdom*. On the other, *Non satis credere*, *want of faith*, or *belief*; ( so *Seneca*, a wise man too, though not so ancient:) *is the original of all mise y*: and one of no less credit, and antiquity, ( some few years abated ) than *Epicharmus*, hath told us long ago, that ἀπιστία, *infidelity*, or *want of faith*, ( his very words, recorded by *Plutarch*; cited by *Clemens Alexandrinus*; τοῖς θείοις τὰ πολλὰ ἀπιστία διαφυγγάνει μὴ γινώσκεσθαι ) *is the cause, that God and his works are not better known unto men.*

WHICH contrariety, not of *opinions* only, but of *events* also, upon which those opinions were grounded, and which occasioned that contrariety; makes me think sometimes the better of those ancient Philosophers, who maintained and argued it at large, that nothing could be certain unto men; and that peremptorily to conclude of any thing, as either true, or false, was great rashness, and ignorance; since that of all those things controverted among men, some boldly affirming, and others as peremptorily denying; there was not any thing for which, and against which probable reasons and arguments might not be produced; which might, if not amount to an absolute *æquilibrium* in the ballance, yet induce a rational man, to suspend his assent. To make this good, how far they proceeded, there be Books both Greek and Latine, yet extant, that will shew: which though written by Heathens, and by many, both Heathens, and Christians

Christians opposed; yet have they not wanted some able Champions, even in our age.

BUT since this is not our business here, and that a perfect *Sceptick*, what ever they may pretend in words, is an impossibility in nature, as by more than one, but St. *Augustine* for one, is well observed; we may certainly conclude, that neither to *believe*, or *unbelieve* ( in things *Natural*, or *Civil* ) is absolutely good, or bad, but as either are guided and regulated, more or less, by reason and discretion: which though they cannot secure any man, the wisest that is, ( such is the condition of mortal man upon earth ) that he shall never be deceived; yet may secure him, that his error shall not be without comfort, that he was not deceived as a fool, for want of wit and consideration: which is the comfort, that Divine *Hippocrates* doth propose unto them, that miscarry a thing he thought very possible ) in a right course, that they miscarry, κατὰ λόγον, that is, (*according to*, or, *for no want of reason*, ) and bids us keep to that still, though again and again crossed, by ill success.

NOW because a well grounded *belief* or *unbelief* ( in things *Natural*, or *Civil*, as before ) are, for the most part, the effects of much observation, and long experience, which many for want of years, ( though supplied in many, by natural pregnancy ) have not yet attained unto: that such as have not, may, if they please, reap the benefit of others observation, is one main end and purpose of this present undertaking. And to prevent all mistakes, which our title might occasion, and the Readers may the better be satisfied, what to expect: First, whereas we say, in things *natural*, by *natural*, I do not only understand such things, which apparently have some ground in nature, and whereof a probable reason may be given; which is the more ordinary notion: But also, as by *Trallianus*, an ancient Physician,

(not

*in things* NATURAL.

( not to name others ) by some very eminent in that art, once to me much commended; the word is usually taken, as when he distributeth, which he doth in every disease almost, his remedies and receipts, into *methodical*, and *natural*; by *methodical*, understanding, *rational*: that is such, of which, or for which a reason may be given, κατα μεθοδον ἐπιστημονικην, as he speaks in one place: by *natural*, those which are supposed to work by some natural efficacy, though the reason, or true cause be, as yet, secret and unknown. Of which nature, he doth make all *amulets* to be, which therefore he calleth φυσικα. or *naturalia*. Of this notion of the word *natural*, St. *Austin* takes notice, in his *eleventh* book *De Doctrina Christiana*, Chap. the 20. as ordinary in his days. For having spoken of *Ligatures*, and *Characters*, he doth add, *quæ miticri nomine Physica* ( in some Editions, *Physicam*, falsly) *vocant, non quasi superstitione, sed natura prodesse videantur*. If therefore we say somewhat, of such also, we do not extend the notion of the word beyond its bounds. · For as *Trallianus*, so other Physicians of his time, and of our time also, as by name, *Sennertus*, do also use the word: *Specifica*, and *Naturalia*, for the same thing. But again, if under the same title, we speak of some things acted, or effected by *spirits*, though the authors, or actors themselves, according to the common opinion, ( contradicted by many ancients ) as incorporeal and immaterial essences, do not so properly fall within the cognizance of ordinary *nature*; yet their operations upon corporeal essences being effected, and brought to pass, ( for the most part at least, as both ancient and late, that have written of these things, are of opinion ) by means *natural*, though to us unknown; may very well be termed *natural* in the latitude of the notion before explained: though to us unknown, I say, as who know yet of nature, in comparison of what we do not know,

know, but very little, as they that have taken most pains in the study of it, acknowledge and lament. Had we added the word *supernatural*, in this place, ( *natural and supernatural* ) it might have been too general, and comprehended *miracles* also, for which we have a more proper place, under the title of *things Divine*. And the word, *Diabolical*, or *Demoniacal*, since there was no need of it, I was willing to forbear.

SECONDLY, I desire the Reader to take notice, that whereas some who have written πεϱὶ πίστεως ἢ ἀπιστίας, ( *of belief and unbelief* ) have chiefly, under that title, insisted upon *trust*, or *trusting*, between man and man, in point of friendship, and ordinary conversation, in contracts and promises, and the like: I meddle not at all with it in this sense ; by *things Civil*, understanding only relations, or histories of things done, or pretended to be done by men; to be seen, or known in the world, not ordinary, and to all men, *credible*.

AGAIN, *Credulity*, oppos'd to *Incredulity*, may be understood two ways, either as a vertue ( for so the word is taken sometimes, by Christian writers, especially ; ) or both *Credulity* ( the most warrantable and ordinary sense of the word ) and *Incredulity* may be taken as two vicious extreams, of what we may call πίστις, in general, taken for a *rational belief*, or, *belief* grounded, either upon ordinary grounds of reason, and probability, which begets, *a moral belief*; or upon such pregnant pressing reasons, as produce a firm assent, answerable to certain knowledge, or science, though not science properly, because not grounded upon the knowledge of the causes. In either sense, *credulity* taken, will fit our purpose well enough: yet of the two, I rather chuse the second, that *credulity* may be taken for a vice ; that so, as all, or most vertues, according to *Aristotle's* doctrine, ( though by some, upon very light grounds,

as

as I conceive, much opposed) we may place this *mean*, or *belief* also in the middle of two vicious extremities. And so is this business of *believing* very well stated by *Plutarch*, in more than one place, and upon several occasions.

LASTLY, whereas my title promiseth the consideration of both equally, *Credulity*, and *Incredulity*; and most of my examples will be found of *Incredulity*, or such as tend to the reproof and confutation of it, I may be thought to have dealt partially, as though I favoured, or less blamed *Credulity*, than the contrary vice. But that doth not follow, neither had I any such respect, in the chusing of my examples. Neither indeed is it absolutely determinable, which of the two, *Credulity*, or *Incredulity*, is most dangerous, or blamable; but as the particular object of either is, so may the one be more or less than the other. But I must confess, the business of *incredulity* did more run in my head at this time, because of the times so set upon *Atheism*, which of all kind of *incredulity*, is the most horrible, and damnable, and most unworthy of a rational man. Now one prime foundation of *Atheism*, as by many ancient, and late, is observed, being the not believing the existence of spiritual essences, whether good, or bad; separate, or united; subordinate to God, as to the supream, and original Cause of all; and by consequent, the denying of supernatural operations; I have, I confess, applied my self, by my examples, which in this case do more than any reasoning; and (the authority of the holy Scriptures laid aside) are almost the only convincing proof; to the confutation of such *incredulity*: in this first part, especially. However, unadvised *credulity* and *incredulity* being considered as two extreams, by the doctrine of contraries, it will follow, that what tends to the illustration, or confutation of the one, doth in some sort equally

equally belong unto the other; and though the *examples*, generally, have more reference to the one, than to the other; the *observations*, upon the examples, shall equally concern them both, which is enough to justifie my Title.

NOW because *credulity*, and *incredulity*, doth properly belong unto such things, as are wondred at, either, as besides the ordinary course of nature; and therefore wondred at, because rare and unusual; or against it, and therefore thought impossible, or supernatural; it will not be amiss in the first place, to consider what those things are, considered in their kinds, or generality, which usually cause admiration. As I go along, I may meet with somewhat, that may occasion some consideration: otherwise, I have no intention, but to name them only.

MONSTERS are the most ordinary subject of their admiration, who are not qualified to admire any thing else, though it deserve it, much more. However, they that have, or shall read the History of *Monsters*, written by *Bauhinus*, not to mention others; may think the better of many things, which before perchance, they thought *incredible*. Though he treat of all kind of *Monsters*, yet *Hermaphrodites* only, are in his Title, as the most prodigious, or most considerable. Indeed, many laws have been made about them, and many cases proposed, and answered, both in the *Civil*, and *Canonical* law. I have read also, of trials, processes, and Judgments against, or concerning them, in several Courts, beyond the Seas; and *Pliny* doth record, that in his time, they were *in deliciis*, not for their beauty, and good parts, I suppose, but (such is the perversity of some) for their very monstrosity. And what if after all this, some men will maintain, that there be no such creatures? One great argument will be; they never

saw

## in things NATURAL.

saw any. Another, there have been some counterfeits. Upon these grounds, who seeth not, how much the History of Nature may suffer, through the rashness and ignorance of some, who affect to be thought wise; for denying what other men believe, the *Continuator* of *Thuanus* his History will tell, what passed in *Paris, Anno Dom.* 1613. about this controversie, if any desire to know.

AFTER *Monsters*, those things I reckon, that happen by natural *sympathies*, and *antipathies*; (though these also, denied by some, who must adventure upon somewhat, that they may be thought some body) and again those things that proceed, from what Physicians call ἰδιοσυγκρασίαι, or ἰδιοσυγκρισίαι, (it is written both ways:) to which *sympathies* may be referr'd, but it extends much further: and again those things that proceed from the strength of *imagination*: concerning all which not only examples and instances, in most books of all arguments, are obvious; but also peculiar books, and tractates, made by learned Physicians and Philosophers, searching into the causes, (though *natural* acknowledged, yet hidden, and secret) so far as the wit of man can reach, are extant: all these, I conceive, to them that search into the works of nature with diligence, offer themselves frequently, as worthy objects of admiration.

ANOTHER great object of *admiration*, is that which they call *occulta qualitates*; to which some *sympathies* and *antipathies*; as also ἰδιοσυγκρισίαι. may be referred; but is much more general, than either. Those *occulta qualitates* have been stiled by some men, who had the ambition to be accounted more profound, and quick-sighted into the works of nature, than others, *asylum asinorum*; or, *the refuge*, or *sanctuary of Asses*; but, in their attempts and endeavours of rendring of reasons, to maintain *manifest qualities*, they, generally, have acquitted

quitted themselves so weakly, so childishly, as by the discourses and refutations of Physicians, and Philosophers, both ancient and late, generally most approved and known, doth appear; that what they thought to brand others with, hath unhappily, but deservedly stuck to themselves, their reasonings, if not themselves, being become the scorn and *ludibrium* of all truly wise, and judicious. So hitherto, I am sure, according to the old Philosophy. But what the conceited omnipotency of *Atomes*, according to the new Philosophy, ( or revived Epicurism ) may do, to satisfie all doubts and scruples, I know not. For my part, I shall not be ashamed to acknowledge my weakness : I have looked into it, with as much candor, and diligence, as in such a case I thought necessary; so far from prejudice, that I would perswade my self, I could not but speed, and find what I sought for : but I have not I profess it ; yet with submission, to better judgments.

TO these *occulta qualitates*, we may add, *influxus cœlestes*, or *influentiæ*; to which I find very learned men, Physicians and others, to ascribe strange effects: Yet there be very learned too, that will by no means admit of such : as learned *Pererius* by name, who doth inveigh against them, as the confusion of all sound Philosophy, and in very deed, the true *asylum asinorum*. Yet, if a man consider of it soberly, and read impartially, what is by very sober men pleaded for them; he may find ground enough, ( it is my opinion ) to believe them : especially, when he doth consider, that *Aristotle* himself was forced, besides his four *Principia*, or *Elementa*, to have recourse to a *quintam essentiam*, ( besides that, which he doth appropriate to the Heavens ) as a more noble cause : yea to *God* himself, in some things, as the immediate cause, operating above *nature*, above *reason* ( humane ) by his meer *Omnipotency*. Whereby *Aristotle*
doth

doth apparently lay a foundation for *miracles*, as we may shew in due place: whereas some conceited foolish men, pretended Christians, but real Atheists, as *Pomponatius* and the like; because they would not seem to depart from *Aristotle's* doctrine, refer all *miracles* to natural causes. Besides it is well known that *Hippocrates* also, doth acknowledge τὸ Θεῖον, in diseases; by which though *Gallen*, and some others understand *ambientem aerem*, only; yet even so, then certainly the *aer* preternaturally, or supernaturally affected, by some divine, or celestial cause; which is the more probable, because in other places he doth speak of the *Gods*, (according to the phrase of those days) very reverently, and doth much ascribe to their power, in those things that happen unto men.

BUT to our *Cœlestes influxus*: though they be granted, yet it is very possible, that many things may be ascribed unto them, which may proceed from other causes. That some men are lucky at Cards, beyond all imagination, or do feats with them, beyond the limits of any supposed activity, or jugling; such as learned *Ragusæus* doth profess in the presence of some others, men of great worth and fame, whom he doth name (*Hieron. Fabritius, ab Aquapendente: Hercules Saxonia, &c.*) to have seen, and admired; I should not, though never so much admired, or *incredible*, ascribe to a *Celestial influence*, though I find a very good Author, whom I ever look'd upon as a second *Aristotle*, (the greatest commendation, I think, that can be given to man, Religion laid aside) in point of sound and solid reasoning; even *Thomas Aquinas*, cited for it, by the same learned Author: whose opinion, in that matter, I much sooner embrace, that such things are done, by contract with the Devil. And yet I have ground to believe, that so much may be done in this kind, by art and cunning;
(which

*Of Credulity and Incredulity,*

( which things are commonly referred to the power of *use and custom*, which will be our next confideration, after this of *influxes* ) fo ſtrange and miraculous, in appearance, that a man had need to be very well verſ'd in ſuch ſpeculations, before he charge any man. And that is, when the caſe is ſo notorious, as no man can rationally doubt; as in that pretended Jugler, who ( related by divers ) before *Charles* the Ninth, King of *France*, made the Rings of a gold Chain, *to leap towards him one after another*, who was at a diſtance ; and after that, made the Chain whole again : which, at laſt, himſelf confeſſed to have done by the help of the Devil; for which he was deſervedly caſt out of the Court, and puniſhed. Learned *Voſſius* hath it too, and quotes three Authors for it, but thoſe three, have it but from one, which kind of quoting is not ſo ſafe, except this very thing add ſome weight, becauſe it hath been believed by ſuch, and ſuch, and not contradicted by any. But, in a caſe of this nature, before ſuch company, and yet of freſh memory, when the firſt relation was made; the teſtimony of one credible witneſs, may be thought ſufficient. But for *Pererius*, why he ſhould be ſo bitter againſt *Celeſtial influences*, ſince he alſo doth grant, and ground upon *occult qualities*, which often are fetched from *Celeſtial influences*, and liable to the ſame inconveniencies, and therefore by ſome; as was ſaid before, who would gladly be thought to ſee further than other men, ſo termed, ( *aſylum aſinorum* ) I ſee no reaſon.

BUT granting theſe *influences*, the great queſtion doth remain, whether they work, *as general* only, or as *particular cauſes* alſo. It is the opinion of ſome very learned, that their power, and operation doth extend even to particulars : as for example, to diſpoſe and to incline ( not compel ) a man, to ſuch and ſuch actions : but of more, that they work only, as *general cauſes* : as

for

for example, why in some ages, men generally have been more inclinable to *superstition*, ready to believe, and to swallow more, than the boldest impostor could invent: in others, more to Atheism and *incredulity*, all upon the senses, and what is visible and palpable, though against all sense and reason. In some, more for strifes, and contention; in others, more for peace, and calmer studies. And what shall we say to that *influence*, that produced in men that frantick humor, the beginning whereof is ascribed by Historians, to the year of the Lord 1260. of wandring about, half naked, and whipping themselves unto bloud? Which though suppressed by authority for a while, sprung up again some forty, or fifty years after, with so much advantage, that most Kingdoms in *Europe*, were over-run with it; and notwithstanding the opposition of Popes, by their excommunications, and other means that were used, continued above 100. years after; as doth appear by a peculiar tractate of *Gerson*, the learned Chancellor of *France*, set out *Anno Dom.* 1460. against it. Thousands in one company, of all kind of people, might have been seen in divers places, thus martyrizing their bodies, by tearing their flesh, and their bloud running; a pitiful sight, in outward appearance, but whether to the greater pleasure of their distemper'd minds, or pain of body, I know not. I have spoken of it, elsewhere, which I shall not here repeat. I quote no Authors: there are so many Historiographers, besides others, that take notice of it, I think it needless. If I may speak my mind without offence, this prodigious propensity to *innovation* in all kind, but in matters of learning particularly, which so many upon no ground, that I can see, of appearance of reason are possessed with; I know not what we should more probably ascribe it unto, than to some sad constellation, or influence. But to conclude this matter of of *influences*, whether of *general*, only; or, of *particular* efficacy also; it is agreed on all hands, that they are secrets of *Nature*, or of *Heaven*, if you will; which none will, upon pretence of any art, attempt to dive unto, but upon a presumption, that the world ( as of wicked men in general, some Philosophers have maintained ) cannot subsist without cheaters and impostors.

ANOTHER great cause of wondring, is the power of *use and custom*: which they, who either by the report of others, creditable witnesses; or by their own experience, have not been acquainted with, and well considered of, must needs ascribe to magick, and supernatural causes many things, which are meerly natural. It is a subject of a large extent, but of excellent use, in divers respects: which made some ancient Fathers, ( not to mention other Authors, of all professions ) upon divers occasions so largely to insist upon it, as they do sometimes. St. *Chrysostom* saith plainly, that there is not any thing of greater power, and which produceth stranger effects, among men: the consideration whereof he doth make excellent use of, in matters of life and religion: which is the reason, that he doth insist upon it so often. Among others, one great use is, to discern some actions, which have been admired, and through ignorance, thought miraculous and supernatural; from supernatural and miraculous indeed: the discerning of which, of what moment it hath been, in Civil affairs, sometimes; and sometimes religious; many pregnant examples might be produced. Another great use the ancient Fathers make of this speculation, is to convince the sluggishness of men, in the pursuit of Heaven, who flatter, or rather fool themselves with a conceit of impossibility of performing what is required, and without which no Heaven can be attained; when they see or may see, such visible examples of far greater performances

for

for a lefs reward, God knows, by conftant endeavours, and refolution. It is poffible, the Reader may light upon a book, tituled, *A Treatife of Ufe and Cuftom.* It is not in the Title, but might have been added (as here) *in things Natural, Civil, and Divine.* That which gave occafion to it, (for I muft own it as mine, though fet out, without my name) was: I was at that time much troubled, and as I thought injured, by what, in the law of this Realm, goes under the name of *Cuftom*; to me, before, little known: and as the bufinefs run often in my mind, (riding efpecially, when I had nothing elfe to bufie my thoughts) it brought in time many things into my mind, which I had read, and obferved, concerning *cuftom*, in general; till at laft it came to this, that was printed. I needed not have owned it, fome may think; and better fo, perchance: yet the thanks I have had for it, from fome, to whofe judgment I could not but afcribe much, becaufe I knew them very converfant in the ftudy of Nature, whereof alfo they have given good proof to the publick; hath made me to adventure upon this acknowledgment. However, were it now to be reprinted, (fuch is the largenefs of the fubject) it might be fitted for publick ufe much more, than ever it was. Now thofe things that are atchieved by Art and Study, though they may feem not fo properly *Natural*, in that fenfe we take *natural* here; yet as they are referred to the power of *ufe and cuftom* (a great myftery of Nature, in our fenfe, and the fubject of much *admiration*, as that Treatife will fhew them, who defire further fatisfaction about it) fo, they properly belong to this account.

I MAY not, in this furvey of feveral heads, which ufually caufe *admiration* (I obferve no order, but take them as they offer themfelves) I may not, I fay, omit the wonders of *Chymiftry*; by fome fo much doted upon,
(right

(right Mountebancks, and cheaters in this) that they would refer all *myſteries* and miracles, even of Religion unto it; and to that end, fetch the pedegree of it from God himſelf, in his holy word, (much profaned and abuſed by their ridiculous, ſenſeleſs applications, and interpretations: wherein, I think, one *Robert Flud*, of this Country, worthily for it chaſtiſed by *Gaſſendus*, hath exceeded, even to the height of blaſphemy; all that I have read or heard of) and after him, from *Adam*, from *Solomon*, by ſundry fabulous forged writings: and whom not? *Trithemius*, that learned Abbot, and a great pretender to Myſteries himſelf, whoſe inventions have troubled ſo many heads, to ſo little purpoſe hitherto; his judgment of it is, that *parum in ſe continet, præter verba, fraudes, vanitatem, doloſitatem*, and the like; which he would have the neceſſary attendants on it. What made him ſo angry with it, I know not. For my part, I am bound to ſpeak of the art it ſelf, lawfully uſed, as by moſt learned Phyſicians at this day, with all reſpect and gratitude, as owing my life, under God, to it. For when (it may do ſome others good perchance, to know it) I was a young *Student* in *Chriſt-Courch Colledge*, in *Oxford*, in a grievous ſickneſs (it was thought, the Small Pox had ſtruck in) I had two Phyſicians, whereof, the worthy Profeſſor, Dr. *Cleyton* was one, the other, a young man, of St. *Magdalens-Hall*, or Colledge, as I remember; by the appointment of my then Tutor, Dr. *Meetkerke*, ſince that, Hebrew Profeſſor in *Oxford*; and afterwards one of the Prebends of *Wincheſter*, of ever dear and honoured memory to me. But my diſeaſe ſo prevailed, it ſeems, that after a fortnight, or thereabouts, having been prayed for in the Church once or twice: at laſt both my Phyſicians came to my *Tutor*, and told him they had done what could be done by art: there was no hope left, but in Gods great power,

power, if he thought fitting: otherwise I had not many hours to live. Having thus taken their leaves, and left him very sorrowful; about one hour after ( this is the account I had from him, by word of mouth, and under his hand too ) the younger Physician came to him again, confirms to him what they had said before, when together; but withal, made a motion, if he thought fit, as in a desperate case, to try some means, which possibly might do more than could be expected, by ordinary ways. At the worst, I could die, but two or three hours before my time. The *Doctor* was at a stand; asked whether he might not send to my friends, before, to *London*; of which famous Dr. *Thory* was the chief, whom I was trusted to, and who took care of me. To which being answered, that before the man could come to *London*, the business would certainly be over; he gave way: and presently, Pills, or Potion, some what was given me, which in less than twenty four hours, ( with Gods blessing ) restored me to sense, and speech; and from that time, I remember well, by what degrees I recovered. For I was brought so low before, that though prety chearful, ever since; it was a whole month at least, after, before I could read in a book, or stand well upon my legs; to say no more. Now, that, what I took, was some *Chymical* composition, my *Tutor* told me, but no particulars of it, which I suppose were not told him. For I never was so happy, as to see, or know him, that had been the Author of so much good, under God, unto me; who I think died soon after himself: ne'r... I so much as give an account of his name, till I... *Doctor's* papers, which at present I cannot. I... averse some are from *Chymical* receipts: which... from meer *Empiricks*, must needs be very dang... but from a man, that is well grounded in the o'd... do strange things. This example therefore I tho... would not be amiss.

## Of Credulity and Incredulity.

I HAVE been much pleased with the relation of divers *experiments*, which I have read in *Quercetanus*, when I have found them confirmed by other sober writers, that were not, or are not, meer *Chymists*. For till then, I think a man may do well to suspend his faith. And I know that *Quercetanus* himself, though very learned otherwise, is suspected sometimes by some, who generally give him good respect, to impose upon the *Credulity* of his Readers. How much more *Crollius*, *Paracelsus*, and the like ? I find learned *Sennertus* charged with no less then *Atheism*, by more than one, for giving too much credit unto him : as particularly, concerning that, which they call, *the spiritual rose*: that is, a rose (and if a rose, why not any other plant, or flower ) by art, reduced into ashes, wherein the substance of the rose shall be so preserved, that with a convenient heat applied, *a spiritual rose* shall arise, and appear in the glass, like in all things to what it was before. Yet this is averred for a truth by some, who profess to have made frequent *experiment* before company. So *Gafarell*, as I find him cited by others : but *Gafarell* is a man of very little authority with me; ( especially in so great a thing ) neither with any man, I think, that loves sobriety. I have ground enough for what I say. Had he, himself no intention to deceive; yet the Authors, whom he doth trust, such as *Galeatus*, *Thevet*, *Cardan*, ( of whom more afterwards ) and his doting Rabbins, sufficiently shew, what a man of judgment he was. In the beginning of that Chapter, where he treats of the *rose*, he tells us of another *experiment*, very well worth the knowing, if true, ( *Cardan* is his Author ) that a knife, being rubbed upon some kind of Loadstone, or a pointed instrument; the body may be cut, or run in, without any pain at all. It may be true, but I would have better authority for it, than *Cardans*; that *mendacissimus*,

*mus*, by his own, and his friends acknowledgment: but more likely to be falſe, becauſe not better known, or more inquired after. But the teſtimony of a learned Phyſician of this Country, confirmed by a noble and learned Knight, doth much more move me. Neither are the arguments, brought againſt the poſſibility of ſuch a thing, by thoſe afore mentioned cenſurers, of any great weight with me. Why ſhould it overthrow all Faith, and all Religion, or be prejudicial to the power of God; as though God, who is the Author of Nature, were not the Author of all wonders, brought to paſs by *natural* means? Indeed, in point of Philoſophy, it muſt needs be very ſtrange, and in ſome manner *incredible*; becauſe of that known Axiome, *A privatione ad habitum*, &c. But to conteſt againſt clear evidence, by Philoſophical Axiomes; is as much againſt Philoſophy, and *Ariſtotle* particularly, as any thing. Neither (if true) doth it abate of the wonder of the *reſurrection*, to me; who ſtill look upon the ſame God, by his power the Author of the one, as well as of the other. Neither is my Faith concerning the *reſurrection* of the dead, confirmed unto me by this *experiment*, (if it be true, which I deſire I may be allowed to ſay, till I have ſeen it my ſelf, or ſee more reaſon to believe it) which I thank God, doth reſt upon better grounds, than *Chymical experiments*; but *illuſtrated*, I will acknowledge, and ſay, not a little. For as here, out of *aſhes*, ſo there, out of the *duſt*: as here, the ſame roſe in ſubſtance, yet a *ſpiritual* roſe; ſo there, the ſame body in ſubſtance; but a *ſpiritual* body: this, by fire; the other, I will not ſay by fire, yet not without fire; *when the Elements ſhall melt with fervent heat*; and *a new Earth*, and *new Heavens* are promiſed. So much for the poſſibility of this noble experiment I can plead: to which I add, that the ſame that deride it, as impoſſible, in point of reaſon;

and, as impious to believe; yet grant the birth, and growing of a Plant in diſtilled water, as poſſible and true, which to ſome others, may ſeem as *incredible*. But on the other ſide, when I conſider, that what theſe write of *plants and flowers*; others, write of *mettals and minerals*, that they may be ſo *reſolved* by art, *ut in vitro inſtar fruticis & arbuſcula, effloreſcant & ſurrigantur*: it makes me to ſuſpect the other the more. For if ſuch things could be done, me-thinks they ſhould be ſeen oftner than they are; or rather, reported to be. It were a ſight for Kings and Princes; not to be done in corners, and by men, who, I am ſure, have been found tripping in leſs matters. I make as much doubt of that which they call, *aurum alatum*, though by ſome averred with much confidence. For if true, the invention and uſe of Gunpowder, would be little regarded, in compariſon.

THEY that write of the wonders of nature, or natural magick, as they call it; bring into this account alſo ſome things that have been done by exquiſite art, apt to cauſe *admiration*, in the beholders, and *incredible*, or almoſt *incredible* to them, that have it by relation only. Though *art*, and *nature* be commonly oppoſed; yet well may ſuch things be reckoned among the wonders of *nature* alſo, in more than one reſpect; whereof one may be, becauſe the Authors of ſuch wonders muſt be looked upon as helped, or fitted by nature, more than art, if by art at all. Such a one is mentioned, a rustick by his profeſſion and education, by *Wormius*, in his *Muſæum*: whoſe pieces were admired by all, and by ſome, he ſaith, thought to exceed bare art. Such were the works of *Archimedes*, that admirable man, whoſe miraculous atchievements, though brought to paſs by Art, (whereof himſelf hath left ſufficient evidences, to posterity) yet so far surpassing the reach and abilities (for ought we can find) of all that have been since him, in so many ages since, that we must needs think there was in him, and his works, much more of *nature*, than *art*. What praise a late Architect (*Dominicus Fontana*) got, for removing one of the *Roman*, or *Ægyptian* rather *Obelisks*, from one side of the *Vatican* Church, where it had stood a long time in *Circo Neronis*, to the other; all books that treat of these things are full of it: as particularly, how long the Pope (*Sixtus* the V.) was, before he could get any body that would undertake it; and how much the work was admired, (and still is) when it was done; what instruments were used; what cost was bestowed, and the like. It was, or is, an entire stone, of 956148 pounds weight: 170 foot high, as some write; but it may be a mistake of the Print: for others, whom I rather believe, say but 107; besides the basis, 37 foot high. The manner, how it was done, is acurately set down by *Henr. Monantholius*, in his Commentaries upon *Aristotles Mechanicks*. But what is this to what was performed by *Archimedes*, in his time? Which things, though of themselves, very *incredible*; yet attested at such a time, and by such witnesses, as they are, one may as well doubt, whether ever there was such a place as *Syracuse*, or such a man as *Marcellus*: not to speak of his own works, yet extant, which they that are able to understand, or part of them, look upon with as much admiration, as ever those works of his were, by them that saw them. I cannot but laugh at the conceit of some men, who think, that the use of Gunpowder was known to *Archimedes*, and that, by the help of it, he did what he did, at the siege of *Syracuse*: such a conceit also hath Sir *Walter Rawleigh*, as I remember, of *Alexanders* time; but upon what grounds, I shall not now enquire. But certainly, *Archimedes* his inventions are much undervalued by them, who think such things could be done by Gunpowder. Gunpowder indeed in a Ship may blow it up, suddenly: out of a Ship, may sink it, in time, if it be not too far. But to hoife a Ship, from the walls of the town, which were compassed by the Sea, at one end; and then to plunge it to the bottom: nay, to make it dance in the air, and twirle it about, to the horror, and amazement of all spectators; and other things, more particularly described by *Plutarch*, and by *Pelibius*; is more, I think, than can be ascribed to the power of Gunpowder. However, the wonder of Gunpowder, is, the first invention, which was casual, except the Devil (which I do not believe, because less hurt is now done in fights, than was, when no Gunpowder was) had a hand in it: what is now done by it, no man doth wonder at: but what *Archimedes* did, was begun, and carried on by Art, and an incomparable brain, or wit, the gift of God, or *nature* only.

AMONG other works of *Archimedes*, one was a glass Sphere; so *Claudian* of it, but, which is more likely, *Lactantius* saith of *brass*: by both it is elegantly described; by the one, in Verse; by the other in Prose. This Sphere represented the *motions* (we may be allowed to speak so I hope, notwithstanding the new, or rather, in this, old revived Philosophy: for all men, I see, are not yet perswaded, nor like to be, to embrace *Copernicus*'s opinion) of the Spheres, and Planets exactly; of the Sun and Moon, especially, from which the division of days, and months, and years doth wholly depend. Here was matter of *admiration*, especially if he were the first, that ever attempted it. Of the truth, or possibility of this, no man doth doubt. But if it be true, which

which is written of another *Sphere*, found in the precious Cabinet of *Cosroes*, King of *Persia*, when he was overcome ( after he had committed many horrible cruelties against the Christians ) by *Heraclius*, the *Roman* Emperor, which not only represented the *Spheres*, and their *motions*, but also rained, lightned, and thundred: as I must acknowledge, that it surpassed that of *Archimedes*; so I shall take the liberty to doubt, whether any such can be made, by meer Art. Yet *Scickardus*, in his *series* of the Kings of *Persia*, doth speak of one of a latter date, made by one *Stafflerus Tubingensis*, not less admirable, which also exhibited a Rain-bow; if many old men ( for, by a mischance of fire, it was burned before his time, it seems ) by him carefully examined about it ( he saith ) may be credited.

I KNOW not by what chance, a Discourse hath faln into my hands, containing an excellent description of some such *Machina*, called *Horologium Astronomicum*, which, as I guess by the last words, was to be seen in *Germany*, in the year of the Lord 1590. The words are; *David Wolkenstein, Vratislaviensis, Silesius; Mathematum professor, & Chori Musici præfectus in Argentoratensium. Academia; Honestissimo & integerrimo viro, Domino Georgio Zolchero, amicitiæ & observantiæ ergo, describebat Anno Dom.* 1590. I will set down ( some perchance will desire it ) the beginning also.

DESCRIPTIO *Astronomici Horologii, &c. Horologium hoc ἀυτόματον est, id est, per se mobile, ponderibus agitatum. Nomen ei indimus ab usu: nempe quia horas, præcipuas temporis partes, annum, mensem, nychthemeron, diem, noctem, horam, minutum etiam, mobilibus statuis, ele. antiquissimis picturis, jucundissima sonorum harmonia, & cantu, discriminat & judicat. Partes ejus sex sunt. Prima continet globum cœlestem, secunda Astrolabium: Calendarium, & orbem horariorum minutorum.* Tertia habet

*habet tres orbes periodicorum motuum; menstrui, horarii, & hebdomadarii. In quarta, Regina considet, &, circum eam, aliquot proceres versantur cum præcone. Extra Regium Palatium, sunt Mars, & Mls, & post hos duos, Angeli. In quinta, sunt duo Angeli, Excubitor, & Gallus. Hæ quinque partes, in aperto sunt loco. Sexta pars, in abscondito est, cymbala continens.*

THUS far the first page, with three lines of the second, written in an excellent hand, distinguished with variety of Incks, (besides the Title-Page, which hath more variety) black, and red: upon pure Vellum; but that it hath received some hurt by Sea-water, as I guess. The whole description doth consist of twenty four Pages. Here indeed, in this whole description, I find nothing of thunder, or lightning: no rain, no rain-bow, as in the former: but so many other things ( *Eclipses* of Sun, and Moon, among the rest ) that if I be not mistaken in the sense of the words, may deserve almost as much *admiration*. I did once conceive, that it was a publick Clock at *Argentoratum*, ( in *Germany* ) famous for some noble pieces of Architecture; but no mention of any such thing hath occurred hitherto to me, that I can call to mind. I have read a description out of *Politians* Epistles, that hath much affinity with this, but that it is not so large, neither doth it mention any Statues, or *Images*, or Musical instruments. *I* doubt not, but some may know more of it, than *I* do, which this, may provoke them to impart.

AND now *I* am upon it, it must be acknowledged in general, that no Science, or Contemplation doth afford more wonders, and more abstract from all materiality, ( *Theology* always excepted ) than the *Mathematicks*, or *Mathematical conclusions*.

*sions*. As for example, (though it be a common example, yet never sufficiently admired) that two lines, bending the one towards the other, may be drawn (still bending, as before) *in infinitum*; that is, to eternity, and yet never meet: This, when a young Scholer in the University of *Oxford*, I was shewed, and sufficiently, by ocular demonstration, as it were, convicted, that it must be so: yet still so strange and *incredible* did it appear unto me, that I could never be satisfied, but that there is some kind of fallacy in that business. I have heard it thus also proposed, which did increase my suspicion the more. A. B. stand at a distance. B. stirreth not: A. maketh towards him. The first day, he goes half the way. The second, another half, of the space that remained, after the first days work, or march. The third, another half of what remained. So the fourth, the fifth day; still one half of the way, or space, that remaineth, and no more. I ask, when shall A. be at his journeys end, and overtake B. I answer, upon the same ground, as before, Never. I would not have these things used, as arguments to confirm the truth of Christian faith, or of any Articles of our faith (I see it is done, by some) that seem most *incredible*. For though assent may be extorted, by apparent irrefragable proofs, and propositions; yet hardly true belief wrought, and obtained. *Gassendus* saith, he will suspend his faith: *adhuc ambigo*, is his word: and gives his reason, Because *Mathematical* (to which, nevertheless, of all humane Sciences, it is acknowledged, that truth doth most properly belong) suppositions may be true in one sense, and not in another. *Chrys. Magnenus*, a great stickler for the atoms saith, *Non eadem est ratio linearum Mathematicarum, & Physicarum*. I hope, then, it will not be required, that *Divinity* shall be

tried

tried by the *Mathematicks*, and made subservient to them; which yet the temper of some men of this age, doth seem to threaten, who scarce will allow any thing else, worthy a mans study; and then, what need of Universities?

BUT, not the *Theorems* of the science, but the works of *Mathematicians*, was that we were upon, as a more proper object ( more visible, I am sure ) of *admiration*, and by consequent of *Credulity* and *Incredulity*. Such were those admirable works of *Archimedes* we have before spoken of, and may have more occasion perchance, in our Second Part: and therefore shall proceed no further in this subject. So we go on.

THERE is not, I think, any thing more liable ( after *monsters* ) to popular *admiration*, than those things that grow in different Climats, or Countries. But, as it belongs to fools and children most properly, to gaze, with no little wondring sometimes, at those that wear Cloaths and Apparel different from their own, or that, which they are used unto: ( some there be so simple, that can scarce believe them real men, endowed with the same qualities of nature, if the difference of apparel be very great ) so truly, to wonder much at any natural thing ; as plants, or beasts, or the like, that are said to grow, or live in any other part of the world; or upon relation, scarce to believe that to be truly existent, though we have good authority for it, which our own Country doth not afford; must needs argue great simplicity and ignorance. What can be more different ( of things that are of one kind ) than *Europian*, and *Asiatick* Wheat, otherwise called *Turkish-wheat*? What if all, or most other things did differ as much, the difference of soil and climat considered ; it were no great wonder, in point of Nature. I have both seen the picture and narration of *Lobsters*, drawing men, notwithstanding

withstanding their resistance, with arms in their hands; into the Sea, to eat them. I will not upon a single testimony, though I have no exceptions against the relator, absolutely believe that it is true: though I believe it possible. A flying Mouse, is no wonder in *England*: why should I wonder at *a flying Cat* ( I do not mean an *Owle* ) if I have good authority for it: I have *Scaligers*, but that is not enough to make me believe it, though he name the place, except he said he had seen it, which he doth not. It is enough for me, that I believe it possible; and if it be true, when I know it, I shall make no wonder of it. Since we know that the world is full of variety, ( none of the least of its ornaments, and an argument of the Creators power, and wisdom ) why should we wonder at all, or make any difficulty to believe, what doth only confirm unto us, what we know, that the world is full of variety? But this kind of *admiration*, or *unbelief*, ( besides them I have spoken of before ) doth naturally belong to them, who never were out of their own Country, nor ever had the curiosity to read the travels of others; upon whom *Seneca* passeth this judgment; *Imperitum animal, homo, qui circumscribitur natalis soli fine*, which I may English, *That man is more an animal, than a man, whose knowledge doth not extend beyond the things of his own Country.* But then, I say, we must have good grounds for what we believe. For to believe every thing, that is reported or written, because it is possible, or not at all strange, in case it be true; doth argue as much weakness, as to believe nothing, but what our selves have seen. But there will be a more proper place for this afterwards. These things here spoken of, might be referred also to the power of *use* and *custom* before spoken of, but in another sense.

OF divers things, which are ordinary objects of *admiration*, and by consequent of *Credulity* and *Incredulity*,
hath

hath been spoken hitherto: but the most ordinary, is yet behind; and that *is*, things that are *supernatural*; of which we may consider two kinds. Some things so called, (termed also *natural* by some, as was said before) because no probable natural reason hath hitherto been found, or given, nor are apparently reducible to any of those former heads, before mentioned: though it is possible, that time, and further experience may discover more, and that be found *natural*, in the ordinary sense; which before was judged *supernatural*. And again, some things, which though called *natural* also, by some; yet, not by ordinary men only, who may easily be deceived; but by others also, men of fame, and approved sobriety and sincerity, whose business it hath been all their life long, (whether obliged by their profession, or no) to enquire into the ways, and works of nature, are deemed and esteemed, the actings of *Devils*, and *Spirits* immediately; or of men and women, assisted with their power, as their instruments. But at this very mention of *Devils and Spirits*, I see me-thinks, not a few, and among them, some, not only in their opinion, but in the opinion of many others, and by publick fame, learned and experienced men; some, to recoil with indignation; others, gently to smile, with some kind of compassion. Now if it may be rationally doubted, whether there be any such thing as *Devils*, or *Spirits*, and consequently such men, and women, as *Magicians*, and *Sorcerers*, and *Witches*; then there is as much reason, to doubt of all those particular relations, which presuppose the operation of *Spirits*, whether by themselves, immediately, or by their agents, and instruments, *Witches*, and *Wizards*. And indeed so we find it commonly, that they that believe

no

no *Devils*, nor *Spirits*, do also discredit and reject all relations, either ancient, or late, that cannot with any colour of probability, or knack of wit, be reduced to *natural causes*; and that they that do not believe *Witches* and *Wizards*, seldom believe that there be *Devils*, or *Spirits*. I might go further, according to the observation of many, both ancient and late: but I will stop there. However, if not all Atheists themselves ( which I have more charity, than to believe ) yet it cannot be denied, but the opinion is very apt to promote *Atheism*, and therefore earnestly promoted and countenanced by them, that are *Atheists*. And indeed, that the denying of *Witches*, to them that content themselves in the search of truth with a superficial view, is a very plausible cause; it cannot be denied. For if any thing in the world, ( as we know all things in the world are ) be liable to fraud, and imposture, and innocent mistake, through weakness and simplicity; this subject of Witches and Spirits is. When a man shall read, or hear such a story, as *Erasmus* in his *Colloquium*, intituled *Spectrum* ( the thing was acted in *England*, as I remember ) doth relate: Who doth not find in himself a disposition, for a while, to absolute *Incredulity* in such things? And the world is full of such stories; some, it may be, devised of purpose, either for sport, or of design, to advance the opinion, in favour of *Atheism*: but very many so attested, that he must be an infidel, as can make any question of the truth. How ordinary is it to mistake natural melancholy ( not to speak of other diseases ) for a Devil? And how much, too frequently, is both the disease increased, or made incurable; and the mistake confirmed, by many ignorant Ministers, who take every wild motion, or phansie, for a suggestion of the Devil? Whereas, in such a case, it should be the care of wise friends, to apply themselves to the Physician of the body, and not to entertain the other, ( I speak it of *natural* melancholy ) who probably may do more hurt, than good; but as the learned Naturalist doth allow, and advise? Excellent is the advice and counsel in this kind, of the Author of the book *de morbo Sacro* attributed to *Hippocrates*, which I could wish all men were bound to read, before they take upon them to visit sick folks, that are troubled with melancholy diseases. But on the other side, it cannot be denied, because I see learned-Physicians are of that opinion, and visible effects do evince it; but that the Devil doth *immiscere se*, in several diseases: whereof Sir *Theodore Mayerne*, ( whom I think for strange and even miraculous cures, I may call the *Æsculapius* of his time, and do no body wrong ) gave me a notable instance, concerning a maid in his house, that had been bitten by a mad Dog, which also died of it: to whom when he came in a morning, with a Looking-glass ( to make trial of what he had read, but not yet experienced himself ) under his gown; before he was in the room, she began to cry out, and told him what it was he had about him. But I leave a further account of it to his own learned and voluminous *Observations*, which I hope they that have inherited that vast estate, will not envy to posterity. Yet I know there be Physicians too, that would make us believe, that bare melancholy; will make men, or women prophesie, and speak strange languages, as Latine, Greek, Hebrew; ( of all which there be sundry unquestionable instances ) but such are looked upon, by others of their profession, the far greater, and every way, much more considerable number, as Hereticks in that point. But because the matter is liable to mistakes, and imposture, hence to infer and conclude, there is no such thing,

thing, as either *Witches*, or *Spirits*; there is no truth, but may be denied upon the same ground, since it is certain, there is no *truth*, no nor *vertue*, but is attended with a counterfeit, often mistaken for the true; as by divers Ancients, both Historians, and Philosophers, is observed, and by sundry pregnant instances confirmed; whereof I have given a further account in my Latine notes upon *Antoninus*, the *Roman* Emperor, his incomparable ( I must except those of our late Gracious Soveraign, and Gods glorious Martyr ) moral *Meditations*.

NOW whereas I said but now, they that did not believe there be Witches, or Spirits, did generally discredit, and reject such relations, either ancient or late, as cannot with any colour of probability or knack of wit, be reduced to natural causes: it is true, generally they do. But see the contradictions, and confusions of a false opinion, and affected singularity. For some of them of a more tender mould, being convicted by frequent experience, of the truth of those operations, by others accounted *supernatural*, or *diabolical*; and yet, it seems, not willing to recant their error of the non-existence of *Witches and Spirits*, which perchance had got them ( the thing, certainly, that divers aim at ) the reputation of discerning able men, above the ordinary rate of men; to maintain their reputation, they devised a way, how not to recede from their former opinion, and yet not deny that, which they thought ( it is their own acknowledgment ) could not be denied, but by *mad-men*; that is, *supernatural* ( generally so called ) operations. How so? Why, they tell us, that all men, good or bad, learned and unlearned; by the very constitution of their soul, and the power and efficacy of a natural faith, or confidence, may work all those things, that we call *miracles*, or *supernatural operations*. This was

was the opinion of one *Ferrerius*, a later, and learned Phyfician in *France*, whom I have had occafion, but upon this very fubject, elfewhere to fpeak of. How many more befides him, did efpoufe the fame opinion, (for he was a man of great credit, as by *Thuanus* his relation doth appear) I know not. Now becaufe I never heard, neither is it alledged by any other, that I have read, that this man, or any that were of his opinion, did ever attempt to do miracles, which certainly they would have done, had they had any confidence in their opinion; May not any man probably conclude from thence, that they maintained, what they knew in their own confcience to be falfe : or by Gods juft judgment, for not fubmitting their reafon to his *Revealed Word*, and the ordinary maxims of Religion, were fuffered to entertain fuch opinions, as muft needs argue fome kind of deliration and infatuation ?

BUT if the Reader will have the patience of a fhort digreffion, I will tell him a ftory, concerning this *Augerius*, or, as *Bodin* writes him, *Ogerius*, which may be worth his hearing; not becaufe it is ftrange, which is not my bufinefs, properly, but becaufe it is not impertinent to what we drive at, *truth*. There was, it feems, at *Tholoufe* in *France*, where this man lived and died, a fair houfe, in a convenient place, which was haunted, and for that reafon, to be hired for a very fmall rent. This houfe, *Augerius* (as once *Athenodorus*, the Philofopher, did at *Athens*) not giving perchance any great credit to the report, did adventure upon. But finding it more troublefome, than he did expect, and hearing of a *Portugal* Scholar in the town, who in the nail of a young boy, (it is a kind of *Divination*, we fhall fpeak of, in due place) could fhew hidden things, agreed with him. A young girle was to look. She told, fhe faw a woman curioufly clad, with precious chains, and
gold:

gold: which stood at a certain piller in the Cellar, (the place, it seems, chiefly haunted) having a Torch in her hand. Hereupon the *Portugal's* advice to the Physician, was, he should have the ground digged, just in that place; for that, certainly there was some treasure there. The Physician had so much faith, it seems, as to believe him, and presently takes care for the execution. But when they were even come to the treasure, as they thought, or whatever it was; a sudden whirle-wind puts out the Candles, and going out of the Chimney, (*spiraculum cellæ,* the Latine Translation calls it: which may be understood of a Store-house, in any part of the House, or a Cellar, or Vault: I live in a House built upon a Vault, which once had a Chimney) battered some 14 foot of battlement in the next house, whereof part fell upon the porch of the house; part upon the said Chimney, and part upon a stone-pitcher, or waterpot, that was carried by a woman, and brake it. From that time, all annoyance of Spirits, ceased in that house. When the *Portugal* was told, what had happened, he said, The Devil had carried away the treasure, and that he wondred the Physician had no hurt. *Bodinus,* my Author, saith, The Physician himself told him the story, two days after; who presently after (*Bodinus,* I mean) went to see the ruines, and found it as he was told. And this, saith he, happened in a very clear calm day, as at the best time of the year, though it was the 15 *December,* 1558. By the Dedicatory Epistle, in my Edition, *Bodinus* first set out his book 1579: *Augerius* died, 1588. There arose some difference, it seems, between *Bodinus,* and this *Augerius,* before he died, as *Thuanus* doth tell us. But whether friends, or foes, (though here, *Augerius* is stiled by him, *Medicus Doctissimus*; and a little before, where he speaks of his opinion,

D *vir*

*vir doctus*) no man, I think, can rationally have the least suspition, that *Bodinus*, upon the very place, where the thing happened, which could not be long concealed from publick knowledge, durst, or could relate it in any particular, otherwise, than as it was generally known in all the Town, to have happened, and *Augerius* himself had made relation to him. And this was the man, who not able otherwise to avoid *Spirits* and *supernatural operations*, which as to the matter of fact, he doth acknowledge, and thinks it a kind of madness to deny them; did take upon him to devise and maintain, that all men naturally, *learned and unlearned*, were in a capacity to do miracles by their faith. I wish the Reader would take the pains to peruse that whole Chapter of his, *De Homerica Curatione*, as he doth call it, to see, how that learned man doth labour miserably to come off, with any probability, with his mad project; which yet, he professeth, he did not hastily, or unadvisedly fall upon; but, *cùm toto animo ac studio omni* [ in eam cogitationem ] *incumberem*, as himself speaketh. A good caveat, I think, to others, how they entertain new opinions. Yet, I cannot absolutely say, that he was the first Author of this mad device. The *Enthusiastick Arabs* long before, ( we have given an account of them, elsewhere ) did broach some such thing; which by *Cornelius Agrippa*, is largely explained and maintained in his books, *De occulta Philosophia*: but neither by the *Arabs*, nor by *Cornelius*, is this power given to all men in general, *learned*, and *unlearned*; but to them only, who by constant study and speculation in these mystical arts, ( in very truth, *Diabolical*, and so acknowledged, in effect, by *Cornelius* himself, in his solemn recantation in his books, *De Vanitate Scientiarum*; though not believed by all men, to have been so sincere, as it should have been ) have refined their Souls to such a degree of perfe-

perfection, as much exceeds the bounds of ordinary humanity. But, neither were thefe ever famed for wonders, or miracles done by them, that I remember, whether *Arabs*, or others. Ancient Magicians, as *Porphyrius*, *Iamblicus*, and the reſt; did profeſs to deal by Spirits: So later Magicians, *Agrippa* and others; and *Trithemius*, in his anſwers to the queſtions, propoſed unto him, as the man then in *Europe*, beſt able to reſolve him, by *Maximilian*, the Emperor, concerning the power of *Witches*, &c. doth much inveigh againſt the malice, wickedneſs, and fraudulency of thoſe *Spirits*. And thoſe few ſet aſide, as *Agrippa*, *Trithemius*, and ſome others (of whoſe great acts neverthelefs, I find but little recorded) it is well known, that ſuch as we call *ſupernatural*, not *Divine* operations, have in all ages, ſince thoſe ancienter Magicians, been wrought by men and women, who were altogether illiterate, and for their lives, moſt infamous.

AS for them, who allow and acknowledge *ſupernatural operations* by Devils and Spirits, as *Wierius*; who tells as many ſtrange ſtories of them, and as *incredible*, as are to be found in any book; but ſtick at the buſineſs of *Witches* only, whom they would not have thought the Authors of thoſe miſchiefs, that are uſually laid to their charge, but the Devil only; though this opinion may ſeem to ſome, to have more of *charity*, than *Incredulity*; yet the contrary will eaſily appear to them, that ſhall look into it more carefully; as by that little we ſhall ſay of it afterwards, any indifferent man may be ſatisfied. And though it is much, that he doth grant, and no ſmall part of what we drive at, when he doth acknowledge *ſupernatural operations*, by Devils and Spirits, as we ſaid before: and that he had not the confidence, though his project of acquitting Witches from all crime, might tempt him to oppoſe himſelf to the belief

lief (grounded upon daily experience) of all ages, of all men, some few excepted; neverthelefs, I cannot but look upon the opinion he doth maintain, as grofs, and notorious *incredulity*; and of very pernicious confequence; and therefore, think my felf bound to enquire into it a little further, before I proceed to other matter.

MY firſt argument, or obſervation ſhall be, *concenſus generis humani*. For, that ſome few here and there diſſent, if any ſhould object them againſt the univerſal conſent of men; he may as well object, that the earth is not round, becauſe there be many hills, and valleys in moſt part of the world. Now this reaſon from the generality of mens belief all the world over, muſt be of great weight to engage ours, except there be manifeſt reaſon to the contrary. *Ariſtotle* doth acknowledge it, a man otherwiſe not over-credulous, or addicted to popular opinions; Ὁ πᾶσι δοκεῖ, τοῦτο εἶναι φαμὲν, faith he: *What all men believe, we may ſay, is truth*. And what uſe hath been made by ancient Heathens and others, of this general conſent of mankind, to prove that there is a God, is well known. It is very uſual with many, when they have ſome ſtrange opinion to broach, to tell us of ſome erroneous perſwaſion, which hath long prevailed among men; as, that thread bare example of the *Antipodes*, which once to believe, was hereſie; to which ſome others may be added. But in this particular, how impertinent ſuch allegations are, who doth not ſee? For it is one thing by ſome authority of man, or probability of reaſon, to be miſled into an opinion, determinable more by ſpeculation, than experience; or, if by experience, yet rare, and difficult, and wherein few men are concerned, as to matter of life: In ſuch a caſe, if the error be never ſo general, it is no wonder. But in a caſe of this nature, as *Witches* (to which we add, *Spirits*,

*in things* NATURAL. 37

*Spirits*, in general, and *supernatural* operations ) which doth mostly depend, especially where learning is not of daily experience, and wherein mens lives and fortunes are so much concerned : to be misled in this, and from age to age, to continue in the error, is a strange thing indeed, if not a meer impossibility. The world is much wider now ( as to Knowledge ) than it hath been formerly : and therefore the consent of it so much the more considerable. I have ( as all men, I think have that are any thing curious ) read several relations of all the known parts of the world, written by men of several Nations, and Professions, learned and unlearned, in divers languages : by men of several ages, ancient and late : I do scarce remember any short, or long, but doth afford somewhat to the confirmation of this truth; but in most, I remember well to have met with very particular accounts and relations of *Witches* and *Sorcerers* ; strange divinations, predictions, operations, whereof the relators, many of them, men of several Nations and professions, Papists and Protestants, who probably never heard of one another, profess themselves to have been eye-witnesses.

NOW if we confine our selves to this one part of the world, which we call *Europe*, to which one part all learning seemeth now to be in a manner confined; which, within this hundred, or two hundred years, hath produced so many able men of all professions ; Divines, Lawyers, Physicians, and Philosophers ; Papists and Protestants; those few men excepted, who may soon be named all, known by their writing, to have dissented ; Who is there among them all, who hath not, *pro re nata*, and as occasion served, born testimony to this truth, or cause ? But how many are there, of most Kingdoms, *Germanes*, High and Low, *French*, *English*, *Spanish* ; not to seek
D 3 further ;

further; of all professions that have written of this subject, pleaded it, by reason and experience, and all kind of proofs; answered all objections, and pretensions: some whereof, learned and grave, have had the examination of persons, men and women accused for those wicked practices in great number. *Nicholaus Remigius*, a man both pious and learned, ( I wish covetous Printers had not bereaved us of his excellent Poetry, in many Editions ) in his books of *Demonolatrie*, doth profess, within the space of sixteen years, to have had the examination of near 2000, whereof 900 were condemned to death. We may say the same, or there-abouts, I think, of *Grillandus*, not to mention others. That so many, wise and discreet, well versed in that subject, could be so horribly deceived, against their wills; or so impious, so cruel, as wilfully to have a hand in the condemnation of so many Innocents; or again, wilfully, in the face of the Sun, and in defiance to God, by so many false relations, to abuse all men, present, and future; what man can believe. Their chiefest evasion, who are, or would seem to be of a contrary opinion, is, what a strange thing a depraved fancy, or imagination is; how easily it may represent to it self Devils, and Spirits; Sorceries and inchantments, and, God knows what: which things, commonly talked of, among ordinary people, especially, as many other things are; though they have no real being, yet may make great impressions in the brain, and offer themselves in sleep, or when the brain is sick, and out of temper, by melancholy especially. Or, if they be of *Wierius* his opinion, what advantage the *Devil* may make of a sick brain, to make silly poor women believe, that they have done things, which they never did, nor could. And this, when they have proved by two or three examples ( or say twenty, or more; for it is no hard business ) they think they have done much.

much. But what reason have they, to think this such a mystery, that none of those, that have had to do with *Witches*, and *Sorcerers*, ever heard of any such thing; and would not well consider it, before they passed any judgment? But what if more than one, ten, or twenty perchance, (it hath been so sometimes) have been actors, or accessories in some one execrable business, and, upon suspition, being severally examined, are found to agree in one tale; to have been thus and thus incouraged, assisted, by *Spirits*; to have acted such and such things; met in such places, at such times; which things, accompanied with notable circumstances, are found upon examination to be true, in all points and particulars? What if others, men and women, be convicted by the deposition of sundry creditable witnesses, upon some sudden quarrel, or old grudge; To have cursed, and threatned, thus and thus; men or cattle; and that it hath happened accordingly: Strange deaths, strange diseases, strange unnatural, unusual accidents, have ensued: can all this be, the effects of a depraved fancy? Or what, when such a house, such a parish hath been troubled with such unusual accidents; if all those accidents, immediately cease, upon the arraignment and execution of some, that are suspected, and have confessed, (though it doth not always so fall out, that they confess, which may be some argument of their repentance, which, I fear, is not very usual) shall we impute all this to a depraved fancy, or imagination: or say, with *Wierius*, that all this is done by the Devil only, to bring poor innocent women to destruction. And that God doth suffer these things, to punish (but more of that by and by) the *credulity* of men? Truly, as I can believe, that some men, innocently, for want of experience and good information, may hold such an opinion, which of the two, they conceive most charitable; so, that any man of ordinary capacity, that hath taken pains to inform himself, can really, without some great and secret judgment of God, persist in it, is to me almost incredible; or not less strange than any of these supernatural operations, which ordinarily cause most admiration.

THEN, if a man consider, what kind of men, for the most part, they have been, who have taken upon them, to oppose the belief of mankind, or universality of men, concerning Witches, &c. some notorious Atheists, as *Pomponatius*, *Vaninius*, &c. others, confident, illiterate wretches, as one of this Country, *Reginald Scot*, and the like; he will think certainly, that if the cause be no better, than the Patrons, it cannot be very good, nor see any reason at all to embrace it. But I must not let *Reginald Scot* pass so, without a further account, for their sakes (if any) that have a better opinion of him, though otherwise, a very inconsiderable man. His book, I must confess, I never had, nor ever read; but as I have found it by chance, where I have been, in friends houses, or Book-sellers shops; and, as the manner is, cast my eyes, here and there; by which perfunctory kind of taste, I am sure, I had no temptation to read much of him. I do not, therefore, take upon me to judge of him, by what I have read of him my self, which being so little, might deceive me; but by what I have read of him, in others, whom I know to have been learned, and judicious, and of great moderation and candor, in judging, even of enemies. This, I hope, I may speak without offence, or contradiction, of one, whose surname, notwithstanding the vast difference of their worth, comes somewhat near (for I know, that observations have been made, even upon names to the others christian-name; and that is, Doctor *Reynolds*, when he lived, as I take it, *Regius Professor*

*feſſor* of Divinity, in the University of *Oxford*: who it seems upon the report the man had got among the vulgar, had the curiosity (a right *helluo librorum*, as any was in his time) to read him. He doth mention him more than once, or twice, in those learned, and elaborate *Prælectiones* of his upon the *Apocrypha*; and not only name him, but takes notice of many particular paſſages, and confutes them; or rather, makes himself and his Auditors (now Readers) sport with them, but always admiring the unparallel'd boldneſs, and impertinence of the man. Of all the books he doth mention, in those large and elaborate *Prelections*, I do not remember any whom he doth censure with more scorn and indignation. Neither is Dr. *Reynolds* the only man I have read, that doth censure him: I could name two or three more, if it were *tanti*, or worth the while. And what might not we expect from a man, who reckons *Plutarch*, and *Pliny* (so I find him quoted) among the Fathers of the Church: and *Leonardum Vairum*, a late *Spaniard*, who hath written three books, *De faſcino*, or *Incantatione*, (I have him not, but in *French*) and stiles himself *Beneventanum, Ordinis Sancti Benedictini,& Priorem Abbatiæ ejuſdem, in Italia*: makes him, I say, either a Proteſtant, or an ancient Father: But theſe things we may laugh at, if theſe were his greateſt errors; concerning which, they that deſire to know more, may find enough in that learned piece before mentioned.

AS I was upon this, and had even written, or rather, (for I had ended this *firſt part*, and was now writing it out, as faſt as my weak condition would give me leave) written out so far: a worthy learned friend, whoſe judgment and communication in all kind of literature, wherein he is very expert, I much value, brought me a book entituled, *A Philoſophical endeavour, in the defence of the being of Witches and Apparitions, againſt Drollery & Atheiſm*, 1668.

Glad

Glad was I, to see the book, who am a stranger to all new books, except it be by some chance, these many years; and I was not long, before I had run it over. I was glad to find, that we agree so well in our account, both in this particular of *Reginald Scots*, and of Witches in general, though in different ways. He Philosophically, and subtilly: I, more popularly and plainly; yet I hope, not less usefully. As for his particular opinions, or conjectures, we may take further time to consider of them. His zeal against the Scoffers and Drollers of the time, as he doth call them; that is, against *Atheism*, which now passeth commonly, but most falsely, and among them only, who want true wit, and solidity; for wit and gallantry, I do much applaud. So much of it, ( the book I mean ) if not to satisfie others, yet my friend, who did help me to the sight of it.

BUT *Wierius* was a learned man, a Physician by his profession, who neither wanted wit, nor experience. They that have read his other book, *De Lamiis*, ( which I never saw ) lay to his charge, that he is not constant in his opinion: sure I am, in his book *De præstigiis*, &c. he doth shew much inconsistency; and sometimes, no small conflict and repugnancy, as a man that is much put to it, and doth not know what to say. For example, where he doth argue, whether men or women, *Sorcerers* and *Witches*, may become unsensible to any torments, inflicted by Magistrates; at first, he doth deliver it affirmatively, that they may; and wickedly, or unadvisedly, ( as elsewhere frequently, for which he is much condemned, and censured by some, to have written more in favour of *Spirits*, than *women* ) doth set down some charms; that ( he saith, or may be so understood ) will do it. But then immediately, he doth propose some things to the end, that what he hath delivered before as true and certain, might be questioned and
. deemed

deemed rather ridiculous and false, than true, or credible. For (saith he, as though any man, acquainted with the world, or the Scriptures, could not have answered it) *all powers are of God*: it is not likely, that God will give so much power to *Devils*, as to hinder the course of Justice. A great argument indeed, of Gods power, and providence over the world, that though he doth it sometimes, to make us the more sensible, and thankful; yet he doth it not often. Secondly, because God, as he is just, will not have wicked actions (a great and invincible argument, that there is a time and place of rewards, besides this present world) to pass unpunished. Yet for all this, his conclusion at last is: (*Sed tamen hominum impietate sic merente, sæpius hæc accidisse fateor*) *that it is so neverthelesss; there be Charms and Spells, which with the Devils help* (*through the wickedness of men*) *will make men and Women unsensible of any torments, be they never so great.* This puts me in mind of what I have heard from Sir *Theodore Mayerne*, (though dead many years ago, yet his memory, I hope, is yet fresh and living: I shall need to say no more) whereof he had been, he said, an eye witness; and what course was then held in *Geneva* (which then abounded with such creatures) for the prevention, or redress of such *Diabolical unsensibleness*, in Witches, and Magicians. I could say more from him; but I will not, now he is dead, give any man occasion to question the truth, either of his, or my relation. But to return to *Wierius*: So much was the man himself unsatisfied in his own opinion, that it is no easie thing for any man else, that reads him, to know what he would have. For, that horrible things are done really, according to the confession of women, accounted Witches; that, he doth not deny: That divers things, by the confession of these women, of the time, and place, and manner, and complices,

come

come to be known, which before were not known, and which upon diligent examination are found punctually true, in every circumstance, according to their confession; he doth not only acknowledge, but doth tell many strange stories himself to confirm it. What then? The Devil, saith he, makes them believe they have done, what himself hath been the true author of; nor could indeed be done by any, but himself. But did ever any man believe, that which Witches did, they did it by their own power? But that they wilfully, and knowingly, to satisfie their own lust, or defire of revenge, or other wicked end, make use of the Devil, to bring such wicked things to pass, which are confessed to be true and real, and wherein they usually are instrumental themselves; as by clear manifest proofs, and evidences ( if any thing be clear and certain in the world, besides their own confession ) doth often appear; this is that which is laid to their charge, and for which they deservedly suffer.

NAY, he doth not deny, but that such as have been bewitched, have been restored by those, who were suspected ( and convicted, some ) to have bewitched them: and yet for all this, bare Phansie the cause of all. I beseech him, What hath he left to us, that we can call *truth*, if this be but phancy? And still the conclusion is, that God doth suffer these things, poor innocent women to perish, for the *Credulity* of men; because they believe that there be *Witches* in the world: So that according to him, not those women, who are suspected and convicted by the Devil, upon their earnest seeking to him, to have done such and such things; but they that are so credulous, as to believe it, deserve more ( though he doth not say it, it doth follow so ) to bear the punishment. And who doth not see, that by this doctrine, the greatest Malefactor, Traitors, Rebels, and the like,

*in things* NATURAL. 45

like, may be accounted innocent? If this be not enough, to shew that the man was infatuated; then hear him plead, that *Witches* cannot be, because it is against the Goodness of God, to suffer, that poor old women, oppressed with misery and age, should fall into the worst of evils, as to become a prey unto the Devil. And again, that if God did give such power to *Witches*, the world could not subsist : That if *Witches* have such power, what need any King, or Prince be at such charge, to raise Armies, to defend themselves, or offend others ; when one single Witch may bring the same things to pass, without such trouble, or cost ? Now the strength of these arguments doth lye in this ; if it be true, first, that women are the only object of Gods Providence and Goodness, and not men : And secondly, because God for reasons best known to him, yet not altogether incomprehensible to man, doth sometimes suffer ( as in *Jobs* case ) some of these things to be, which we may believe, and yet believe that not one hair of our heads can perish, to our prejudice, without Gods permission : that God, I say, because *sometimes*, is therefore bound to suffer them *always*, and hath given the Devil absolute power over the Earth : which things, if ridiculous, and impious ; so certainly must the opinion be, that is grounded upon them. But if all this reasoning will do nothing ; yet *Wierius* hath another refuge; though, we *see* these things, ( which we think a good argument of truth in most other things ) yet we must not *believe them*, but rather think that the Devil hath bewitched our eyes to represent unto us things, that are not *really*, than to believe, that women can be so cruel. So he professeth of himself; *Tam enim id existit inhumanum, tetricum, & crudele, & creditu difficile, ut si vel meis intuerer hæc oculis*, &c. Yet of men, he will believe any thing, it seems. by
those

those sad stories he tells us of Sorcerers, whom he doth detest to the pit of Hell; but of women ( *Solomon* did not find it so, nor the Author of *Ecclesiasticus* ) we must not believe any such thing. My opinion, ( to end this discourse ) concerning the man, is, His Prince, and Master, whose chief Physician he was, had been wrought into that belief by some, ( as always here and there some have been of that opinion ) before *Wierius* had any thing to do with him; that it was so, and so, in the case of Witches, just as *Wierius* doth endeavour to make good, in his book: who also ( his Prince ) what he believed, took a pleasure ( if not, pride ) to discourse it publickly. All this, I learn from *Wierius* his *dedication*, and some passages of the book: my opinion is, that to gratifie him, was the chief ground of *Wierius* his undertaking, who probably by what we have observed, would not have engaged himself into such trouble of spirit, and mind, to oppose the publick belief, without some great provocation. This is a charitable opinion, the Reader will say, if he consider, what is objected unto him by others, to prove, as was intimated before, that what he intended, was not so much to favour *women*, as the *Devil* himself, with whom, it is to be feared, that he was too well acquainted; as ( besides other pregnant arguments ) *Cornelius Agrippa* his disciple, and bosom friend, according to his own relation and acknowledgment. But enough of him.

TO others, that are of his opinion, or perchance deny *Magicians*, as well as *Witches*, I would have them to consider, that if there be really such, as the world doth believe; who ( whether men, or women ) by entring into covenant with the publick enemy of mankind, and by the mischief they do, not to particular men, women, and children only ( not to mention dumb creatures, which are made for the service of man ) but even ( God permitting )

ting) to whole Towns, and Countries, by Fires and Pestilences, and otherwise, as the most approved Historians, and Physicians of these times, who have taken great pains to search into it, and give such reasons as few, I think, will undertake rationally to refute, do assert and maintain: If such, I say, really, who for those reasons, deserve no less than the *Devil*, to be accounted the enemies of mankind: what may we think of those, (though some, I believe, through ignorance, and for want of due information) that become the Patrons of such? And if there be laws against calumniators, and false witnesses, and those that go about to take away the good name, even of private men and women; what punishment do they deserve, that dare publickly traduce all the venerable Judges of so many Christian Kingdoms, as either ignorant wretches, or wilful murderers?

BUT all this while, we have said nothing, from the authority of Gods *Holy Word*, by which, besides some pregnant examples of Witches, and witchcraft in the Scriptures, all Sorcerers and Magicians; all *Witches* and *Wizards*, with much exactness distinguished and enumerated, are condemned to death; and their sin set out, as the most hainous of sins, in the eyes of God; and for which more than any other, the wrath of God comes upon the children of men, to the utter destruction of whole Kingdoms and Countries. This indeed I should have begun with, and might have contented my self with such authority, had I to do with Christians only. But I know what times we live in: we may thank these late confusions, the fruit of Rebellion, and a pretended *Reformation*, for a great part of it. But they that are true Christians, need no other proof, I am sure. Others, if rational, and not too far ingaged into *Atheism*, have somewhat also to consider of, if they please.

I THINK I have spoken of most of those general heads,

heads, under the *Mathematicks* (as by the rest, many particulars, which I do not mention) comprehending the *Opticks*, and all manner of glasses, by which strange things are performed: most of those general heads, I say, *natural*, and *supernatural*, which usually cause *admiration* among men; and thereby become objects of *credulity* and *incredulity*; Civil, and Divine only, which we refer to their proper places, excepted. I shall now in the next place give some Instances, first in things meerly *natural*, as generally understood; then in things *supernatural*; or, in *Trallianus*, and other ancient Physicians, their sense and notion, which we have followed in the Title; *natural* too, but as *natural* is opposed to *rational*: which things, intended for instances, shall be such, which I, upon grounds of reason, as I conceive, profess to believe; though by many, who suspect the relations, not credited, or thought impossible. After which instances, I shall annex some *directions*, or *observations*; with some examples of some things, which but lately generally credited, have proved false, which I think may be useful.

MY first Instance shall be concerning those men and women, who have been reported to have lived some years without either meat or drink: except *air* should be accounted meat, as to *Chamelions*, and some other creatures it is generally (though denied by some, I know) supposed to be. The truth is, that having had occasion sometimes, not otherwise very forward to tell strange things, though never so true, in ordinary discourse, yet upon occasion, supposing this to be no such strange thing, because I had read so much of it, but might be believed; I did once adventure, in very good company, a learned Physician being then present, to mention such a thing: but I perceived it was entertained, as a thing not *credible*; especially, after the Physician,

tian, in very deed an able man, whom I did not defire to oppofe in a thing more properly belonging to his cognizance ; had paffed his verdict upon it, that it could not be. Yet now, I will fay, upon the credit of fo many good Authors, and the particular relations of fo many examples, delivered with fo many circumftances, wherein no miftake, or impofture can rationally be fufpected ; that I do believe it, that divers men, and women, but more women, than men, have lived divers years, ( fome to their lives end, others for fome years only, and then returned to eating ) without any bodily food, ordinary or extraordinary, liquid or folid ; yea, I believe it, as I believe that I my felf, with ordinary food, and Gods blefling, have fo many years above 60. lived hitherto.

BUT here, before I proceed, left any, now that mocking and fcoffing at Religion, and the Scriptures, is fo much in fafhion, fhould take any advantage, to flight and deride Religious, or miraculous fafts, fuch as are recorded in the Scripture: I muft profefs, and declare in the firft place, that I never met with any relation, true or falfe, of any man or woman, that ever did, or could, by any art, or ftudy ; ( though, by the Devil, I think, fuch a thing might, God permitting without any prejudice to *religious* and *miraculous fafts* ) bring their bodies to any fuch thing. But fo many, as I have read of, were fuch, who either after fome great and tedious difeafe, or fome natural operation of a proper temperament, or conftitution of body, not voluntarily, but againft their wills, came to this ftrange pafs. The want of which right information might make fome, whom *Joubertus* doth mention, and ftile, *men for their fimplicity, and piety* ( except he fpeak it ironically ) *venerable*; to difcredit, what otherwife, upon fuch evidences, they would have believed. I remember well, that when I was a young Student in

E the

the University of *Oxford*, I had often a book in *Quarto* (as we call them) in my hands, which also had the picture of the party cut to the life, which did contain a very particular relation of one of these: which because I never did meet with since, (it was in one of the Booksellers shops, not in any Library) I make this mention of it here, so far as I can remember. But divers others have written of it: among others, *Joubertus*, before mentioned, a *French* Physician; against whom one *Harvy* appeared, to shew the impossibility, in point of nature; who, by more than one, I believe, (for *Raphael Thorius*, Doctor of Physick, whom I may not mention, without honour, both for his worth, and for particular obligations; lent me a little *French* book in defence of this subject, which he accounted a very solid piece, by which this secret of nature came first to my knowledge) by more therefore than one, I believe, but by one, who was most taken notice of, *Franciscus Citesius*, the then *French* King, and *Cardinal Richelew*'s Physician; a very learned man was answered: who also wrote the story of one of these foodless, or if we may so call them, Aerial Spiritual creatures, which he calls, *Abstinans Consolentanea*: the book Printed in *Paris*, 1639. But besides him, I have also one, *Paulus Lentulus*, a learned Professor, he was then, *Bernæ Helvetiorum*, who hath written the History of one himself, and collected several relations, most, by men of note, as *Langius*, *Hildanus*, and others, (not omitting *Citesius* before spoken of, but contracted) concerning others, not a few, in other Countries. This book hath the attestation and *Encomium*'s of many learned men prefixed: and hath the picture of one of them also; yet I cannot believe, that it is the book I saw in *Oxford*, which, as I remember, gave account of one only, and was, I think, a thicker book. Truly, it would be hard, if not proud and insolent,

## *in things* NATURAL.

lent, (Saint *Auguſtine*, in the like caſe, faith *impudent*) to queſtion the faith, or judgment of ſo many credible men, (ſome, of eminent fame) of divers Nations and profeſſions. But that which makes the caſe indiſputable, is, that ſome of theſe, whoſe ſtory is exhibited, have been long, or long enough to find the truth, kept and obſerved by Divines, Phyſicians, Magiſtrates: one, by *Maximilian* the Emperor, his great care, and particular appointment, (whoſe ſtory is written by more than one) to ſee, whether there could be any fraud, or impoſture. And beſides, the very ſight of ſome of them, might have converted, or ſilenced at leaſt, the moſt *incredulous* obſtinate creature in the world; their ſtomack, and bellies, whereof nature had no further uſe, being found ſo ſhrunk, that it was impoſſible to think, that meat and drink could there find a receptacle.

I WAS once kindly entertained at a place, (in *England*, but where, or by whom, except I had the conſent of them, to whom I profeſs to owe much reſpect for their kindneſs, the Reader muſt excuſe me) where after I had been ſome days, upon ſome information concerning a Gentlewoman, that had ſome relation to the houſe, though not then in the houſe, who was ſaid to live without meat; I made bold to ask my friend, (a noble Knight) the Maſter of the houſe, what he knew of it. His anſwer was, that ſhe had been his houſe-keeper, one month, he ſaid, as I remember, and ſat at his table every day, but had never ſeen her eat. This did ſet an edge upon my deſire, and curioſity, to enquire further. This Gentlewoman had married one of his Sons, who lived and kept houſe by himſelf there alſo have I been kindly entertained more than once) not many miles off. He was a Scholar, and a very ingenuous Gentleman, and one, who himſelf was as curious to underſtand as much

much of nature, as by ordinary study and curiosity can be attained. His answer was, that ever since (some years, I am sure) she had been his wife, he never did observe her to eat otherwise, than that sometimes, once in a week perchance, in handling of dishes, she would seize hastily upon some one bit, which her *phancy* more, than her *stomack*, was tempted with. I make no question, but if faithful *observations* were duly made, which was the way in ancient times, of all that hapneth extraordinarily in this one Country of *England*, we should not need be beholding to strangers so much, or at least, would find less cause, in many things, to reject and contemn their relations, as *incredible* and fabulous. Sure, I am in most books that I have read, to understand what is not ordinary in the cause of nature ; I find *England* often named, where I can find or hear of no *Englishman*, to attest. In this very particular I am now upon, I have read of some, I am sure, reported to have lived in *England* without either meat or drink ; I know not how long, of whom I have read nothing in *English* Histories. But I shall not trouble my self to find where, having said enough to satisfie them, who have not, by some solemn vow or resolution, made themselves impenetrable to reason. Yet, the story of an *English* woman or maid, that lived, I think, twenty years without eating, written by *Roger Bacon*, the Reader may find, if he please, in the *Collection* before mentioned, for the truth whereof; though I doubt not the possibility, except otherwise confirmed, I will not engage. But whereas he doth fetch the cause from Heaven, or *Heavenly influences*, if he be in the right in that, this example will not so properly concern us, who pretend in this particular to nothing, but natural causes. I know there be also who ascribe it to the *Devil*; neither will I deny the possibility of such a thing. However, when

*in things* NATURAL. 53

when natural caufes may clear the bufinefs, except fome unnatural circumftances, as fometimes it doth happen, perfwade to the contrary ; much better it is to let the *Devil* alone, than to fly to him for fatisfaction.

BUT to return to our relations: I have faid it before, and fay it again : No man I think that will take the pains to read the books I have mentioned, with all the particulars which they contain, but will, what ever opinion he was of before, acknowledge himfelf fatisfied of the truth, as to matter of fact. As to poffibility in point of nature, I will not be fo peremptory, though I acknowledge my felf very fully fatisfied, by thofe learned Tractates that have been fet out about it, that it may be. Now that any ( women moft, to whom this hath happened ) fhould after long ficknefs fall to this, and fo continue, dull, heavy, confumptive in their bodies, and fome without motion; and fo, after fome years, die ; though ftrange even fo, yet I do not fee much to admire, but that it fhould fo happen unto any ; who neverthelefs for fome years have continued frefh and vigorous, with a good colour, and without any abatement of flefh without, or any other notable alteration ; and have returned in time, to eating and drinking again, as other folks ; as I think it happened to her, that was kept by *Maximilian*'s order ; is that I moft wonder at, and wherein we might with more probability fufpect a *fupernatural* caufe, though herein alfo, I fubmit to better judgments, and believe as they do, that it may be, naturally. The matter is fully difcuffed by *Sennertus* alfo, a man of fo much authority with me, and with all men, I think, whom new difcoveries have not fo befotted, as to think nothing right, but what is new ; that he alone might go a great way to perfwade me.

E 3 *Marcellus*

*Marcellus Donatus* alſo, *De Med. Hiſt. mirab. lib.* 4. *c.* 12. is very full upon it: and hath many inſtances: this among the reſt: *That a certain Prieſt did live* 40. *years in* Rome *with Air only, as by the keeping of Pope* Leo, *and divers Princes, and the Narration and Teſtimony of* Hermol. Barbarus, *is moſt certain.*

HOWEVER, I am not ſo addicted to any cauſe, that I would allow of any indirect ways, to maintain it. To prove the *poſſibility*, among other arguments and inſtances, that are uſed, I ſhall here take notice of one, and what I have to except againſt it: not hence to infer againſt the cauſe it ſelf, any thing, for which there is no juſt reaſon, this being but a remote and inconſiderable proof, in compariſon of ſo many more pregnant and direct evidences: but to take this occaſion, by the way, to ſhew, how teſtimonies ſhould be examined, before we yield much to their authority. It is alledged by more than one, that there is a people in the North, about *Muſcovia*, who conſtantly from ſuch a day in *November*, to ſuch a day in *April* following, hide in Caves of the Earth, and continue all that time without any food, but ſleep. Now that this was averr'd to *Henry* the *III.* King of *France*, when in *Polonia*, by men of great quality, who lived in, or about thoſe Countries, and might eaſily know the certainty, with great aſſeveration; this indeed, I believe, and is of great weight with me, (though I would not, upon no greater evidence, preſs, or perſwade any other) to work ſomewhat towards a belief. *Sennertus*, I find, dares not peremptorily affirm it, for a truth; or much truſt to it, for an evidence; as having much greater, and more wonderful things, which no man, he ſaith, can queſtion, to prove the poſſibility of living, without eating, or drinking. Yet it doth appear by his words, though he feared it would ( *multis fabuloſum videri* ) by many be ſlighted

as

as a fable, yet that himself did much more incline to believe it, than not. And there be other relations of those Northern people, believed, I see, by sundry grave and learned men; which, to be compared, might seem every whit as strange and *incredible*. But because I do not make it my business here, to undertake for the truth of it, as I before professed; nor have any intention to entertain my Reader with strange relations, more than shall be necessary to my principal end; I shall willingly forbear them, or reserve them to another place. That which I have to except in the relation of this story is, that two Authors are named, *Gnagninus in Muscoviæ descriptione*; and *Sigismundus Baro, in Hebeirsten, in itineratio*: as two several Authors, and two several testimonies; whereas if we examine those Authors, they will appear in this, but one, not only by the words, which they borrow the one from the other; almost the same, in both: but also by *Gnagninus*, who at the end of his *Description*, doth make honourable mention of *Sigismundus*; whereby it doth appear that he had read him, and borrowed of him. But, what is worse, upon further examination, it will appear, that this *Sigismundus Baro*, saith no such thing at all himself, but hath that passage *verbatim*, out of an *Itinerarie* of a nameless Author, written in the *Ruthenick*-tongue: translated, or part of it, by himself, and inserted in his own *Commentaries*: and moreover, that he had, with all possible diligence ( as he professeth, Page 89. of the *Antwerp* Edition, *Anno Dom.* 1557. ) inquired of those *hominibus mutis*, and other, *morientibus & reviviscentibus*; those sleepers in Caves of the Earth before spoken of; yet professeth he could never meet with any, that could say he had seen it himself, but only heard it from others: and therefore saith he, ( *Ut aliis ampliorem quærendi occasionem præberem* ) to the end, that others might

might further enquire, not as believing it himself, or commending it to others for a truth; he was willing to let them know, what he had found in the *Itinerary*. It is almost incredible, what a wrong to *truth* this manner of citing of witnesses and testimonies hath been in all ages, when three or four, sometimes four or five, or more, are cited, as several witnesses, who upon examination prove but one, and perchance, not so much as one, good, or clear witness. But I have done with my first instance or example: which concerned things *natural*, as ordinarily taken; and though store of such offer themselves to me; yet, because I have reason to make what haft I can, being every day, by much weakness summoned, or put in mind; I will proceed to instances in things *supernatural*, which will better fit my design.

MY second instance therefore shall be out of *Seneca*, who in his fourth book of *Natural Questions*, which doth treat of *Snow*, *Hail* and *Rain*: in his sixth Chapter, relates rather as a *tale*, than a *truth*, (so he doth profess, at the beginning) what he found recorded, and believed by some others, to wit, that there were men in some places, who by observing of the clouds, were able and skilful to foresee and foretel, when a storm of Hail was approaching. *Cleonis* was the place, by him named; which was then the name of more places than one: but by what he saith of it, it should be a Town of the *Peloponnesus* (now *Morea*, under the Turk) of no very great fame, or name. But it seems, whether by the nature of the Climat, or somewhat else, *natural* or *supernatural*; very subject to storms of Hail, by which the fruits of the ground very commonly destroyed. It did so trouble them, that after many endeavours, it should seem, to prevent their loss, they at last found a strange remedy. First, it must be believed, according to the relation, that

that by diligent obfervation of the clouds and other temper of the skies, in fuch ftorms, which, to their great grief and damage, were fo frequent among them; fome men had attained to that skill, that they could, as was faid before, foretel a ftorm. Of thefe men, fome were chofen and appointed, as publick officers, (therefore called χαλαξοφύλακες; that is, *obfervers of the Hail*) to give warning to the people, who upon that warning did haften to kill, fome a Lamb; others, according to their abilities, *Pullum*: fome young thing or other: probably, a *Chick*: the bloud whereof was offered, as a Sacrifice. But if any were fo poor, or by chance, fo deftitute at that time, that he had neither *agnum* or *pullum*: why, then his way was to prick one of his fingers with fome bodkin, or writing-fteel (as the fafhion was then) that had a good point, and that bloud was accepted for other; and fo the ftorm certainly diverted. In the relation of this, *Seneca* doth ufe fome merry words, which have deceived many, (which hath made me the more willing to take them into confideration) as though it were far from him, to believe fuch an abfurd and impoffible thing. *Grant*, faith he, *there were fuch men, that could forefee and foretel a ftorm: What relation have the clouds to bloud; or, how can fuch a little quantity of bloud, as a Chicken, or a prickt-finger can afford, fo fuddenly penetrate fo high, as the skies, to work fuch an effect?* Yet if a man doth well obferve his words, it will appear, that *Seneca* did more incline himfelf to believe it, and fo doth propofe it to us, rather as a thing true, than otherwife. For after he had faid, that men in the examination of the caufe, were divided; fome, as became *very wife men* (that is his word) abfolutely denying, that any fuch thing could be, that men fhould covenant with the Snow, and with fmall prefents pacifie tempefts, (though, faith he, he, It is well known, that *the Gods themselves are overcome with gifts: for, to what end else, are all their sacrifices?*) Others thinking, that there was in bloud, naturally, some kind of efficacy to repel, and avert a cloud; he doth further add, what he knew would be objected by others; but how can, in so little bloud, be so great force, as to pierce the clouds, and to make them sensible of its power? After this, knowing, and tacitly grounding, there was no arguing the possibility of a thing by reason, against certain evidence; for which in this case there was so much to be said: *How much more safe, and ready would it be,* ( saith he ) barely *to say, It is a lye, an arrant lye; it cannot be.* And then go on: But at *Cleonis,* they were wont to punish them severely, who had charge to prevent the tempest, if through their negligence, either their Vines, or their Corn had suffered. *In our XII. Tables also,* ( the old *Roman-*law ) *there was a law against them, who should by any kind of inchantment, hurt, or destroy other mens Corn.* To what end all this, think we, but to make it appear, that if *evidence* would carry it, there was enough to perswade us, the report of *Cleonis* was true enough. Yet after all this, fearing he had gone too far, to expose himself to the *ludibrium,* or derision of those *sapientissimi,* or *wonderful wise men,* who would believe nothing to be true, ( the clear profession of the *Epicuraeans* of those days ) the cause whereof they could not understand; to make some amends, he ends his discourse in the reproof, as it were, of *rude ignorant antiquity,* that could believe such things, as that there were *Charms* or *Spells* for the Rain, to be procured, or put back: which, saith he, is so clearly impossible, that we need not go to Philosophers, to know their opinion.

AS for *Seneca*'s meaning, whether I be in the right, or no, I shall not think my self much concerned; let
every

every man after diligent perusing of his words, judge as he pleaseth. Though this more, to make my interpretation of his words, more probable, I have to say, that it doth appear by other places, how fearful he was to utter any thing in this kind, that was not generally believed, though himself, in all probability, made little or no question of the truth. See but immediately before, how tenderly he doth propose, and not without an *Apology* for himself, lest he might be thought seriously to believe it, ( which also made *Ovid* so fearful, though himself an eye-witness, to write it ) that the Northern Seas are wont to freez, or to congeal, in the Winter-time. Let also *Pliny*'s words be considered, concerning this very thing ; not the place, but the thing : *There be Spells against Hail*, saith he, *and Diseases*, and ( *ambusta*, which he also calls, *ambustiones* ; that is, πυείσυμα ) *burnings* : *some of which have been tried* : ( or, by experience, approved true ) *Sed prodendo, obstat ingens verecundia* : that is, but to set down *particularly, a marvellous shame* ( or *fear* ) *doth hinder me, as well knowing the different opinions of men. Let every man therefore think of these things, as himself pleaseth*. So *Pliny* : whereby doth appear, that he durst not speak what he thought, and believed, lest he should undergo the reproach ( those *wonderful wise Epicureans* ; *Pliny* himself, a great favourer of their Sect; being very numerous, and in great credit in those times ) of a writer of tales. But, as I said before, let *Seneca*'s meaning be what it will ; as to the thing it self, though I will not undertake for the truth of it, according to every circumstance of *Seneca*'s relation, partly because I never saw the Records of that City my self, which haply *Seneca* did ; and partly because *Plutarch*, who doth mention those, Χαλαξοφύλακες, or *observers of Hail*, doth not name any place, and instead of the bloud of a *Lamb* or *Chick*, doth mention

mention another kind of bloud : yet that there is no such *impossibility* in the relation, but that it might be very true ; so far I dare undertake, and I hope to make it good. Neither will it appear *incredible* to any man, who instead of a *natural*, will but allow us a *supernatural* cause. But first let us see what we can say, for the truth, or probability of the *fact*, or thing ; and then let the Reader judge, what may probably be the *cause*. It seemeth that very anciently, such an opinion hath been among men, *Romans* and *Grecians*, that by some *Magick* or *supernatural* art, ( for the *Devil* was not so well known, in those days, though *Dæmons*, which was an ambiguous word, as elsewhere I have shewed, were ) strange things might be wrought, as in the air, so upon the land, to further or hinder the fruits of the Earth. *Empedocles*, anciently, a notorious Magician, became very famous for his skill in that kind, ever since he helped the *Athenians*, when by unseasonable winds, all their Corn was like to miscarry ; as *Laertius*, and others, bear witness : from which time and thing, he got the title of κωλυσανίμης, or *wind-stiller*. Among other things, it was very generally believed, that *Witches* and *Magicians* had a power, or an art, to transfer both the crop and fertility of one field to another. *Messes hac atque illac transferunt diris tempestabibus, omnesque fructus, paucorum improbitas capit* ; saith the Author of that Poem, or *Comedy*, ancient and elegant, commonly called *Querelas* : quite different from that in *Plautus*. And *Tibullus* long before, to the same purpose ; *Cantus vicinis fruges traducit ab agris*. One *Caius Furius Cresinus*, a *Roman* of a mean fortune, whose grounds were observed to thrive so beyond measure, that he did reap more *ex agello*, or a little field, than his rich neighbours did, of sundry large ones ; was accused, that he did *fruges alienas pellicere veneficiis* ; that is, *that by witchcraft he*

*did*

*did rob other grounds, to enrich his own.* It came to a trial, but he came of with great honour. *Pliny* is my Author.

BUT, by the way, it will, I hope, be no digression, to take notice of another story of his, which will not be impertinent to our present discourse, concerning this anciently believed *tranflation* of the fruits of the Earth, from one ground to another; and very pertinent to our main subject, of *Credulity* and *Incredulity*, of which *Pliny* doth afford more examples, than any other Author I know; and is very often wronged, and censured by men, through *Incredulity*, grounded upon ignorance. Many fabulous relations he hath, I know, from all kind of Authors, which himself made no other account of, for the most part. Nay, I am sure, he doth sometimes reject that for fabulous, which upon better confideration, will appear true enough. We may therefore think ourselves beholding to him for the knowledge of many true things, which, if because accounted by him fabulous, he had taken no notice of in his Obfervations; we had never known. But, however those things may prove, or be judged, which he had from others; it can hardly be shewed, that he records any thing of his own time, or upon his own knowledge, that can be proved a lye: & it is well known, that being a man of great wealth, and dignity, wilfully and willingly he did adventure his life (and lost it, we know, in that adventure ) the better to learn the truth, and, if possible, to discover the cause of some strange things : So heartily was he addicted to the study of *Nature*, and therefore more unlikely, he would wilfully, do the truth of Nature so much wrong, as to violate and defile it ( willingly and wittingly ) with fabulous narrations. But now to the story which himself doth call, ( *Prodigium super omnia, quæ unquam credita sunt* : ) *A prodigie beyond all prodigies,*

*prodigies, that ever were believed*; and yet delivered by him, as a true story. In *Nero's* time, he saith, it so happened, that a whole Olive-field was transferred, or carried to the other side of the high way, and the ploughed ground, that stood before in the adverse side, set in the room. He doth not ascribe it to any witch-craft: though it be so apprehended by some, that tell this story after him: as *Ludovicus Vives* by name, for one. It is much more likely, that it happened, if true, (as I think very reasonable to believe) by some strange Earthquake, or motion of the ground, in those parts, occasioned by subterraneous winds, and vapours. Who hath not heard of Trees, and Rivers, removed from their proper place, and placed elsewhere, by Earthquakes? But if any be so *incredulous*, as not to believe *Pliny* in this: what will they say to *Machiavil*, an Historian without exception, that I know of, whatever his religion was; who tells us of a storm in *Italy*, by which, besides many other wonders, ( I have not the original *Italian*) *Tecta, quæ templis inædificata erant; the roofs of Churches*, ( he names two ) *integrâ compagine, ultra milliare inde confedere: were removed whole and entire; above an Italian mile*: *l.*6. *p.* 3478. He doth indeed leave it free to the Reader, whether he will impute this strange accident to a *natural* or *supernatural* cause; and to us, and our purpose, whether *natural* or *supernatural*, is indifferent. So much to give some-light to that part of *Seneca*, that mentioneth, according to the phrase of the *XII.* Tables, the *inchanting* of grounds, or fruits of the ground.

NOW to return where we begun; Extraordinary storms of Hail; very prejudicial to the fruits of the Earth, which seemed supernatural; in these days *Seneca* speaketh of happening very frequently: ( I am much deceived, if *Geneva*, which in *Calvins* time was much infested

fested with *Witches*, hath not formerly known such *acci-dents*) Country people sought for remedy to such, as did deal in those things; by whom they were taught Rites and Sacrifices; as also *Spells* and *Charms*, which proved very helpful, and therefore used very frequently. In so much, as they that did write of *agriculture*, or, *De re rustica* in those days, did not think they did acquit themselves of what they promised sufficiently, if silent in these things: as particularly may appear by *Columella*, (not to mention others) not inferior unto any that hath written of that subject, either ancient or late; in his Tenth book, whereof he hath some receipts, not much unlike this in *Seneca*. Certain it is, that *Spells* and *Charms* were in such credit in those days for such uses, that even *Constantine the Great*, a Christian Emperor, when he made Laws against *inchantments*; he doth except those, that were for the preservation of the fruits of the Earth, and those that were made, or used against *Hail*, particularly: *Cod. l.* 9. *tit.* 18. inscribed, *De Maleficis, & Mathematicis*; which, according to the stile of those days, was as much as *magis*. In the fourth Chapter, or Paragraph, *De magia*; these words are; *Nullis vero criminationibus implicanda sunt remedia, humanis quæsita corporibus, aut in agrestibus locis, innocenter adhibita suffragia*: (Some might by that word perchance, understand *Ecclesiastical prayers*; but here of necessity, *Magical Spells and Charms*, must be understood, which he doth excuse only, for the good that they do) *ne maturis vindemiis metuerentur imbres, aut venti, grandinisque lapidatione quaterentur: quibus non cujusquam salus aut æstimatio lederetur; sed quorum proficerent actus, ne divina munera, & labores hominum sternerentur*. I think I shall not need to English this, because the substance of it is already expressed. Neither did this Law die with *Constantine*; for it was renewed

by

by some Emperors after him, though at last, as it well deserved, repealed and abrogated. And God forbid, any such thing should ever be allowed in any place, that pretends to Christianity. For besides that we must not *do evil that good may come of it*; where such wicked practices are suffered, though some present benefit may be reaped for a while, yet the curse of God will be found, sooner or later, to light upon the place; and for some benefit, unjustly purchased, many mischiefs, (if not utter destruction, through Gods just judgment) will ensue. However, that the opinion of mischief, done by *Witches* and *Magicians*, by storms of Hail particularly, did continue long after *Constantine*'s law was repealed, may appear by laws made against them in after ages: as particularly by *Lodovicus*, King of *France*, and Emperor of *Germany*, his *Additions* to the *Capitula* made by him, and his father *Charles* the *Great*, *Add. II. c.* 18. *de diversis malorum* (so printed, but *Magorum* certainly is the right) *flagitiis*.

I THINK by this that hath been said, it will not seem strange, that any Town, in those Heathenish times, should have such officers, as from their office should be called Χαλαξοφύλακες, or *Hail observers*: especially, when *Seneca* doth in a manner appeal to publick records. But that such a device, the *bloud of a Lamb*, of a *Chick*, or a *prickt-finger*, should have such operation, as to prevent the danger; may be a wonder indeed, yea, an *incredible* thing to them that do not know, or believe there be such creatures, as *Devils* and *Spirits* in the world; whose delight is, to abuse mankind with such fopperies, that whilest men ascribe the efficacy to some outward things, they may less suspect themselves, or be suspected by others, to work by unlawful means, and get an ill name, if no other punishment for it.

*LEONARD Vair*, in his book of *Charms*, hath

a

a relation of a strange custom, in some places, very well known to him, it seems; for he speaks of it with much indignation; ( in *Spain* or *Italy*, we may be sure ) which custom is; when Country-people will drive Grashoppers, or any such hurtful Vermin ( frequent in that Country, probably ) out of their grounds; they hire a *Conjurer* for Judge, and two Advocates; the one to plead the cause of the Vermin, the other of the people, which solemnly performed, at last, sentence of *Excommunication* is pronounced against the Vermin. Thus the Devil, by his instruments, *Conjurers* and *Sectaries*, doth endeavour to bring the most solemn Ceremonies of the Church, even the Sacraments ( whereof examples in books of this argument are very obvious ) into contempt. *Vair* doth not tell us, with what success: but by what we shall observe in due place, as occasion doth offer it self; the Reader will yield it very probable, that it is not, sometimes at least, without success; and how little reason any man hath to be scandalized at such things, shall be fully argued, before we end this first part. But it would please some, better perchance, to hear of somewhat meerly *natural*, that should have, or be reported to have the same effect, which we ascribe to the power of *Devils* and *Spirits*. I have some Authors for it, but believe it who will, ( though I profess to believe much of the vertues of Plants and Minerals, if Coral may be reckoned among them ) that *red Corals* have the same property: and that in *Germany*, many husbandmen, upon approved experience, will after sowing, here and there, but especially in the borders of their grounds, scatter some little broken pieces of *red Coral*; and by that means preserve their own from all hurt, when their neighbours grounds, round about, are much annoyed by the violence of either Hail or Thunder. My Author, as I take it, is a *German* himself; he

F might

might eafily have known the truth. He makes himfelf a great *peregrinator*, to fatisfie his Curiofity, or improve his knowledge in *natural* things. Such a thing as this, me-thinks, had he had any hopes to find it true, might have been worth his labour, though he had rode many miles, and he might have had the thanks and bleffings of many for fuch a difcovery, had it been certain. This makes me very much to fufpect, if not affirm, that it is but a tale. I have read of women too, fomewhere, who upon fuch occafions, ufe to caft up falt in the air, which is more probable: but with what fuccefs, or upon what ground, I can give no account.

BUT if after all this, not yet fully fatisfied with fuch inftances, as the old known world hath afforded, we will take the pains, to fearch the Records of the new world, there we fhall meet with *Seneca's* cafe very punctually; the *bloud* of men offered unto Devils (their Gods) to preferve their Corn, and other fruits, from Hail-ftorms, and Tempefts. Witnefs *Petrus Martyr Mediolanenfis*, *De Infulis nuper inventis*; whofe teftimony, not to feek further, we may reft upon, as a very credible witnefs.

BUT to proceed, and fo to end this particular, which *Seneca* gave us the occafion of; That Devils can raife ftorms and tempefts (if God permit) by their own power and skill, when they pleafe; they that believe the Hiftory of *Job*, will make no great queftion: and if *Devils*; *Witches* alfo by his power; as all that have written of *Witches*, who believe there be fuch, averr, and give many inftances. As for rain, mentioned by *Seneca*, (though his words found otherwife to me, than to any by whom I find him quoted: let the Reader judge by what I have faid of it before) as, *the dotage of antiquity*; as of Hail, fo of Rain, I find none that have written of *Witches*, and believe them, but determine it affirmatively, ly, that the Devil hath the power of that alſo, God permitting, when he will. To paſs by ordinary inſtances: *Dion Caſſius*, a very ſerious Hiſtorian, hath a relation of plenty of rain, in time of greateſt neceſſity, by which a *Roman* Army, was as it were, miraculouſly preſerved; procured by *Magick*. Which, with *Baronius*, I ſhould be very inclinable to believe to have been done by the prayers of *Chriſtians*, as under *Aurelius Antoninus*; acknowledged even by Heathen writers; it once happened: But that the Chronology will not, I doubt, agree: Chriſtianity was not ſo ancient in thoſe parts, I believe. We have now gone through all the particulars of *Seneca*'s relation: I ſhall only add, I do not believe, that *Cleone* ( for the word is differently written ) by the ſcituation of the place, was more ſubject to *Hail*, than any other place; but the *Devil* by ſome chance of opportunity, having once got this ſuperſtition there eſtabliſhed, he would be ſure they ſhould not want occaſion to continue it; which muſt be, by frequent Hail threatned; and probably he did ſo order it, of purpoſe, in the air, that they might eaſily ſee, without any Conjuring for it, when a ſtorm was coming.

IN the next place, I ſhall take notice of a relation in *Philoſtratus*, ( an Author, though fabulous in thoſe things, that concerned his main deſign, to make a God, of a *Magician*; yet for ſome ſtrange relations, once ſuppoſed falſe, now approved true, well deſerving to be read ) and his conceit, or Comment upon the relation. The Relation is this, how *Apollonius* being in Priſon by *Domitian*'s command, and one of his legs fettered; *Damis* that attended him, began to be much out of heart, and doubtful of the iſſue. Whereupon *Apollonius*, to revive him, ſhewed him his leg out of the fetters; and when *Damis* had ſufficiently viewed it, looſe, and free; of his own accord he put it into the fetters, or ſtocks flocks ( *διομὸν* ) again. Whereupon *Damis* doth infer, that surely, because he did it with such ease, without any *previous prayer* or *sacrifice*, that he must be more than a man. Now, that this might probably be done by *Apollonius*, we may believe, since he did much more afterwards, which by *Christian* Fathers, and *Historians* is acknowledged, when being brought out of prison, as a criminal, to the Court-*hall*, or place of Judgment, *Domitian* being present, he vanished out of sight, and was at the same time seen far from the place, but not in prison any more. The relation then admitted, or supposed: what is *Philostratus* his descant upon it? *The simpler sort,* saith he, *ascribe such things* is γίνεται, to *Witchcraft* or *Magick*: πεπόνθασι δ' αυτὸ ις πολλὰ τῶν ἀνθρωπίνων· that is, ( not as the Latin interpreter, though not much amiss to the sense, *Quas ad plurimas rerum humanarum proficere arbitrantur* ) *and so they judge of many other things, that happen in the World among men.* He goes on: *The publick wrestlers and fencers, out of a greediness to be victorious, they have a recourse unto this*: ( *Witchcraft* or *Magick* ) *but the truth is, they are not at all the better for it, when they have done*: *but if by chance* ( or providence: ἀπὸ τύχης, so is the word often taken, as I have shewed elsewhere by some examples, to which many more may be added ) *they happen to prevail, wretched men* ( κακοδαίμονες ) *bereaving themselves of the praise, ascribe it to the arts.* *And in case they be worsted,* ( ἐπαίρουσι ορᾶν: what that ὁρᾶν makes here, I do not understand: till some body tell me, I shall make bold to read, ἀπίστα δ' αυτῇ οὐδ' ἡττώμενοι. "Αρην or ἄρην. 'Ει γὰρ τὸ δεῖναι ἔθυσα) *yet will they not mistrust the art. Fool, will they say: for had I but offered such a sacrifice, or burnt such incense, I could not have missed of the victory.* And so he goes on, that it is so with *Merchants* and *Lovers*: and how they suffer themselves to be cheated by these *Sophisters,* as he

*in things* NATURAL. 69

he calls them. They that will read this Author, may not truſt to the Latin Tranſlation; no, nor to the Greek Text, as now printed. I wiſh ſome body had undertaken the printing of it, in my time; they might have had it more correct and intelligible, in many places, than it is, in any Edition I have ſeen. But, to the buſineſs. He would not have it thought, that *Spells* and *Charms* can do any thing: there was a reaſon for it. He knew, *Apollonius* did deal in ſuch things, as could not be aſcribed to *natural* cauſes: ſo that he could not avoid the ſuſpition of a *Magician*, if there were any ſuch thing as *Magick*. Now, if once granted, that all, who pretended to ſuch things, were but *impoſtors*, and could do nothing, really; then it muſt of neceſſity follow, that *Apollonius*, what he did; did by *the finger of God*, and was a divine man. Though we deny not, but there have always been, and are now; in *England*, I believe, not a few; *London* eſpecially; *Morlins*, and others, who have a way to cheat and abuſe ſilly people; (whether rich or poor, I call them ſo, that are ſo eaſily caught) making them believe, they can do great things, whereas, in very deed, all they do, (except they deal by the *Devil*, as *Apollonius* did) is but cozenage and deluſion: yet this diſcourſe of *Philoſtratus* notwithſtanding, if we ſearch the Records of Antiquity, we ſhall find, that in thoſe days, and before, as it was very ordinary for them, who did ſtrive for victories publickly, either in the *Circus*, by racing, or any way elſe, by any kind of game or exerciſe; to apply themſelves to *Witches* and *Magicians*, that by their help, they might be ſure of the game; ſo, not unuſual alſo, for men to prevail, by thoſe arts. Which gave occaſion to *Conſtantius*'s law, *De maleficis comprehendendis*; where learned *Gothofred* his note is; *Agitatores equorum plerique*, &c. that is, *Moſt horſe-racers of thoſe times, by*

F 3 *magical*

*magical arts*, at times, did hinder their adverſaries horſes, and made their own ſwſter, as *St.* Jerome *in the life of St.* Hilarion; Arnobius, contra Gentes, *and* Caſſiodore *in the third of his* Varia, *bear witneſs.* So he. We ſhall have a proper place afterwards, to conſider of St. *Jeromes* words here cited, which are very pregnant, and appoſite to prove the thing; but otherwiſe, might cauſe further doubt and wonder, and therefore muſt not be paſſed over in ſilence. But beſides thoſe quoted by *Gothofred*, there be others of as great, or greater antiquity, and authority, that bear witneſs to the ſame truth. *Ammianus Macellinus*, in his 26. Hiſtory, doth record, that one *Hilarius*, a horſe-racer, was put to death by *Apronianus*, then Governour of *Rome*, a man, he ſaith, of equal integrity and ſeverity; for being convicted, to have ſent his ſon to a *Magician*, to be taught by him, (*ſecretiora quædam legibus interdicta*) *certain ſecret Spells and Charms* ( ſo I take it ) *by which without any mans knowledge, he might be aſſiſted, and enabled to compaſs his deſires, in the way of his profeſſion.* St. *Auguſtine* alſo writeth of himſelf, that at a time, when he prepared to make a party in a ſinging-prize or match, upon the Theater, ( not then, a Prieſt, or in Orders, you may be ſure ) an *aruſpex* ( or *Magician*: ſo taken ſometimes) offered him for a good reward, to make him *victor*: which he profeſſeth he did abhor, and deteſt. But I muſt not conceal from the Reader, that *Galen* whoſe judgment, in ſuch a caſe, muſt needs be very conſiderable, ſeems to deride ſuch things, and particularly, that by ſuch devices any man ſhould be enabled, ( ἐκτὸς γὰρ αὐτῶν ᾗ γελοία, κρατῆσαι τῆς ἀντιδίκους, ὡς μηδὲν ὅτι τὸ ἐναντίον δυνήσασθαι φθέγξασθαι, &c. ) *to confound his enemy, in publick Courts and places of Judicature, and to ſtop their mouths, that they ſhall not be able to ſpeak.* He doth indeed; but then it was, when in general he denied all
*Magical*

## in things NATURAL.

*Magical* or *Supernatural* operations, and, as a *rational* Physician, and *Naturalist*, in which profession he was accounted the wonder of his age, he thought himself bound to deny, whatsoever had not, as he speaks in more than one place, Ὀυδένα λόγον ἰατρικὸν: *a probable reason to satisfie a rational man.* Yet the same man afterwards, upon further experience, and better consideration, fearing also ( probably ) the reproach and derision of men, for his obstinate *incredulity*, did nobly recant, and acknowledge his error, as we shall shew afterwards.

BUT to go on as we began: we read besides, that at the *Olympick* games, the greatest and most solemn conflux of mankind, that hath been known, either before or since; and the records whereof, were accounted most authentick; a certain *Milesian* of known valour or ability, being to wrestle with an *Ephesian*, he could do nothing, because the *Ephesian* had about him, Ἐφέσια γράμματα, that is, certain Spells or Charms, so called, *The Ephesian letters*: which being suspected, and taken from him, he was thrown by his adversary, no less than thirty times. So *Eustathius* upon the 19. *Odiffie.* *Suidas* hath the same relation; but there, the Text both, and the Translation had need to be corrected: a little will do it, ( τεσσαρκοντάκις for τεσσάκοντα ) that sense may be made of it. That there be, even now, *Spells* and *Charms*, when God is pleased to give way, ( which in all things, wrought by the Devil, must always be understood ) to make men *invulnerable*, no man, I think, upon the attestation of so many creditable witnesses, can rationally doubt. Learned *Sennertus*, in his book *De vulneribus*, begins his 24. Chapter thus; *Cum nihil hodie*, &c. that is, *Whereas there is nothing more ordinary, now adays, among Souldiers, than by certain Pentacula, and Seals, and Characters, to fence themselves, and to make them-*

## Of Credulity and Incredulity,

*selves inviolable against all kind of arms*, and *musquet-bullets*, &c. and so far was he from suspecting, that any body that knew any thing of the world, would make a question of the truth of it, that omitting that disquisition, as needless and ridiculous, he presently falls upon that, whereof only he thought question could be made; *An liceat Christiano*, &c. *Whether it be lawful for a Christian by certain Amulets, or Seals, fastned to the body, or the like, to make himself inviolable to any kind of arms.* Some take upon them to limit, how far the *Devils* power, in point of reason, may extend in this kind; as I remember a learned man doth, who hath written the life of *Monsieur de la Nove*, a *French* Gentleman of great fame. So doth *Sennertus* too : he tells of many particular cases, for which no reason can be given, but experience; wherein, and whereby the power of those Spells is eluded or frustrated. But I think the truest limitation, is, *so far as God will permit, or give leave*. For I doubt not, but the Devil can do much more, as he is a Spirit, by his own skill and power, than to preserve a single man, even from Canon-shot. It is much more strange, which yet I believe true, that whole Armies of men, ( God then, not without good cause certainly, permitting ) have been defeated by his power, as by several Historians and others, the relation whereof, because obvious enough, I shall here omit, is averred : and some others made victorious as strangely : in all which things, though set on work by men also, I look upon him, but as Gods executioner; without whose leave and permission, whatever his power be, by his nature, he cannot hurt the meanest man. They that desire to be further satisfied in this particular, may read *Delrio*, the Jesuite, if they please; in his *Magical Disquisitions*. Yet I will not say, that I believe every thing, that he doth propose as true : it may be his faith, doth in some
things

things extend much further than mine: but I would have the quality of his witnesses well considered; and if they will not (I think they do) avail to a certainty in this point; there be others that may be consulted, whom no man, that I know, hath gone about to contradict, or challenged of falshood, except it be in the way of those *incredulous wife men*, of whom *Seneca* speaketh, (*Mendacium est: fabula est*) *it is a lye: it is a lye. I will not believe it.* But I name him before any other, because every where to be had.

I HAVE already gone further than I needed, to make good my censure of *Philostratus*, or *Damis*, in *Philostratus*, his false and deceitful judgment, concerning the power of *Magick*, to offend, or to defend, in several cases, which hath occasioned us, all this discourse. The Reader I hope will acknowledge himself satisfied, that he was in the wrong, if he did think so, really.

NOW as I have hitherto argued against *Incredulity*, in this particular; so will I also give some examples of too much *Credulity*, in the same business, as I conceive, and why I think so. A learned man that hath written, *De Idololatria Magica*; *Photius*, saith he, *in Olympiodoro narrat.* No, not so, but, *Olympiodorus, in Photio*: it is not *Photius*, that is the Author of the tale; he saith nothing of it; but *Olympiodorus*, barely; whose words about that, and divers other things, he doth, as out of other Authors, only transcribe. Well, what saith *Olympiodorus*? That in *Rhegium*, over against *Sicily*, there was a *Magick*-Statue, or a Statue made by Art-*Magick*, to avert the burnings of Mount *Ætna* in *Sicily*, and to keep the Islands from the invasion of barbarous Nations: which Statue being broken by one *Æsculapius*, Governor of it under *Constantius*, the Emperor; the Island was grievously annoyed by both; those *burnings*,

and

and the *Barbares*. As much is said by the same Author, of three other Statues, to secure the Empire from the eruption of the *Barbares*. That the said learned man gave some credit to this, as that such Statues were made, and that they were effectual to that end, may be gathered by his words. *Postea Diabolus, &c.* But I will not much stand upon that: it may be he did not intend it. Before I pass my judgment, concerning the thing, as to the efficacy of such Statues: I must acknowledge, that I easily grant, that such Statues made by *Art Magick,* and to such ends, have been anciently. For besides what is here related by *Olympiodorus*; *Gregorius Turonensis*, Bishop of the same Town, in his History, *lib.* 8. *Cap.* 33. where he describes a general conflagration of the City of *Paris*, (but not comparable to that of the City of *London*, of fresh and horrible memory) which happened in his time; at the end of that Chapter, he hath these words, *Aiebant hanc urbem consecratam fuisse antiquitus*, &c. that is, *It was reported, that this Town had formerly been consecrated, that no fire should prevail in it, no serpent, no glis,* (a Dormouse properly; but I take it here for a Rat; I have some reason for it; but I will not stand upon it) *should be seen*. *But now lately, when a Vault belonging to the Bridge, was cleansed, and the sullage, that filled it was carried away; a brass Serpent, and a brass Rat were found in it: which being taken away, both Serpents and Rats, without number, have appeared; neither hath it been free from the violence of fire.* So he besides: *Leo Affricanus* in his Ninth book, of the description of *Africa*, where he treats of the River *Nilus*; out of ancient writers of those parts, doth relate, that in such a year of the *Hegira*, such and such being Governours; there was in the rubbish of an *Ægyptian* Temple, found a Statue of Lead, of the bigness (and form, I suppose) of a *Crocodile*, graven with *Hieroglyphick*

*phick* letters, and by certain conſtellations contrived againſt Crocodiles, which being broken in pieces by command of the Governour, Crocodiles began to lay wait for men. But again: the Author of the Geography, commonly known by the name of *Geographia Nubienſis*; in high credit with all men, that are ſtudious of the *Arabick*-tongue, in his fifth part of the third *Climat*, (for ſo he doth divide his book) *Of the Country Hems*, ſaith he, *the Metropolitan Town is Hems*, (whether *Emiſſa* or *Hemeſa*, of the Ancients, I am not now at leiſure to conſider) *Which by witchcraft and inchantment is ſo fenced, that no Serpents, or Scorpions can have entrance, and in caſe any be brought to the Gates, they die preſently*. Then he tells us of a *horſe-mans Statue*, ſet upon a *high* arch in the middle of the Town, turning every way according to the wind: and of the picture of a *Scorpion*, in one of the ſtones of the arch: to which painted, or carved Scorpion, if any man, bitten by a *Scorpion* or *Serpent*, apply dirt or morter, and afterwards, that dirt or morter, to his wound or bitten place; he is preſently cured. But this is beyond my ſcope, as well as my belief. But of the horſe-mans Statue, or picture of Scorpion, in the wall; being ſo confirmed by other parallel ſtories, I think it may be believed. Had we any certainty of the Ancient *Palladium* of *Troy*, I ſhould have begun there. But out of all queſtion, we may conclude, that ſuch Magical Statues have been found in more than one place: and not improbable, that the *Devil*, as he is a great emulator of Gods works, but not his holineſs, might have a reſpect to the *brazen-Serpent*, ſet up in the wilderneſs by Gods appointment. But of the efficacy of thoſe Statues, according to relations, we may very well make a queſtion: neither will Hiſtory make good, if well examined, all that is written of them. Neither is it probable, that the *Devil*, who can do nothing to annoy

annoy or protect men, without permission, can warrant any such things, as are reported, for the time to come, except he could beforehand by some *natural* or *supernatural* observations of his own (as in many prophesies of his, concerning things to come) find out the mind, or counsel of God in those particulars; or that God, or some good Angels subordinate to God, and privy to his will and determination in those things, had revealed it unto him; neither of which is very likely. And that which makes it more unlikely, is, that even those, who to become invulnerable, have had recourse to the Devil, or his agents, and have enjoyed the benefit of their purchase for some time, even to admiration; yet have found themselves, on a sudden destitute of it, to their great astonishment, and have miserably perished in their confidence, as is observed by more than one, who have written of that subject. How then should he be able to warrant any Town or City, and make his promise good for many ages?

WHAT I intended, to wit, a full consideration, or refutation rather of *Philostratus* his assertion, is, I hope, sufficiently performed.

OUR next instance shall be from *Josephus*, the *Jewish* Historian, highly esteemed, both by *Romans* and *Grecians*, and by one that could judge of good books, as well as any man of this, or former ages, stiled, *Diligentissimus, & φιλαληθέστατος omnium Scriptorum: The most diligent and greatest lover of truth of all writers*; sacred always excepted, we must understand. This *Josephus* in his Eight book of *Jewish* Antiquities, and second Chapter, where he treats of *Solomon's* wisdom, and exquisite knowledge of Nature; following the tradition of the *Jews* of those days, who because they were great *exorcists* themselves, and dealt much in *Spells* and *Charms* of all kinds, (so that from them the Heathens received divers,

*in things* NATURAL. 77

divers, extant in their books to this day) to countenance their unlawful practices, did perswade men, that *Solomon* was the founder of what they falsly called, *Natural Magick*: to magnifie this Art, and the power of it, *Iosephus* doth there produce a notable instance, which is this: How, that on a time, himself being present, one *Eleazer*, before *Vespasian*, and his *Sons* (or *Children*) and the chiefest Officers of the Army, did cast out *Devils* from several that were possest; and to satisfie the company, there was no jugling in the business, commanded the *Devils*, as they went out, to do somewhat, which might witness the presence of a *supernatural* power. To bring this to pass, this dispossession I mean, besides words, there was some other mystical action: that was, the applying of a certain ring to the nose of the possessed, under the seal of which ring, a piece of root was inclosed, which was believed (so reported, at least) to be of singular efficacy to drive out Devils. The name of the root is not there set down by *Iosephus*; but in another book, *De bello Iudaico*, lib. 7. Cap. 23. he doth name it, *Baaras*, and withal doth tell strange things of it, what danger it is, to pull it out of the Earth, except such and such ceremonies and cautions, which I forbear here, be used. Now that in all this *Iosephus*, though his report, to some may seem, both ridiculous and *incredible*, and is, I know, by some rejected as meerly fabulous, which made me pitch upon it the rather; yet that in all this, he doth deal *bona fide*, truly and sincerely: as I believe my self, so I hope to give good and convincing reasons, why others also, who pretend to reason, as the trial of truth, should believe. First, that such a thing was really done before

*Vespasian*,

*Vespasian*, the *Roman* Emperor, as he relates it; they that know that *Josephus* was a man as nobly born; so of great credit at the Court, and in great favour with *Vespasian* himself, how can they rationally doubt? He must be supposed more than a mad man, that durst write such a forged story, and attest persons of that quality for the truth; had it been a thing of his own devising, nay had he lyed in any circumstance of it. As for that he writes of that *root* or herb, that it hath such properties, such vertues, how to be pull'd out of the earth, and where to be found, &c. whether true or no, must not be laid upon his account, as I conceive, because in that, trusting the relation of men, whom he took to be real honest men in their profession, and to work by natural means, himself professing no skill or insight in that art; it is enough that in all he saith of it, there is nothing, but what was generally believed, or at least reported and famed, not among the *Jews* only, but *Grecians* also, and others that were *Gentiles*. The name of the herb, he saith, was *Baaras*: and what is that, (from באר or בהר: I need not tell them, that have any skill in the tongue) but ἀγλαόφωτις in Greek: which herb is acknowledged by all, or most that write of herbs. *Josephus* saith of it, it will with some adjurations, expel *Devils*: *Pliny* saith, or *Democritus* rather, in *Pliny* it is a Magical herb, which *Negromancers* or *Magicians* use to raise *the Gods*: that is, in the phrase of our times, *Spirits*. *Josephus* saith, there is great danger in the pulling up of it. One way he doth mention, is, by uncovering the root so far, that it may have but little hold in the ground, and then tying a dog to it, so that the dog may easily draw it out with him, when he thinks to follow his Master going away, as he followed him thither. But if the report be true, the dog comes short of his reckoning, or rather doth much more than what he thinks he
doth.

doth. For when he thinks to follow him, he doth his Master a better service; he dieth for him, who otherwise (if the report be true, as before) could not have out-lived the boldness of his attempt. A strange story, but not of *Josephus*'s contriving, nor by *Josephus* only believed. The very same, as to the substance, is recorded by *Ælianus* also: *De Histor. animal. lib.* 14. *cap.* 27. more fully, and, as his manner is, with studied elegancy. He doth also give it another name, taken from this very ceremony, or action, κυνόσπαςος, that is, *dog-drawn*. The Latin interpreter doth somewhat contract the relation, for which I do not, seeing he hath all the substance, much blame him, it being almost impossible to express all in another tongue without an unpleasing redundancy, except the sweetness (next unto sweet musick, to curious ears) of the *collocution* (a grand mystery of the so much admired *Sophisters* or *Orators* of those times, their Rhetorick, as elsewhere I have declared at large) could have been exhibited also. But again, *Josephus* saith, the herb grew in *Judea*: *Democritus*, in *Pliny* saith, in *Arabia*: but this is easily reconciled, and is done very fully, by learned men: and had *Democritus* said in *Ægypt* or *Ethiopia*, there is enough besides, to satisfie any man, that *Baaras* was a known herb, to those effects by him mentioned, among men of that profession, whom *Josephus*, (a learned pious man, but herein too *credulous*, but not the first or only pious and learned, that hath been deceived in such) accounted holy religious men, but in very truth, no better, (as how many at this day) than cheaters, and impostors, to what they pretended; by some others, of those times, who had considered of it better than *Josephus*, rightly called, *præstigiatores* and *magi*. Now *Josephus* so far acquitted, that he had no intention to deceive, but was deceived himself by others; if any will be so curious, as
to

*Of Credulity and Incredulity,*

to know what truth there is, or then was, for the reports concerning that herb; that there is such an herb, which for some kind of *resplendency*, may be called *Aglaophotis*, is by all *Botanicks*, or *Herbarists* I have seen, acknowledged. And if it be a kind of *Peony*, as is averred by divers, which against the falling-sickness is known to be of excellent vertue, it is less to be wondred, that for this very reason, it was first supposed to be of some vertue against *Devils* and *Dæmons*, the nature of this disease being somewhat *extraordinary*, and by some formerly supposed to proceed from some extraordinary cause; for which reason it was also called, ἱερὰ ῥίζα, or, *morbus sacer*, *the sacred disease*; and not only supposed to proceed, but also certainly known sometimes to be accompanied with *extraordinary supernatural* effects; yea plainly, *Diabolical*: whereof I have given some instances in my Treatise of *Enthusiasm*. So far the mistake then might be tolerable: but for the rest, the danger of plucking it out of the ground with the root, and the means used to prevent it, this by the experience of best *Herbarists* of these days, being found false, and fictitious; we must look upon it, as the meer invention of Magicians and Impostors to inhance the credit of their Drugs, and to serve the Devil by the increase of superstition; whereof examples are so obvious ( in great Towns, as *London* especially ) as no man needs to wonder at it.

BUT yet let us see, what may be said, even for that, not altogether improbable perchance; so they that are not so much experienced, will the better know by this example, how to examine the truth of things, and to distinguish between *certainty*, and *probability*, or *possibility*. Do not we to this day find things, which they call *Empirica* and *Specifica*, in the writings of very sober Physicians, that may seem as strange? As for example,

The

The rindes of the root of *Elder*, pull'd off from the upper part, shall purge by vomit: from the lower, by stools. The brain of a Ram, with some other ingredients, a good medicine against madness; provided that the Ram be a *virgin Ram* (*virginity*, an ordinary caution, in diabolical exploits, to blind the world, as afterwards shall be observed) and that his head be cut off at one blow. I find this in *Sennertus*: the other in *Anatomia Sambuci*, printed in *London*: where the Author thinks, but doth not affirm, that this happily may be ascribed to some *Idiosyncracy*, either of the body of the patient, or of the humor, that causeth the disease; or perchance, to the strength of imagination. And even *Galen*, such an hater of all that resented of any superstition, and rigid exacter of reason; he recanted afterwards, we shall shew; but even whilest he was so, in his Tenth book, *De compositione Pharmacorum*, where among others, he doth set down a remedy against the stone in the bladder; *This remedy*, saith he, must be prepared with a kind of *religious observation: For the ingredients must be beaten, or bruised in a wooden-mortar with a wooden-pestle; and he that beats, must not have any Iron about him, either in his fingers, or shooes*. And this he calls a *mystery*, which he saith he learned from a Rustick. But should I here take notice of those strange things, and wonderful effects of herbs, which no less a man than *Matthiolus* tells of, in his *Dedicatory Epistle* to his *Herbal* for truth; what hath been written of the herb *Baaras*, would be acknowledged very *credible*, in comparison, I dare say. Yet I believe our modern *Herbarists*, that experience doth teach them the contrary. Well, but doth it follow necessarily, that if it be not found so, now: therefore it was never so? Yes, if we stick to the true reall nature, or natural effects of the Herb.

G          But

But who knows, but that the Devil might abuse the Magicians of those days, in that kind, making them believe, that those strange effects (for of that I make no question) did proceed from the natural properties of the very *herb*, thus and thus observed; which doth not hold at this day; as I dare say there be many superstitions about Herbs and Plants, now in force among men of that wicked profession, which were not known in former times. There is nothing in all this, but is very *possible*; and if I said *probable*, it might be justified. But considering how many things in this kind, are to be found in the books of old Magicians, as *Democritus*, and others, which upon trial, even in those days, were found false; and because we would not multiply wonders, where there is no necessity, that when there is, as we conceive, we may speak with more authority, and be believed; I shall rather stick to my former judgment, that it was but a fiction of the *Magicians* of those days, to add credit and reverence to their art.

BUT now I turn to the men of these times; the *wits*, as they call themselves, and by some others, for want of real wit, and good learning, are so *called*; who because they believe nothing but what is palpable and visible, deny therefore *Spirits* and all *supernatural* effects; and consequently the truth of all relations, wherein *supernatural* causes are ingaged; what will these men say, to this of *Josephus*? That he did invent what he recordeth to have been done, before such witnesses? What reason can they give, for such a senseless supposition? Or that the eyes of so many were deceived, who thought they saw, what was not truly and really to be seen? But then how deceived; by what means, *natural* or *supernatural*? It poseth me to think what they can pretend, why we should not *believe*. Yet I will suppose that somewhat they will say: if nothing else, yet this, that it is an old
story

story, and therefore they are not bound to believe it. A worthy answer for men that pretend to *reason*. But I will see, if I can fit them with a later, to the same purpose, and as irrefragable, as I account that old.

*ANDREAS Laurentius*, a late and learned Physician, well known to the world by his writings, in his book *De Strumis*, or *Kings Evil*, printed in *Paris*, *Anno Dom.* 1609, and dedicated to *Henry* the Fourth, of late Glorious memory; in his first book, ninth Chap. where he treateth of the power of the *Devil*, to cause, or to heal diseases, at large; he hath there this story: *The most Christian King*, saith he, (the very same to whom the book is dedicated) *did see a Rustick* (or Country Clown) *Who by the incense, or smoak of a certain herb, in a moment, as it were, would cure all that were sick of the Kings Evil. He made them vomit, so that they did cast much pituitous stuff, and with it certain little creatures, which he said* were the (*germina*) *buddings* (or *seminaries* perchance) *of the disease. This I have heard more than once from the Kings own mouth, When he did enquire the reason from me. Besides the King, Monsieur de Lominie,* one of the Kings Privy Council: *Monsieur de Frontenae: Francis Martell, chief Chyrurgion to the King, and divers others of the Kings bed-Chamber, did see the same. I always was of opinion, that it was done by the Devil. Neither was I deceived in it: for this Rustick some few days after vanished, and from that time, though by his friends, and those of his house, sought far and near, was never heard of.* So he. Good, and unquestionable witnesses I hope, the King, and so many others of his Court, men of credit, and of all men (the *Chyrurgion*, at least) best able to judge.

LET this be compared with *Josephus* his relation: which shall we say is the strangest? This I think. What then shall we say, is there any such thing in the world, as Truth: or such a thing in the Heavens Firmament, as a *Sun*? If so, then let us account, though *strange*, yet not *prodigious* those things, which are known so often to happen: but those men not so *strange*, as *prodigious*, who what all men see, would make us believe they do not see, or though they see, yet will not believe.

BUT now we are upon it I will run through some other instances: I shall not be long upon them; but they shall be chosen instances, that nothing may be left for the cure of those men (a hard cure I must confess) who love their disease, nay are proud of it, for the most part, as knowing they owe the reputation they have (among the vulgar) of *wise men*, unto it, more than they do, or have cause to do, unto any thing else. I speak this of the most. If any truly discreet and wise, and learned I must add, be of the same opinion too, we must needs look upon it, either as a judgment, or some natural distemper of the brain; for which I have the warrant of a learned Physician before spoken of, and one of their own sect in part; who though he did not believe *Devils*, because he did not see them; yet what he saw, and had often seen, or had been often seen by many others, whom he believed, (what we call *supernatural* operations) he pronounceth them *mad*, that did not believe. It may be the number of instances and testimonies of several men, of several nations, in cases or diseases of a several nature, may do what any one single or double evidence, though never so clear, could not.

*ANTONIUS Benevenius*, what I have seen of him is but very little in bulk, but very considerable; and I see he is in good credit with all Physicians, for he is often cited by them with good respect. Nay, if I be not mistaken in *Sennertus*, lib. 1. Part. II. cap. 31. where he treats of the *Epilepsie*, he hath been set out with the *Scholia*'s of learned *Dodoneus*, which must be no small honour

## in things NATURAL.

nour unto his book. I have been beholding to it elsewhere: and therefore shall give him here the first place. Well, in that little book of his, *De abditis nonnullis ac mirandis*, &c. in the 26. Chapter he hath this story. A Souldier had an arrow shot through the left part of his breast, so that the iron of it stuck to the very bone of his right shoulder. Great endeavours were used to get it out, but to no purpose. *Benevenius* doth shew, that it was not feasible without present death. The man seeing himself forsaken by Physicians and Chyrurgions, sends for a noted *Ariolus*, or *Conjurer*: who setting but his two fingers upon the wound, with some *Charms* he used, commanded the iron to come out, which presently without any pain of the patient, came forth, and the man was presently healed. *Vidimus*, he saith: *we did see it*: but I do not approve of his censure at the end, that two were *damned* (the Patient and the Conjurer) for this Act. It was possible, the Patient was not so well instructed, how unlawful it was to seek to the *Devil* for help; how much better for a Christian, though he suffer never so much, whereby he is made so much the more *conformable* to Christ his Saviour, to die. Or perchance not sufficiently instructed, that such a cure could not be wrought by such means, without the *Devil*. There be strange things written of the herb *D. Ctamnus*, which if he had read, or were told, he might think the man had the right way to use it, which all men perchance have not; nay, we need no *perchance*, if all that I have read of it, both in ancient and late Authors, be true. Besides, God might be so merciful unto him, that he might heartily and with many tears repent of what he had done in the extremity of his pain. The *Conjurer* also, who

can

can absolutely say, that he never repented? Not in the ordinary way of the world only, with a simple *Lord have mercy upon me*, when he was at the last: but time enough to make his repentance real, and sincere? Though I must needs say, I think it is very seldom, that God doth grant true repentance unto such, who wilfully and deliberately have put themselves into the hands of the *Devil*, and either *directly* ( as many do ) or *tacitly*, which must be supposed, have abjured any right, or pretention to Gods mercy.

MY next instance shall be out of *Zacutus Lusitanus his Praxis Medicinæ admiranda*; a book of great credit with all I have met with, but those who will admit of nothing for truth, ( an effect of their ignorance many times more than *incredulity* ) but what their little reading, and scanty experience hath commended unto them for truth. Which, I doubt, is the case of not a few in these days; who to avoid labour, and to cover their ignorance, would gladly reduce all medicine to some few, whether true or pretended, and by most believed true, revelations of these later times. *Galen* and *Hippocrates*, ( I have heard it my self ) what should they do with them? The course of Physick is now altered, by late discoveries: there is no more need of them. Ignorant wretches, and unhappy they, that fall into such hands. But I have done. *Zacutus* his relation is this: A young Gentleman, of a comely shape, and of excellent parts, was so passionately in love with a fair maid, of a noble parentage, about eighteen years old; that he had no rest, neither night nor day, very near unto distraction. But when by reason of the inequality of their birth, he found nothing at her hands, but contempt and scorn; enraged, he applies himself to *Witches* for revenge. They according to art, make a picture or image rather, of her, in wax, which when pricked, with some Charms, and

and imprecations; at the same time the party was seised with such horrible torments in all parts of her body, that she thought her self pierced, or run through with some sharp weapon. It was not long before divers Physicians (the best that could be had, we may presume) were sent for, who at first thought those horrible accidents must proceed from some distemper of the womb. But after they had observed, that all remedies they had applied made her worse, rather than better, they absolutely pronounced her disease, to be no *natural* disease, and that she was either actually possest by some evil Spirit, or infested and infected by some of their creatures. In which judgment, see God would have it to prevent the contradiction of some confidents, which in all places are to be found; when she began to cast out of her body lumps of hair, (*tribulorum fasciculum*, I know what it may signifie besides, but I would not make the matter more strange than it must needs) others of thistles, needles; then a black lump in the form of an egge, out of which, when dissected, came flying Ants, which did cause such a noisom stink, that no body was able to abide the room: they were much confirmed. But at last, reduced to great extremity, and at the point of death, with much difficulty, being in a *syncope*, she vomited a certain creature, of the bigness of an ordinary fist, of a black colour, long tail, hairy all the body over, like a mouse; which being fallen to the ground, did with great swiftness run to and fro the room, and then died. The Parents astonished with this horrible case, and seeing their child forsaken by Physicians, they have recourse to all the *Witches*, *Sorcerers* and *Magicians* the Town or Country yielded. Among all these, one was found, who did with no small confidence, upon condition of a good reward, undertake to make her well, if they sent for him, when she was in a fit. It was agreed: being in a fierce fit, he is called: who, (*Zacutus* then present, he faith of himself) after he had applied a very white paper to her pole, in which two letters only (T. M.) were written, and an Asses hoof half burned, and chanted to her ears some words, (*Zacutus* did not hear them it seems) she was presently free from all evil, and so continued for the time to come. *Morbi ergo trans naturam*, &c. that is, *Difeafes therefore befides nature, as after* Fernelius, Carrerius *upon* Galen *de locis aff. difp.* 37. *doth vigorously argue must be cured by remedies that are not natural.* So *Zacutus* concludes, as he did begin, making that, by his title, the very drift and purpose of his narration. I hope he did mean well, but with, he had spoken more warily. For first, were such cures never so certain and ordinary, yet are they impious, and unlawful; as not *Divines* only, the most and best approved, but also learned *Phyficians* well determine and conclude. True it is, there is a story of a *Difperfation* granted by Pope *Nicolaus* the *V.* to a Bifhop very dear unto him, which may seem to cross what we say, if Popes might not erre, and do wickedly, as well as other men. For the Bifhop having been bewitched unto a grievous disease, of which he could not after many endeavours be cured by any natural means; a *Witch* offered her self, and upon condition she might be allowed to *bewitch* her, that had *bewitched* the Bifhop unto death, (which she said was in her power to do) undertook to cure him. Whereupon the Pope being sued unto for a *Difpenfation*, he granted it, and the bufinefs was done, the first *Witch* died, and the Bifhop was restored. *Sprengerus* as I take it, who was an *Inquifitor* for all such bufineffes at *Rome*, was the first that made it publickly known. Scarce any body that writes of this subject of *Witches*, and their power, but takes notice of it from him. And as yet, I have not found it contradicted by any,

any, that I can remember. Neither do I remember that *Delrio*, in that bulky book of his *Difquifitions*, takes notice of it any where; which we may be sure he would not have omitted, to vindicate the Pope, had he known how to excuse it with a good conscience, or how to censure it without offence. But the truth is, though he take no direct notice, and durst not apparently justifie it, yet that it made him write more favourably of such cases, than otherwise he would have done; for which he is justly blamed, and as solidly refuted by learned *Sennertus. lib.* 6. *p.* 9. *cap.* 8. I cannot but suspect. Yet as to this particular case, what he thought of it, he doth, without any particular mention, tell us freely enough, when he doth limit his *licenfe* or *difpenfation* ( which he doth allow ) with this *provifo*, that if help be required, or admitted from such; yet of no other than the very *Witch* or party, that hath done the mischief. For which, though he gives a very good reason, yet he concludes but timorously, *Quare raro admodum*, &c. *It muft be therefore but very feldom, if ever, lawful, to require the help of another Sorcerer,* [ *or Sorcerers* ] *but only from him* [ *or her* ] *who is the actor of the mifchief.* But *feldom,* if *ever.* Now here, in the Bishops case, it was required by the Bishop, and indulged by the Pope, that a *Witch*, by bewitching her to death, that had done the mischief, might do the cure. Was not this example, think we, in the mind of *Delrio*, when he so wrote; and was not he put to it shrewdly between fear on the one side, and conscience on the other? But how more they, between such manifest *evidences* on the one side, and an obstinate and resolved *incredulity* on the other, who after all this will tell us, dare tell us, there is no such thing, as *Witches* or *Sorcerers* in the world? Well, it was so it seems in this particular: the *Witch* that had done the hurt must perish, or the Bishop

Bishop could not be cured: but left the Reader should mistake, that it is always so, he may learn by another instance.

*LEONARD Vair* in his book of *Charms*, before mentioned, hath a story of a woman, which though she passionately loved her husband, yet when he came to approach her as her husband, she was affrighted with such horrid phancies and apparitions; and if much urged, suffered in her body such strange symptoms or accidents, that she became an object of no less horror, than pity, to all that saw and heard her. Her husband was one, that this *Leonard* ( no mean man, for his worldly estate and credit in the world ) had a great affection for: and was not wanting to him, in the best advice, or assistance he could give him. But all to no purpose. They continued in this forced kind of *continence*, from the first of their legal matrimony, three whole years: at the end of which, the *Witch* that had out of meer envy and malice bewitched the woman to this unusual kind of affliction; whether procured, or of her own accord I know not, because my Author doth not tell me, came to the house, absolved her; and from that time they lovingly and comfortably enjoyed one another. My Author doth not say *he saw it*, the woman, I mean, in her fits: neither was it fit he should be admitted to see; which himself, I dare say, ( a pious honest man, his book speaks him ) would have refused, had he been desired. But how every thing did pass, he did not want good information, we find by the account he doth give us, and the circumstances of fact, as he doth relate them, fitter to be read in him, than related by me, in the judgment of any indifferent Reader, may amount to a *Vidimus*. It will be found in his third book of the said Treatise, of my *French* Translation, Page 502, &c.

BUT secondly, *curantur*, *Zacutus* saith, as if it were
very

very certainly feafible, at any time, which is moſt falſe; and though his words ſeem to imply ſo much, yet I hope and believe it was not his meaning. For though God, for ſome reaſons permit ſuch things ſome times; and one reaſon certainly is, that men generally ſo inclinable to *Atheiſm*, might certainly know, if not wilfully blind, that there is ſomewhat beſides fleſh and bloud, and what may be ſeen with bodily eyes (that is, ordinary nature) to be thought on; yet I am very confident, that not one in a hundred, nor a thouſand perchance, that ſeek to *Devils* and *Witches*, doth ſpeed, or obtain what he doth deſire; not becauſe the *Devil* doth want power, or will, but becauſe God doth not permit. Nay, many certainly, when they have done what they can or could, to be acquainted with *Devils*, yet have miſſed of their deſires, which might be a juſt judgment of God, ſo to harden them the more in their *Atheiſm*, and other wickedneſs; or an act of his providence perchance, to prevent the miſchief that they would do, had they ſuch an aſſiſtant. Whereof we have a notable example in that monſter, *Nero*, who as *Pliny* relateth, having with care and great longing, applied himſelf to the beſt Magicians of his time; yet God would not permit (*Pliny* was not ſo well perſwaded of the gods of his time, as to ſay ſo) but would not, I ſay, permit, that they could do any thing before him, for the credit of their profeſſion; whereby *Nero* grew very confident, and upon that very ground, many were then, and have been ſince, that there is no ſuch thing as *Magick*; and that all that profeſſed it, were but cheaters, and impoſtors. We might alſo ſay ſomewhat of *Julian* the *Apoſtate*, one of the greateſt followers of *Magicians*, when *Magick* and *Necromancy* was in higheſt requeſt, that ever was; as all writers, Chriſtians, and others acknowledge. Yet for all that, how long he reigned, and how he died, we know. But yet

yet more particularly, we have heard of one Bishop, who sped (as to this world, wretched man) in the hands, or by the hands of a Witch: But *Bodinus* will tell us of another Bishop, whom he names, with all his titles and dignities; and he saith he was present with one *Faber*, a learned Physician: when one of that profession did take upon him to cure him of a Quartan Ague; which neverthelefs, for all his confidence, he could not do. But this is but one for another, becaufe it offered it felf fo opportunely: but I believe, as I faid before, that many more, without number, miscarry, either seeking to no purpose, or when they have found whom to treat with, finding themselves cheated and frustrated.

BUT to return to the relation it felf, wherein I would leave nothing disputable; I observe in it an *Image* or *picture* of the party to be tormented, made of wax. I observe it, becaufe I know fome, who question not the power of *Devils* or *Witches*; yet in this particular are not satisfied, how fuch a thing can be. For there is *no relation or sympathy in nature*, (faith one, who hath written not many years ago) *between a man and his effigies, that upon the pricking of the one, the other should grow sick*. It is upon another occasion that he speaks it; but his exception reacheth this example equally. A wonder to me, he should fo argue, who in many things hath very well confuted the *incredulity* of others, though in fome things too credulous himself. If we muft believe nothing but what we can reduce to *natural*, or, to fpeak more properly (for I my felf believe the Devil doth very little, but by *nature*, though to us unknown) *manifest* caufes, he doth overthrow his own grounds, and leaves us but very little of magical operations to believe. But of all men, *Cardan* had leaft reafon to except againft this kind of *Magick*, as ridiculous or *incredible*, who himself is fo full of *incredible* ftories in that kind, upon his own

credit

credit alone, that they had need to be of very easie belief, that believe him; especially when they know (whereof more afterwards) what manner of man he was. But I dare say, that from *Plato*'s time, who among other appurtenances of *Magick* doth mention these, κἠεπα μμμήμετα that is, as *Ovid* doth call them, *Simulachra cerea*, or as *Horace, cereas imagines*, (who also in another place more particularly describes them) there is not any particular rite, belonging to that art, more fully attested by Histories of all ages, than that is. Besides, who doth not know, that it is the Devils fashion (we shall meet with it afterwards again) to amuse his servants and vassals with many rites and ceremonies, which have certainly no ground *in nature, no relation or sympathy* to the thing, as for other reasons, so to make them believe, they have a great hand in the production of such and such effects; when, God knows, many times all that they do, though taught and instructed by him, is nothing at all to the purpose, and he in very deed is the only agent, by means, which he doth give them no account of. *Bodinus* in his Preface to his *Dæmonology*, relateth, that three waxen-*Images*, whereof one of Queen *Elizabeths*, of glorious memory, and two other, *Reginæ proximorum*, of two Courtiers, of greatest authority under the Queen, were found in the house of a Priest at *Islington*, a *Magician*, or so reputed; to take away their lives. This he doth repeat again in his second book, Chap. 8. but more particularly that it was in the year of the Lord 1578. and that *Legatus Angliæ*, and many *French*-men, did divulge it so; but withal, in both places he doth add, that the business was then under trial, & not yet perfectly known. I do not trust my memory: I know my age, and my infirmities. *Cambden*, I am sure, I have read and read again: but neither in him, nor in *Bishop Carletons thankful remembrancer*, do I remember any such thing. Others may perchance. Yet in the year 1576. I read in both, of some pictures, representing some, that would have kill'd that glorious Queen with a Motto, *Quorsum hæc, alio properantibus* ! which pictures were made by some of the conspiracy for their incouragement; but intercepted, and shewed, they say, to the Queen. Did the time agree, it is possible these pictures might be the ground of those mistaken, if mistaken, *waxen Images*, which I desire to be taught by others, who can give a better account.

MY next and last instance, in this kind, or matter of *Cures*, shall be out of the *Observationes Medicæ*, of *Henricus ab Heers*, Domestick Physician, not many years ago, to the *Elector of Colen*: a man of no small credit in those parts among the better sort, especially; but no friend to *Empericks*, among whom he reckoned *Van Helmont* as one of the chief. But I shall not interpose my judgment in that. Of *Heers*, I dare say in general, not to meddle with those things that properly belong unto a Physician to judge of; that he doth write as a sober, learned, and ( which is the Crown of all ) pious man. The subject of his eighth observation, is a very strange story of a young maid, that was bewitched by one of that wicked crew; which being found by the consequents of the presence, or absence of the *Witch*; she was laid hold of, arraigned and convicted ; and for that, and many other things of the same nature done by her, as she confessed, deservedly put to death. But with the *Witch*, ( as she her self at her death, had foretold it would be ) the pains of the miserable girle did not expire, but continued at least one year after. So long is expressed, how much longer I know not. *Heers* had the keeping of her a good part of the time. In the mean time, such strange things happened unto her, and such strange things came out of her, that her keeper did verily believe, and did endeavour to perswade divers others,

who

who were admitted daily spectators, (Scholars and Philosophers, or Naturalists, among the rest) that not the maid really in her body, did suffer those things that did appear unto them, but that their *fascinated* eyes (as it doth happen sometimes) did falsly represent unto them things which had no real being. But did not long continue in that opinion, being convicted by manifest experience, as he doth relate, to the contrary. The particulars are so many, that I must desire the Reader, if so curious, to take them from the Author himself: who in the relation is so put to it, to protest and to apologize for himself, that I doubt he had not been much acquainted with such cases, by his own experience, or read much in others, that write of them. *Quæ tunc viderim, audiverim,* &c. *What I then saw, heard, handled, because I know there be many that will not believe,* &c. *So God bless me, I shall write nothing, but what I have seen.* And again, *I do most conscienciously,* (or, *by what is most sacred*) *and all my domesticks are ready with me most solemnly to take their oaths,* &c. But yet of all particulars, the last of all seemeth to me most observable, and that is, a *natural receipt*, commended and approved by more than one before, men of credit and learning, which he will tell you, it was a long time, though he did use all possible endeavours, before he could procure to remove or cure such kind of witchcraft: but at last he got it, and it wrought the desired effect. For the maid, he saith, with the use of it, perfectly recovered. He doth make us believe, he hath given us the receipt clearly expressed, which to understand he was long puzled. If so, he hath deserved well of posterity, and deserves the thanks of the present age. However, it is very possible that what he found effectual, and some others before him, to such a purpose, may fail sometimes; which in things of such an abstruse nature, and which depend

of

of many circumſtances, it is no great wonder that it ſhould be ſo, when we ſee that ordinary Phyſick doth not always produce the ſame effects in all bodies; no, nor in the ſame ſometimes.

NOW of theſe receipts (this, upon this occaſion, to direct the *belief* of others, not much verſed in ſuch things) that pretend to ſome hidden, but *natural* vertue; therefore, as we had it before by ſome called, *natural*, κατ' ἐξοχὴν, or *eminently*: ſuch as keep to things meerly *natural*, as *herbs*, *roots*, *ſtones*, and the like; and are not accompanied with any words, or ſpells, pronounced or written; nor contain rites and ceremonies, as many are; I know not, if we allow, as all ſober men muſt, of *occult qualities*, I know not, I ſay, why we ſhould ſuſpect our ſelves, or make others ſcrupulous of ſuch: eſpecially when commended unto us by perſons, that are not at all ſuſpected, and that they are known to have been effectual, I will not ſay always, but ſometimes. I am not therefore of their opinion, I muſt confeſs, who confine us to thoſe things, for which a probable reaſon may be given, from the nature of the ingredients, or ſimple materials. But on the other ſide, where there is any juſt ground of ſuſpicion, it muſt be conſidered alſo, that it may be the craft of the Devil, or his inſtruments (*Witches* and *Magicians*) to aſcribe cures to things *natural*, as the means, to draw us on by degrees; when thoſe *natural* things ſignifie nothing at all really; and all the operation doth proceed from a more myſtical and concealed cauſe. But again, no queſtion, I think, is to be made, but that the Devil and thoſe that work by him, to inhance the credit of their art, or power, where they are allowed, diſguiſe ſometimes the operations of things meerly *natural*, of purpoſe, with ſuperſtitious rites and ceremonies, which of themſelves do nothing; though probably without them,

thoſe

*in things* NATURAL.

those natural things would not prove efficacious in the hands of them, that had them from such masters; nor yet in the hands of others perchance, through the ignorance or omission of some small circumstance, which in point of very nature, may much alter the case. However, in process of time, it is likely that such and such things came more generally, (as many of those *naturalia* or *specifica* are) to be known to be efficacious to such ends, which were at first as great secrets, prescribed by those masters, to them that did apply themselves to them. For otherwise, how they should come to the knowledge of men, (though some, by some casualty might, I confess) were hard to guess. Of this nature I suspect something may be found in *Trallianus*, than whom, I think, no man (those that profess such things under the *Devil* their Master excepted) hath more of these *Naturalia* or *Specifica*, for all kind of diseases. A strange thing, that a man in his profession, and the rational way, so learned and useful, as I have heard some eminent Physicians attest, besides what *Fererius* and others write, should give credit to so many tales, as he that reads must needs suspect, or rather absolutely pronounce of many, or most of them. Yet is he not content to set them down barely, to satisfie the curiosity of some, as he doth sometimes profess; but many times doth commend them, as approved by certain experience. Other ancient Physicians have, I know, some; but so many as *Trallianus* hath, and so confidently proposed, I think not any. Yet that he was a *Magician*, or did work at all by the *Devil*, of whose nature, and properties probably he knew little or nothing, I do not believe: but if his *naturalia* did prove so effectual, as he would make us believe, I must suspect nevertheless that the Devil had a hand in the operation of many of them. And should any man, acquainted with the mysteries of our faith & the Scriptures,

H so

go the same way, to advance the credit of such remedies. I should believe him either a *Magician*, or as bad as a *Magician*. But even among Christians, ( profest Christians at least ) as elsewhere, so in *England*, there be I doubt too many, that are not so tender-conscienced, as to stick at those things, or enquire after the lawfulness of the means, ( through ignorance, and want of good information, some, probably ) may they but compass their desire, either of profit, or of ease. A very good friend of mine, a serious man, and a good Preacher, told me this story, as very well known to him. A friend of his, he said, having been long troubled with an Ague, and probably tried many means without success, either went to, or lighted upon an Apothecary ( he named him, and the place of his abode ) who undertook to cure him, and to that end, delivered unto him six very small rouls of paper, rouled up very close, and bid him eat them. But he before he did execute what was injoyned, had so much curiosity or boldness, as to look into one of them first, then into another, and lastly, into a third; in all which, he found no more, than this written, *Do well*, or, *All is well* : so reported unto me, uncertainly ; but one of the two, certainly. Having satisfied his curiosity, and happily thinking there could be no *Magick* in this, he did what he was bid, that is, eat them. Whereupon he was surprised with great pains, the like whereof he had not felt before, for a while : but afterwards, was altogether free of his disease. Whereof having given an account to his friend, or Physician, what he had suffered first, and how free afterwards; Then I will warrant you, said he presently, you did open some of the papers ; and so many papers, as you opened, so many fits you had, I believe, of those pains, which his friend told him, was very true. At the same time, one that was present, but not so well known to me, told a

story,

story, that had much affinity, and I am much deceived, if I have not read somewhat printed that hath more: but one will serve our turn of this kind. For though I may perchance believe my friend, as he believed his, that it is true; yet to commend it to the Reader, as an absolute truth, I dare not, but upon a probable supposition of the truth, the opening of the papers, and what ensued excepted, I should not much wonder at the possibility of the thing, in point of nature. For a strong confidence, if the Apothecary did well act his part, or *imagination* may do much: it is a common observation, and examples every where are obvious.

NOW to proceed, I have given, I think, a sufficient account of the power of Magick in point of Cures, which by some, besides them that deny all *supernatural* operations, is not believed, but more, I believe, for want of diligent enquiring into the thing, then through meer *incredulity*. I have made choice of such instances, against which what rationally can be excepted, I cannot so much as imagine. But I will yet oppose *incredulity*, in another kind of *supernatural* operations, by instances as irrefragable as the former; and to them that think themselves concerned in the true sense of the Scriptures, more considerable. *Psalm* 58. verse 4. and 5. it is written: *They are like the deaf Adder, that stoppeth her ear: which will not hearken to the voice of the charmers, charming never so wisely.* Besides, *Ecclesiastes* the 10. verse the 11. *Surely the Serpent will bite without enchantment, and a babler is no better*: and again, *Jeremy* the 8. and the 17. verse: *For behold I will send Serpents, Cockatrices among you, which will not be charmed, and they shall bite you saith the Lord.* For the first place, it were no hard matter to interpret the words of the *Psalmist*, as spoken *proverbially*, without any consequence of a supposition of the truth, or reality of the thing, in matter

of fact. For many things are thus spoken *proverbially*, which they that speak have no intention to assert as true, or perchance know, or believe at last, to be most false. So *Cygnea cantio* : *Sirenum cantus*, and the like; for which perchance somewhat may be said, but not believed I am sure, by all that use the speech. Or if I compare a woman to a *Circe*, or a man to *Proteus*, or to aggravate any burden, say it is heavier than that of *Atlas* ; no rational man will hence conclude, that *I* believe that such have been really. But the two other places are more positive, and cannot so well be evaded. Yet *Valesius*, not to name others, a very learned *Spaniard*, in his books, *De Sacra Philosophia*, hath taken great pains to perswade men, that these things were spoken not *proverbially*, but mystically, and *allegorically*; and though He deny not *supernatural* operations by *Devils* and Spirits, whom he doth not at all doubt of: yet as to this particular, of *inchanting by magical Words*, he doth altogether deny, as possible, and whatsoever is alledged by any ancient or late writer to that purpose, he doth reject, as meerly fabulous. It seems by *Pliny*, that learned men of old, have been very much divided in their opinions about this matter ; insomuch, that he dares not take upon him to decide it, but leaves it free to every man to believe as they shall see cause : His words, ' elsewhere produced by me, in a proper place, very notable and applicable to many occasions, are, *Maxima quæstionis, & semper incerta est, valeantne aliquid verba & incantamenta carminum*; and again more particularly, *Varia circa hæc opinio, ex ingenio cujusque vel casu, mulceri alloquio foras: quippe ubi etiam Serpentes extrahi, cantu cogique in pœnas, verum falsumne sit vita non decreverit*. So he. We shall give light to those words, *cogique in pœnas*, afterwards : We have given the substance of the rest before. Now for my part, partly upon what I have seen
my

my felf, but much more upon the teftimony of others, who profefs to have feen it, and give a particular account of every circumftance; men all generally well accounted of; I do profefs that I know not what to believe in the world, which I cannot fay I have feen my felf; if I may not believe this, and commend unto others, for a truth. If *any thing*, *I* fay, which *I* cannot fay, *I have seen my self*: which would be a ftrange kind of *Incredulity*, and worthy to make a man unworthy of the fociety of men, of whom, even the beft, and moft creditable, he can entertain fo bafe an opinion: Neither can it, *I* think, enter into the heart of any man, to be fo miftruftful, but theirs only who are confcious unto themfelves of their own bafenefs, and make no other difference between *lying* and *speaking truth*, but as either beft fits their prefent occafion. As for *Valefius* his opinion, though a learned man, and for ought *I* know, pious and wife; yet it is no wonder to me, that any one man, though pious and learned, fhould fall into an opinion very *paradoxical*, and contrary to moft other mens belief: efpecially in a thing of this nature, which moft depends of experience. *Pliny* hath fufficiently warned us againft this fcandal, or exception, when in this very cafe, he tells us, that men are apt to believe and frame their opinions, according as they have found; or, by their particular experience: an excellent obfervation, and, as *I* faid before, applicable to many things of good moment, whereof *I* have given examples elfewhere. *I* am very confident, that it was not *Valefius* his luck, to meet with any man (much lefs two or three, or more) whom he accounted pious and judicious withal, that could fay, he had feen the thing done, with his own eyes, and in the prefence of many others: but more probable, that he had met with, or heard of fome cheaters and impoftors in this very cafe, whereof it were no very hard thing, *I* believe, to find inftances & examples:

and when a man hath once framed to himſelf an opinion, and pleaſed himſelf ( as we are too apt ) in his invention; it is no eaſie thing, ( ſuch is the infirmity, even of the beſt of men ) to get him out of it. But *Valeſius* hath been, and his reaſons fully anſwered and confuted by more it may be, but by one I know, very learned and judicious ; and with ſo much reſpect and moderation, as that *Valeſius*, I think himſelf, would have thought himſelf, had he read him, rather beholding to him, than otherwiſe, of whom alſo I ſhould not be afraid, or think it any diſcredit ( ſuch an opinion I have of his real worth and learning ) to borrow ſome inſtances, in ſuch a caſe, more to be reſolved by *inſtances*, that is *experience*, than any thing elſe. But that my curioſity hath been ſuch in this particular, that I think ( without pride or bragging ( be it ſpoken ) I could have furniſhed him. Which I may ſay alſo of what he hath written of, and upon *Joſephus* his place, before examined, very accurately and learnedly: let the Reader, upon comparing, judge, as he ſhall pleaſe. But I have not yet, though before I have, upon another occaſion, named the man: It is Doctor *Reynolds*, Royal Profeſſor in *Oxford*, when he lived: and the book his learned *Prælectiones*, before named alſo. A pity it is, as he doth complain himſelf more than once, that the condition of thoſe *Prælectiones* was ſuch, that he was forced oftentimes to repeat the ſame things, which is able to make thoſe, that have not patience, nor know how to value ſuch ware, to be ſoon weary. His chiefeſt inſtances, beſides *Fernelius* and *Matthiolus*, their opinions in the caſe, upon certain proof and experience are, the firſt, *Baptiſta Mantuanus*, a known Phyſician, in his notes, or obſervations upon *Avicen*, which he doth call *Lectiones*: whoſe words are; *Ego mihi credite, vidi meis oculis*, &c. that is : *My ſelf with mine eyes, you may believe me, have ſeen it, a certain*

*certain man who when he had made a circle* (*cumque signaret*) *and drawn some characters about it, and uttered some words, he did call together above a hundred Serpents.* So he. This indeed *Montanus* doth not relate to the same end that I do, to prove that there be supernatural operations by the intervention of Devils and Spirits; but he, to prove the strength of *imagination*. For he was, it seems, of the opinion of some *Enthusiasts Arabs*, as *Avicenna* and some others, embraced by some professing Christianity also; who did ascribe so much to the strength of *imagination*, as if Rain, and Thunder, and even Earthquakes might be caused by it. Certainly, they that did believe this, really, had a very strong *imagination*. How comes it to pass, they never did none of those miracles? But for a further resolution, or refutation of this, if any desire it, I refer them to learned *Fyenus* his excellent Treatise, *De viribus Imaginationis*, well worth the reading, written in the old *Aristotelean* way; though he do *Aristotle* some wrong, unwillingly I believe, when he doth say, that *Aristotle* he believeth, did write of the strength of the *imagination*, no were, but *Problem. l.* 10. *c.* 12. a great mistake. But to our purpose. *Remigius* his relation, which is not in *Reynolds*, is more strange, and not less credible, I think. *I have seen a man,* saith he, *who from all the neighbourhood* (*or confines*) *would draw Serpents into the fire, which was inclosed within a Magical Circle; and when one of them, bigger than the rest, would not be brought in, upon repetition of the Charms before used, he was forced, and so into the fire he did yield himself with the rest, and with it was compassed.* So *Remigius*. By this, what *Pliny* meant, by his *cogique in pœnas*, may be understood. But I must conceal nothing from my Reader. They that should see my *Remigius* would easily believe that I have read him over, more than once, by my noting and scribling in most pages of it. Yet at this time, *I* must confess, *I* could not find this passage, where *I* thought it most probable it would be found. And that which makes me somewhat suspitious is, that *I* find much of this relation, set out with more florish, as acted elsewhere: which *I* confess is very possible, that what the *Devil* hath done in one place, he may do in another. And this *I* find in an Author, who professeth to have travelled the greatest part of *Europe*, to satisfie his curiosity: and to speak truth, for the bigness, *I* have not read stranger things in all kinds in any book: but this of Serpents, he doth relate from others, of what credit *I* know not; he doth not say he did see them himself. And therefore the Reader may suspend his belief, as to this particular relation; if he please, till he or *I* have found it in *Remigius*. Yet withal *I* must say, that the same Author, but now spoken of, though he doth not attest this relation of Serpents, as a thing seen by himself; yet another he doth, ( *Vidimus* ) his word, which in point of the creatures charmed, is as different, as *Serpents*, are from *Flies*; in all other things have much affinity: *Hercules* Πδιοπλ⊙, is the title of the book: one *Joh. Exnestus Burggravius*, the Author: these two particulars of Serpents and Flies, page 68. and 77. My Author for *Remigius*, is one that calls himself *Philippus Ludwigus Elich*, in his *Dæmonomagia*: who is very full of quotations, out of good books, *I* confess, but otherwise, whether sober or no, when he wrote; he is so full of extravagancies, *I* do not know. But again, *Remigius* and *Burggravius*, their relations agree very well; but that they do not agree in the place, which is no argument against the truth; some may think it a confirmation of their relations, because as *I* said before, it is very possible the same thing in substance might be acted, as most other things are, in different places: But *Delrio*, in whom though diligent

*in things* NATURAL. 105

gent and copious enough, *I* find none of thefe, nor a word of *Valefius*, he hath an example which he calls *celebre exemplum*, as known unto all men, that feek after thefe things, and uncontrollable; fo I underftand him; but of a quite contrary event: for there the *Magician* was kill'd by the Serpent, who laft appeared, who probably might be the *Devil* himfelf: but enough of this.

MY next inftance (in *Reynolds* alfo) or teftimony, is of *Andreas Mafius*, that excellent *Commentator*, and learned Divine, who being intreated by *Witrius*, to explain unto him the true notions of the *Hebrew* words, wherewith all kind of *Witchcraft* is expreffed in the Scriptures, when he comes to the word חבר, which properly fignifieth *incantare*, or *to inchant*; he doth add: *Et ego vidi*, &c. *I alfo have feen them, who with words* (or *charms*) *could ftop wild beafts, and force them to await the ftroak of the dart: who alfo could force that domeftick beaftly creature, which we call a Rat, as foon as feen, amazed and aftonifhed to ftand ftill, as it were immovable, until not by any deceit or ambufhes, but only ftretching their hands they had taken them, and ftrangled them.* So learned *Mafius*. Some Reader it may be that is not *incredulous*, for want of due confideration, will be aftonifhed at thefe things, that fuch power fhould be given unto man, or *Devil*. But they fhould rather make this ufe of it, that if fuch power even *Spirits* have, that are Gods creatures, and fervants; which both good and bad are, though againft their wills; what may his power be, who is the *Creator* of all things; and how inexcufable they, who in fome articles of our faith, ftick at fome things, as impoffible to God? And if they believe,

(they

(they do, if true Chriftians) that one Angel, at Gods command, deftroyed in one night, *one hundred fourfcore and five thoufand men*, why, a wonder unto any, that a man, by the help of the *Devil*, who is a rebel-Angel, fhould have fuch power ( God not hindring) upon dumb creatures, whether fierce or tame? The *German Piper*, I think, there be but few, but fometime or other have heard of, who having agreed with the Town, or Village, at a certain rate, to deftroy all the Rats, which did much annoy the place, and after performance, was denied, and laughed at: drew by his mufick all, or moft Children of the Parifh, or place, after him; who ( if a true tale ) were never heard of. It is related by many for a truth, and faid by fome, to be left upon the records of the place or Country. But I will not trouble my felf to feek my books or papers for it, at this time. Enough hath been produced of later times, which I think unqueftionable, and I have yet more to the fame purpofe. I remember well, that many years ago, Sir *Henry Wootton*, being then *Provoft* of *Eaton-Colledge*, he did tell me, that fome body, whether Englifh or Outlandifh, did offer unto him to deftroy all the *Moles* of the Country for I know not what compafs of ground: but this, not by any charm, or incantation, he faid, but by a fecret of nature; becaufe the Moles, at a certain time of the year, it was their nature and cuftom, to gather together in one place, and then, what to be done, I know not: he told me more, but this is all I remember. But I have a ftory of a later date, which though for fome reafons I am fomewhat fhye to come to: Yet, becaufe in two feveral places in my *Notes* and *Obfervations* upon *Diogenes Laertius* lately fet out, and in thofe *Obfervations* upon the *Pfalms*, and *Proverbs*, the importunity of Printers, when I was not very well furnifhed, either with books or leifure; but worft of all, of will, ( when nothing

could

could be expected to be acceptable, and welcome, but what relished of schism and rebellion) extorted from me: but because in those two several places I have touched upon it, I desire I may have the liberty to relate it here at large.

IN the year of our Lord 1648. I then lived in *Sussex*, some three miles from *Chichester*, under the protection, not out of any love to me, who was looked upon as a desperate malignant; but out of a respect to my wife, between whom, and his wife, there was some relation of kindred; but under his protection, whom I dare not name; but a man of very great power, at that time; I wish he had made better use of it, than generally he did: though I never heard that he did much inrich himself by it, which many others did, who had less power, but were more covetous. I must acknowledge, not knowing at that time, where to dispose my self more commodiously, I was much beholding to him: and it did much conduce to my peace and quietness, as being of that profession and party, then sufficiently hated and persecuted; that he would do me the favour, and honour sometimes, as to come to my house. One time (I can tell the very day, it was the 11. of *February*) he came, and brought with him a Gentleman, his wives own father, and of kin to mine, who had been not long before Sheriff, as I remember, of *Sommerset shire*, and suffered much by the times, for his loyalty. They came on horseback, with divers servants, among whom, because the chiefest of the company had lately bought a *Barbary*-horse, to whom he did not think convenient, as yet, altogether to trust himself, was one *John Young*, a known horse-courser of that Country. Whilest we were above, in the best Room I had, and the Servants in the Kitchin by the fire; my son (the only I then had, or since have had; some 12. or 13. years of age) comes in, with his
Mastiff,

Maſtiff, which he was very fond of, as the Maſtiff was of him: *John Young*, to make himſelf and the company ſport; What will you ſay, Sir, ſaith he, if I make your dog, without touching of him, lie down, that he ſhall not ſtir? Or to that effect. My ſon, for it was a Maſtiff of great ſtrength, and courage, which he was not a little proud of; defied him. He preſently to pipe, and the Maſtiff ( at a diſtance ) to reel: which when the boy ſaw, aſtoniſhed and amazed, he began to cry out. But the man, fearing ſome diſturbance in the houſe, changed his tune, or forbare further piping, ( I know not which ) and the dog ſuddenly became as well and as vigorous as before. Of this I knew nothing, till the company was gone. Then a maid of the houſe obſerving that I much wondred at it, and wiſhed I had ſeen it: O Maſter, ſaid ſhe, do you wonder at it? This man doth it familiarly, and more than that, the fierceſt horſe, or bull that is, if he ſpeak but a word or two in their ears, they become preſently tame, ſo that they may be led with a ſtring; and he doth uſe to ride them, in the ſight of all people. This made me the more impatient; and ſo it was, that being invited thither to dinner againſt the next day, I thought long till the time was come, and had not ( the next day ) been long there, but told the Maſter of the houſe, before much company, that were then preſent, what I had heard of the man, and how deſirous I was to be further ſatisfied; That ſhall you ſoon be, replied he: and preſently ſent one for him. But anſwer was brought he was gone abroad, but they thought he would not be long away. This very delay, though but for ſo ſhort a time, troubled me, which whether obſerved or no; Well, well, ſaith the Maſter of the houſe, I will give you ſome ſatisfaction, in the mean time, by one ſtory I ſhall tell you. This man, ſaid he, was once in company, and being in the mood

( or

( or to that effect ) began to brag, what he could do to any dog, were he never so great or so fierce. It hapned, that a Tanner, who had a very fierce Mastiff, who all the day was kept in chains, or musled, was in the company, who presently ( not without an oath perchance, it is too usual; good laws against it, and well executed would well become a Christian Commonwealth ) offered to lay with him ten pounds he could not do it to the said dog : that was, without any force or use of hands to lay him flat upon the ground, take him into his arms, and to lay him upon a table. *Young* hapned to be so well furnished at that time, that he presently pull'd out of his pocket ( I think I was told ) ten shillings. The Tanner accepts; the money on both sides laid into the hands of some one of the company, and the time set. At which time, to the no small admiration, certainly, of them that had not seen it before, but to the great astonishment, and greater indignation of him, that had laid the wager; with a little piping the party did punctually perform what he had undertaken. But instead of the ten pounds he expected, being paid only with oaths and execrations, as a *Devil*, a *Magician* : after some expectation, a suit was threatned or commenced. The conclusion was, that the business being on both sides referred to arbitration, and this very Gentleman that told me the story, chosen and agreed upon for one; of ten pounds, five ( if my memory fail me not in any particular circumstance, as in the main, I am confident it doth not ) were given him, and there was an end. Then they began to tell some other of that company, besides horses, what he had done to fiercest bulls, before great company, and some persons of quality : but withal, what one bull, more refractory than the rest, had done to him; carried him, against his will, into a deep pond, where he was in some danger, but at last, had his will of him also, as well as of the rest. Whilest they were speaking, in comes *John Young*.

*John*, faith the Master of the house, here is a Gentleman, at whose house you were yesterday: he is very desirous ( to satisfie his curiosity, and to no other end ) to see some of your feats. I was sitting by the fire, ( it was cold, and I was not very well ) but turned and fixed my eyes upon him, and he his, as earnestly upon me. I told him what I had heard of him, and that it would much satisfie me, to see that done with mine eyes, which, I knew, by some was thought impossible. Whereupon the man, still earnestly looking upon me, began a discourse, how that all creatures were made by God for the use of man, and to be subject unto him; and that if men did use their power rightly, any man might do what he did. I must confess, I did wonder not a little to hear a man, whom by his profession, and his countenance, you would hardly have thought able to read ( and whether he was, I do not know ) to speak so Philosophically; especially after. I remembred what I had read in *Cornelius Agrippa*, that famous, but learned *Magician*, to the same purpose, *D: occulta Philosophia lib.* 3. *cap.* 40. *Quod un'cuique homini impressus est character*, &c. where he begins : *It is approved by good experience, that man naturally hath an inbred power in him of binding and commanding*, &c. and yet, it is far from my thoughts to think, that ever the man heard so much as of the name. But after I had heard him a-while, I did adventure to desire him, that I might hear some of his piping. He, as one that made very slight of it, took a little stick out of the Chimney, most of the company being busie in discourse, one with another, not regarding what passed between him and me ; and did begin to make some kind of noise, wherein I did not think there was much musick. But this I observed, ( the Reader may laugh, and I know it might be a chance ) that whilest he was piping, which was not long, a Cat that was in the Chimney-corner,

ner, came towards him, and looked upon him, in that posture of body, that I could not but take notice of it. But, by this, Dinner was brought in, and the room with guests and servants, pretty full. The man promised me he would come to my house, and I to him, he should not lose his labour. I trusted to it, and forbare any further mention of him, whilest I was in the house. But when returned to my own, I expected, day after day, and no news of him. I sent, as opportunity offered it self, messages unto him: promises were returned, but no performance followed. At last, after I began to suspect the man avoided me, I made two journeys to *Medhurst*, some seven miles from mine own house, where I was told, or not far off, he did live; but for ought I could do, I never had the sight of the man ever since, and I think he died before, or soon after I left the Country. Upon enquiry, all that I could learn is, that he had learned it of his father, who they said, drove the same trade before him.

IF the Reader have received any satisfaction from this story, I am glad of it. If not, to make him amends, I will tell him another, I cannot say more true; but he will perchance, because better attested, and from the place, and occasion more noble; whereof a *Bull* is a considerable part. And this, not because I desire to please his ears, (which is far from me) but to vindicate a truth of such consequence, which cannot (except Scripture authority will be thought sufficient, which in this particular seems to some doubtful) be better vindicated, than by experience. After the death of Pope *Leo* the Tenth, and before *Adrian* the sixth, his successor, was chosen, (being then absent) and come to *Rome*, there was, it seems, besides other confusion, by strife and divisions, a grievous Plague at *Rome*: which did so amaze the people, being otherwise, by other evils,

much

much annoyed and perplexed; that having tried other usual means to no purpose; at last, they had recourse to one *Demetrius*, a *Grecian*, and noted *Magician*, who was said, and attested by some, to have done wonders in that kind, in other places. The man, with much confidence, undertook the business, promising to clear the City, not for the present only, but for the time to come also. This to bring to pass, (for a good reward, we may be sure) he requires a bull to be brought to him: a black bull it must be and a very fierce one, they say it was: but he after some charms, made him gentle and patient enough, so that he suffered his horns to be cut off, without any resistance. What I chiefly aimed at, is at an end: but if the Reader desire to know somewhat of the issue, truly I am at a stand in that. *Quercetanus, de peste*, relates it out of *Paulus Jovius*, whom I have not; *Pestem Romæ grassantem, sedatam fuisse incantationibus cujusdam Demetrii*, &c. that is, That *the Plague, raging in* Rome, *was asswaged by the inchantments of one* Demetrius, *&c. Delrio*, the Jesuit, out of *Grillandus*, saith nothing of the Plague, (*Delrio* doth not, whether *Grillandus* doth, I know not; I have him not at this time) but only of the Bull (which he calls, *ferocissimum taurum*) how he was calmed by Magick-art, and led by a string, hundreds of people following, and for this very act, *Demetrius*, as a notorious inchanter, cast into prison. But *Gilbertus cognatus*, (him I have) who very largely doth tell the story, and by some prayers I have of his in another book, seems to have been a very religious man, and was then at *Rome*, as I take it: by him, indeed the Plague is mentioned, a very sad Plague, and the confusions of the City at that time fully set out: the *Magician* also hired, the Bull required and tamed: all this he hath at large: but not that the Plague was thereupon asswaged or removed: though it seems the people

## *in things* NATURAL. 113

of the City, had so good an opinion of the man, after he had done his feats, that when cast in prison, by authority, as a *Magician*; he was violently delivered by them, and set at liberty. And *Cognatus* doth add, that from thence, he went into a certain place, where the Plague was, and that it was said, he had, by his art cleared it; but, said only: whether truly or falsly, he doth not tell us. *Onuphrius*, in the life of *Adrian* the sixth, doth mention the Plague, but nothing else: neither indeed was it for the credit of the place, or people, he should. For *Cognatus* writing to his friend about it, begins, *De Græca illâ* ( the *Magician* that was imployed was a *Grecian*, I told you before ) *superstitione, quæ Romam, Anno* 1522. *invecta fuit, scribere volens, vereor,* &c. that is, *Purposing to write of that Greek superstition, which was acted at Rome, in the year 1522. I have reason to fear, that neither I shall acquit my self, as I ought, and that both to you, and other Readers, the thing will seem incredible. For such is the indignity of the thing,* &c.

WELL, I think we may take it for granted if certain and approved experience, can make any think indubitable, that by *charms* and *inchantments* many *supernatural operations*, are brought to pass: and if such approved testimonies of fresh memory were wanting, yet to me, as to many others I suppose, the testimony of so many ages, grounded upon common experience, would be a sufficient evidence. After the Scriptures, *Homer* for his antiquity, of all Authors now extant, is most considerable; whose testimony is ordinarily produced, as indeed very pertinent and emphatical: So is *Plato*'s, in more than one place: So *Pindarus*, and divers others, whom I pass by, because every where to be found. Physicians and Philosophers, if not all, yet not a few, did allow of them; and the laws of Princes some-

I                          times

times did, and sometimes not; but those that did not, and were most severe, but not unjust against them, ( as indeed they were, sometimes ) they are as good evidence, in our cause, to prove that such things were practised, and found available, as those laws, that did favour them. *Ammianus Marcellinus*, whose judgment we need not much stand upon, as long as his testimony, for the matter of fact, is good : in his History of those times, when himself lived, doth record it, as an example of great cruelty, that some were proceeded against in his time, as great malefactors, because they had made use of *anile incantamentum, ad leviendum dolorem*; and in another place, that *a certain Magistrate*, ( *anum quandam simplicem*, &c. ) that is, *Did put to death a simple* ( or *innocent* ) *old woman, which was wont with smooth* ( or *harmless* ) *inchantments, to cure intermitting Fevers*, ( or *Agues* ) *after that the same being sent for, had healed his own daughter*. A cruel thing indeed, that he should use her help, or art, to cure his own daughter, and afterwards put her to death, for curing others, and making a practice of it : except we understand it so, that this man in authority, not fully satisfied that such a thing could be; that is, *that charms and inchantments* were of that power, and having such an opportunity to know the truth, having a daughter sick in the house, he made use of her ; and finding that she was a *Witch*, indeed, and dealt in those things, which by the laws of those times were strictly inhibited under pain of death ; so he put her to death, notwithstanding that ( against his expectation perchance ) his daughter had reaped the benefit of her unlawful profession. And yet let us observe by the way, that if he did it of purpose, to make trial, and to know the truth ; besides that he made himself obnoxious to the law, for trespassing against it, under pretence of trial, and finding of transgressors ;

which

which I believe the law did not allow: he might also have missed of his end. For it was possible, that she that had cured many by those unlawful courses, might not cure all, though she used the same means. For still we must presuppose the concurrence of Gods will and permission, without which nothing lawful or unlawful can be done: besides, what may also be alledged from natural hidden causes: and there be store of instances to that purpose, that effectual charms, in, and by the same hands are not always effectual. But again, *Wierius* would say, that the *Devil*, to mischief a poor innocent old woman, did so contrive it, that her charms should be effectual at that time, though in very deed, all that she did, did contribute nothing really to the cure, whereof himself was the immediate and only author. So far we may admit, that the charms of themselves were nothing, but as they were made effectual by him. But the woman therefore, that did apply her self to the *Devil*, and entred into covenant with him to such and such purposes; or, say she made no direct covenant, yet used an indirect way, by the laws of the land severely interdicted; she innocent, and no *Witch*, but in conceit? Who seeth not, I have said it before, and say it again, how by this device any malefactor may become innocent? But of *Wierius*, and his opinion, before sufficiently.

WHAT *Ammianus* doth call, *anum simplicem*, I understand *a white Witch*, as in some parts of *England* they are called; that is, such as are generally, by the common people, supposed to do no hurt, but much good; to distinguish them from ordinary mischievous *Witches*. When I lived in *Sommerset-shire*, where, as soon as by years capable, by the *Collation* of *Lancelot Andrews*, then Bishop of *Winchester*, (whose name will be in honour, and his books in request, as long as good learning, and true piety both, which of late hath suffered

great

great detriment, are in credit in *En land* ) I had a *Living*; I became acquainted with a very pious and hospitable Gentlewoman, one Mistress *Still*, the widow of Bishop *Still* his eldest son, as I take it; and by her, with another of the Bishops sons, yet living, for ought I know: a Gentleman of excellent parts; but, I think, better known unto most, by a strange infirmity he had, for which many that had seen him abroad, as I have often seen him, and once at my house, would have sworn he had been bewitched; yet natural, and contracted, as I have heard, by some hurt in his back-bone, through the unruliness of his horse, when he was upon his back. But this story, now to be told, I had from him. I wish I could relate it in his words, for he was an excellent speaker: There was in his fathers time, whilest a Parson of some Living there, in that Country, such a creature, which for the good she was supposed to do, and good only, had got the name of a *white Witch*; and was by many, who were not sensible of the hurt she did, by drawing so many into *condemnation*, and *the snares of the Devil*, who did use her help; magnified and admired. It seems the woman did not want, either tongue or boldness, to justifie her self, and her proceedings, when occasion was; and had got the reputation, among many, not only of a *cunning*, but also *religious* woman. Whereupon Doctor *Still* was desired by some of better judgment, to admit her to some kind of conference, that the people, if possible, might be undeluded. But he, for good reasons, I make no question, refused it: yet was willing to repair to the Parish, where she lived, and publickly out of the Pulpit, declare his opinion concerning such practices, which he hoped, would do as well, or better; which was kindly accepted. The *Sunday*, or *L rds-d.y* ( which some affect to call the *Sabboth-day*, but not so properly ) being come, which he had set and
promised,

promised, he went: Any body may suppose well accompanied, with friends and servants. The horse that he did ride, was his own ordinary Gelding, to which he was accustomed. But when near the place, (town or village) the horse began to rise, and to cast, in a strange manner, which he never was known to do before: and his carriage was so impetuous, that no-body could come near the rider, who was supposed to be in very great danger, as they were all in great amazement. But at last, there being some kind of *Cross* or *Market-place*, with a stone-ascent to it, not far of; the horse carried him up thither, and then stood stock still. The *Doctor* had no hurt, but could not for a time, but be very sensible of what he had suffered by such violent concussion (or *succussion* more properly) in his body: and by the strangeness and unexpectedness of it in his mind; so that of necessity he was forced to turn back, and they that expected him, were disappointed. What become of the creature afterwards, either I never knew, or have forgotten. The *Doctor*, we know, continued in good credit, and became afterwards *Bishop* of the place. I have done with my story, which for the substance, as related unto me, I dare warrant true: but if mistaken in any circumstance, I desire the Reader to consider, that it is almost half a hundred years since it was told me. I know there be many, so little grounded in the true faith and mysteries of *Godliness*, that at the hearing of this (if they believe it) they will be ready, either to quarrel with God Almighty, for suffering; or to interpret this permission of his, as a kind of justification of the woman, and her practices. But we shall meet with such objections, in another place, before we end this first *Part*. I shall say no more here, but this: How can they so much wonder at this, who know, that God in all ages hath suffered, sometimes, as lately amongst us, eminently a wicked cause to prosper: and Godly men, his faithful Ministers and Servants; yea godly Kings and Princes (whereof our late most pious *Soveraign*, a rare example) to fall into the hands of the wicked? That the Church of God in general hath been ever subject to the opposition and persecution of the *Devil* and his instruments; and more particularly, that St. *Paul*, though a *Saint*, so dear unto God, met with an *Alexander*, who *greatly withstood him*; and that, when he would have come, once, twice, to the *Thessalonians*, who perchance needed him as much, or more, than the Doctor was needed in that place (Town or Village) whether he was going; *he was hindred by Satan*?

BUT now I am in *Sommerset-shire*, before I leave it, I beg the liberty of another relation, which though it be not much to my main purpose, yet because I have not hitherto, to my best remembrance, met with it elsewhere, or not so fully as I wished, I would preserve the memory of it to posterity. And first of all, I will here insert it, as it came to my father (of bl. m.) from a very good hand, which no man, I dare say, will except against; then I will perfect it (if not much mistaken) with such *additionals*, as I learned in the Country, when I lived there.

ΣΥΝ ΘΕΩι (It was his fashion so to begin almost every thing, that he wrote: I hope there is no *superstition* in it, the great μορμολύκειον, or *terriculamentum* of this *Atheist cal* age. Ancient Christians, instead of it, used ordinarily *the Cross*: there was no *Popery* then:) *Rem miram mihi narrabat hodie, Dom. Episcopus Eliensis, Sanctæ pietatis Antistes. Dicebat se accepisse à multis, sed præcipue à Dom. Episcopo Villensi nuper mortuo, cui successit Dom. Montacutus: evenisse ante annos circiter XI.* (he did write this in the year of the Lord 1610. or 1611.

as

as I guess : for I find no date ) *in urbe Wella, sive ea dicenda, Wella, die quadam æstiva, ut dum in Ecclesiâ Cathedrali, populus sacris vacabat, duo, vel tria tonitrua inter plura audirentur, supra modum horrenda, ita ut populus universus in genua pæ ipsum, procumberet ad illum sonum terribilem. Constitit, fulmen simul cecidisse, sine cujusquam damno tamen. Atque hæc vulgaria. Illud admirandum, quod postea est observatum à multis, repertas ess. Crucis imagines impressas corporibus eorum, qui in æde sacra tum fuerant. Dicebat Episcopus Vellensis, D. Eliensi, uxorem suam (honestissima ea fœmina fuit) venisse ad se, & ei narrasse pro grandi miraculo, sibi in corpore impressa signa extare; quod cum risu exciperet Episcopus, mox nudato corpore, ei probavit verum esse, quod dixerat. Deinde ipse observavit sibi quoque ejusdem manifestissimam imaginem impressam esse, in brachio, opinor: aliis, in humero, in pectore, in dorso, aut alia corporis parte. Hoc vir maximus, Dom. Eliensis, ita mihi narrabat, ut vetaret de veritate historiæ ambigere.*] *Ex. Advers. Is. Casauboni* N. 4. *fol. antepenult.*

THE summ is, That at such a time (some eighty years ago, or thereabouts) a strange thunder, for the terror of the noise, hapned in the Cathedral of *Wells*, in *Sommerset-shire*, as the people were there at Prayers or Sermon: which made them fall all upon their knees. That afterwards, it was observed, that a Cross was imprinted upon the bodies of all, or most there assembled; of the Bishop, and his vertuous wife particularly.

I WILL not take upon me absolutely to determine, how these Crosses might come: I should not make any great wonder of them, no more than I do of those stones, which by the pious and learned compiler of *Musæum Veronense*, are called *Crucis Lapilli*; and fully described by him: which I do not find adscribed to any other, but a natural cause. Learned *Remigius*, I remember,

member, hath an obfervation, that very frequently, thofe bodies, that are ftruck with Thunder, are found marked with figns, refembling the impreffion of nails; which they that are fimple, faith he, fuppofe to be the *Devils* claw, whom they believe to have hoofs and nails, not ordinary. But this, as well he might, he doth laugh at and proceeds to the inquifition of a *natural* caufe, out of *Ariftotle*, and others. But I will not tranfcribe, where there is fuch facile excefs.

I AM a great admirer, I profefs it, of a ftone, which is not very rare. Many call them *Thunder-ftones*. I have them of divers forms, (as to the bignefs, or whole body) which in fome is perfectly *Oval*: in fome more *round*; in others *pointed* or *pyramidical*: fome for the length, not unlike a *helmet*; and fome very *flat*, which have fomewhat of the refemblance of a *heart*, divided in two. And this is obfervable in fome of them, that the lines not going through the body of the ftone, (not vifibly at leaft but ending foon, they reprefent a perfect *Star* or *Afterick*, as ufually painted; curioufly fet out in feveral rows of little points. But this (the occafion of this fhort digreffion) is effential to them all, that are perfect, not broken, I mean, or wore out: They have five double lines, made of two diftinct rows of pricks, or full-points, as it were; but with great variety. For in fome, every row is double, very artificially fet out. The points in moft, are, as it were, denied in the ftone: in fome others, extant, or eminent: but ftill five, curioufly drawn from the top, and all (or moft of them) meeting in one *center*, which is, as it were, a *navel*: which *navel*, as alfo the *vertex*, or very top, feemeth in fome of them, to be a body by it felf, or a different piece, and feparable from the reft; but clofely joynted, or joyned. I have fought into them, diligently, that write of ftones; but hitherto,
found

found but little, that satisfies me. They are not of the nature of ordinary stones, I am sure; but, as I conceive, owe their original to some kind of generation. Learned *Wormius*. who hath made a great collection of them, in his *Musæum Wormianum*, doth tell us, it is the opinion of some, that they ingender, even whilest stones; which his own observation, that he hath some, which have other little ones annexed and as it were proceeding from them, doth make the more probable: to him, at least. *Nec certè omninò abnuere possum*: he saith of himself. Most, that write of them, tell us, that by *Pliny*, they are called, *Ovum anguinum*, or *Snakes-egge*. It may be so; but what reason might enduce them, to think so, I must confess, that as yet I am to seek. His description is; *Vidi equidem id ovum mali orbiculati modici magnitudine crustâ cartilaginis, velut acetabulis brachiorum polypi crebris, insigne Druidis*; which before I take upon me to translate, I must understand better, than I do. Sure I am, here is no mention of the five *lines*, or *tails*, as *Gesnerus* calls them, the most eminent thing in these kind of stones. Besides, whether a true *ovum anguinum*, or no, the trial is, saith *Pliny*, *Si contra aquas fluitet, vel auro vinctum*: Will these stones do so? I have so little belief they will, that I never yet could be so idle, as to make trial. But again, he writes of them as *stones* or *eggs* rather, ( for he doth not at all, in all his description, make them to be *stones*, or call them so ) *of great worth* and rarity; which, if these kind of stones be not much rarer in *Italy*, than they are in *England*, cannot be true of them. Nor even so neither. For *England*, where they are so common, being then in the power of the *Romans*, they could not be very rare at *Rome*, if in any request. He tells of many strange, or rather admirable qualities, which the *Druids*, and *Magicians* reported of them; but not as believing them. However, if that be true, he

seems

seems to report in good earnest, that a *Roman* Knight, whom he names, was put to death by *Claudius*, for having one of them about him, when he was in suit of law, hoping by the help of it, to become victorious; it will follow, that this Snakes-egge was accounted a *magical* thing, which will agree well enough with those things, that are written, and by some believed, of the vertues of these *Thunder-stones*. But this is not much, to perswade me, that they are the thing intended by *Pliny*, by *ovum anguinum*, when so many other things are against it. Let me add, that the figures of these *stones*, set out by *Wormius* and *Gesnerus*, though they agree so well, that a man may suspect, they had them the one from the other; yet not very like, in either of them, to those stones that I have. For whereas their figures between the lines, are *scabrous*, or full of little *protuberances* or *eminences*, like little warts, as *Gesnerus* calls them; mine are smooth in those *interstices*, one or two excepted, which might contract their ruggedness, from the ground, where they did long lie. I have one so smooth, that one half of it is perspicuous or *pellucid*, and doth represent within, some kind of circles or *tunicles*, like Onions-coats; which also hath this singular, that in one side of the circumference, it hath a little round excrescence, as it were a Wen, or a Wart, but smooth. The truth is, the figures in *Wormius* do not agree with his description. The *description* tells us, that the *lines* or *tails, ab apice, in basin*: from the *top*, to the *navel*, as I call it; or as he, not improperly, (alluding to the *modiolus* of a wheel, where the *radii* meet, and are fastened) *modiolum*, do *excurrere*: the figure fetcheth them from the *basis*: which is so main a difference, that *Gesner* by that chiefly doth distinguish them from the true, or supposed, *ovum anguinum*, or *Snakes-egge*: by some supposed to be a *Toads*, and by others, the egge of a *Tortoise*.

*Tortoise.* And as to the stones, which *Wormius* under one figure, and under one kind, by the name of *Brontia, Thunder-stone*; or *ovum anguinum* doth describe; *Gesner* hath the figure of them in another place, ( page 166. of my Edition ) under no certain name: and Chapter 3. p. 59. &c. under the title of *Brontia, Ombria,* and *Ceraunia*: which are the right figures of the stones, which ( but with much more variety ) I have, very well, and fully enough described by *Wormius*. But it is time I should end this, occasioned meerly by the mention of *Thunder,* & *Thunder-marks*; and some kind of affection I bear unto these stones, which seem to me to promise somewhat more than ordinary, and worthy to be enquired after. As old as I am, I could be content to be carried a good way, ( for go I cannot, I am sure ) to learn somewhat of them, not so much of their *vertues,* as of their *production,* which to me seems a great secret of nature. Yet when I consider, that nature doth seem to take some pleasure in those kind of figures, which consist of five divisions, as by the *Stella marina,* ( not to speak of *five fingers,* and *five toes* in man: besides what in divers other creatures is answerable to either: *five senses,* &c. is another thing, because not apparent externally ) a Sea-fish: *stella Solis,* &c. described and figured by *Bellonius,* and others; and by those prety stones, ordinarily known ( and so described by *Gesner, de fig. lap.* p. 37. &c. ) under the name of *asteriæ, astroitæ,* &c. as also by the *pentaphyllum,* whereof there be many kinds and the like: ( to all, or any of which, whether the *Pythagoreans,* by their myftical *quinary,* by them called ὑγεία, which consisted of three triangles, joyned or interlaced into five points, or angles, described by *Lucian,* had any reference, I shall not now inquire ) and again, that some Naturalists by many pregnant instances, do maintain, that neither Sea, nor Land doth produce any thing, but

but is imitated and reprefented in fome kind, by fome kind of *foffile* in the bowels of the Earth : ( whence fo many bones of Fifhes, yea whole Fifhes, imperfect, as to the form, but perfect ftone, are found, and digged up out of the Earth, even upon high hills, far from the Sea : fome my felf have, and look upon, when occafion offers its felf, with pleafure, and admiration ) thefe things confidered, I think it is poffible, thefe ftones may be nothing elfe, ( but even fo, well deferving fome kind of admiration ) but fome kind of *foffiles* ; nature aiming by them at the reprefentation of fomewhat that doth live, or grow, either in the Sea, or upon the Land. But I forget my felf.

BUT now to return to our *Wells* Thunder ; the *additional* of the relation, which I have promifed, is more ftrange to me, than any thing in the faid *relation*; if it be true. For fince no mention of it is made in the exhibited *relation*, I cannot abfolutely fatisfie my felf, that it is true; much lefs can I warrant it to others. This premifed, that which came to me, whileft I lived in that Country, from fome others, who pretended perfect knowledge of the thing, is this : A certain man, they faid had been not long before inducted into a *Benefice* in that Country, of whom there was a report, ( but no proof) that he was addicted to the black Art. This man being fummoned, as the fafhion is, by authority, to Preach in the *Cathedral*, took his Text : *Thou God of Spirits* : ( I was told no more, as I remember ) out of *Numb.* 16. 22. or 17. 16. and whileft he was in his difcourfe about *Spirits* ; ( of purpofe it may be, to confirm the opinion of fome, that he had to do with them, thinking thereby, to be looked upon as an extraordinary man ; though perchance no fuch thing really ) this ftorm of Thunder hapned. Concerning which, I have now, befides the *relation*, delivered *bona fide*, what my memory

ry afforded unto me : which perchance may receive some illustration from what, not out of my memory, but out of my book, whereof I keep such things, which I have by the relation of others, and would not forget ; 1 have yet to say. However, if there be any mistake, rather than his name should suffer, from whom I had it, I will take it upon me : He was one of the Clergy, and a frequent Preacher in this *Cathedral*, to their very good liking, that could distinguish ( which few do or can ) between *sense*, and *sound*: solid good matter, I mean, and a plausible voice and delivery, which hath been treated of at large by me, with an accurate examination of the natural causes, in another book. I shall not conceal his name to any that have known him : to others, it is needless. The account of my book is this : 17. *Iul. Anno Dom.* 1638. of Mr. *&c.* That about some thirty years ago, when he was a young Scholar in *Trinity*-Colledge [ in *Cambridge* ] as they were in the Hall, at the Greek Lecture, the Reader then reading upon *Aristophanes* his Νεφέλαι, ( he thinks ) and perticularly treating of the word κεραυνος, ( that is, *Thunder* ) there came a sudden clap of Thunder, that struck them all down, and some a good space from the place, where they stood : astonished all, and deaded one, for the space of six hours, who also continued lame of it, for three months after : and split one of the main rafters of the roof, in two, *&c.* there being no appearance of any Rain, or Thunder before.

THUS *verbatim*, as I entred it in my book, how long after, I know not; but probably not long after. However, I cannot promise I have exhibited his own words, and therefore if there be any impropriety, or mistake in the exposition, I desire, that may be imputed unto me. Now supposing this, as I believe it true, I do not propose it, as a matter of great admiration : but
well

well worthy of confideration, and which may give fome light to fuch accidents. For, among fo many daily events or accidents, which have nothing in them, but what is ordinary; what wonder is it, if by meer chance, as in the cafting of many ftones at random, fomething happen that is not ordinary? It is poffible, a blind man, if he fhoot often, may hit the mark, when an expert fhooter may mifs, if he fhoot but once or twice. Such a Thunder, I am fure, was nothing but ufual enough; efpecially, if at a feafonable time of the year, as this probably, becaufe nothing obferved to the contrary. And that at fuch a time, when fuch a *Lecture* was read, which treated of, or mentioned *Thunder*; if there were no more in it than I have heard, that is, that, not the perfon reading, nor, any then prefent, were juftly fufpected; fuch a thing fhould happen, might be a chance. Neither fhould I make much more of the former *relation*, if the fecond part of it, whereof I have no certainty, be not as true.

NOW to *enchantments* again, the validity whereof, becaufe, of old, fo controverted, that *Pliny*, as before obferved, thought no age would, or could decide it; and of late there have not wanted learned fober men, who have maintained the contrary opinion, though I have been long upon it, from *men* to *beafts*; not *Serpents* only, ( juftified by the Scriptures ) but *horfes*, *dogs*, *bulls*; and all this by certain undeniable inftances, fufficiently proved; I will yet before I end this fubject, inftance in fome other kind, not yet fpoken of, which, as the humors of men are, may perchance affect fome Readers as much, or more, than any of the former inftances.

THE hunting of an inchanted *Hare* I have read, by an excellent pen: who doth acknowledge never to have feen it himfelf, ( his *hunting* was after books, he faith of himfelf,

himself, not Hares: it was mine too, when I was able )
but doth set it out upon the credit of divers Huntsmen,
as a thing not at all to be doubted of. I wish it were
not true, but I doubt not, but there be too many in the
world, who would make no scruple to go to the *Devil*,
not for their profit only, but also for their *sport*, and
meer divertisement: and that others there be, who to
satisfie them, who have more conscience, will devise
somewhat to make them believe it is lawful enough,
though done by the *Devil*, being done but for *sport*: or
if that will not do it, that such a thing may be contrived,
without the *Devil*. Let a man but once begin to indulge
against his conscience, by degrees he will stick at nothing. *Ο ῥυπῶν, ῥυπωσάτω ἔτι*: it is a just judgment of God,
whereof this age doth afford many sad examples. My
Author doth stile himself, *Prædicateur du Roy*. [ *Essay
des merveilles de nature*, &c. *par Revé Francois, Prædicateur du Roy: à Rouan* 1626. ] If so, me thinks it
would have become well a man of that profession, to
have said somewhat, whereby it might have appeared
unto the world, that he did not allow of such practices,
as lawful. Truly, one great reason that hath moved
me to take notice, is, to shew my detestation, of what
my Author doth leave without censure. This that follows, is more harmless I hope, because I have read of
strange things, that dumb creatures, even wild beasts
are capable of, by the industry of man: I have read a
relation, whereof *Julius Scaliger* is the Author, of a
tame wild-Boar; or if that found too much of a contradiction, of a wild Boar, by art and industry so tamed,
and disciplin'd, that he would hunt with the Dogs, as
skilful and obedient as the best of them, and do his Master very good service. *This, to some may seem *incredible*: but to them that have not read, what fiercest beasts,
by art and industry ( who therefore have been by many
supposed

supposed not altogether destitute of reason ) have been brought unto. Yet I would not warrant, but that this fierce Boar, by nature, might return to his nature, some time or other ; or, at least do some acts of a fierce beast. But for *Agrippa*'s black Dog, though denied by some, who would have us to think well of him, ( *Agrippa*, I mean ) because they do, as *Wierius* and some others; yet upon the attestation of so many others of better credit, I cannot but think of it, as a creature of another nature.

NOTHING now remains, and that too before promised, but to consider of *Galen*'s opinion, and what may *rationally* be objected from his authority. For that such a man as *Galen*, a right ingenuous man, a lover of truth, as I always accounted him, who lived to be a very old man, and consequently not less experienced, than he was learned ; that he should in all those books of his, now extant, as often as occasion offered it self, declare himself as one who gave no credit at all to such things, and made no better account of them, than arrant jugling ; I look upon it I must confess, as a weighty objection. To this we might answer, that though *Galen* was a man of great authority, yet he was but one, to whom the authority of many famous Physicians in his time, or soon after, not to speak of those before, might be opposed. It is the priviledge, if not affected humor, of some great men of real worth ; who also know themselves to be so, in the opinion of the world, to hold some *Paradoxes*; and perchance being unadvisedly fallen upon them in their younger years, they think it ( a great error ) against their credit to acknowledge it, when they are old. Besides, what if *Galen* thought those things, not altogether false perchance, yet dishonourable to his profession, and of evil consequence to mankind, by reason of the increase of impostors, and impostures, if credit

*in things* NATURAL.

dit were given to the validity of *inchantments*; in point of *cures* especially? And that this may not appear a suspition without all ground, doth he not in his books *de Compos. Medicum, l.b. 3. cap. 2.* where he treats of the Cures of the *Parotides*, reject *Archigenes* his advice, of añointing the place infected with the bloud of a *mustela*, upon this very ground, because such prescriptions, if received, would be prejudicial to the art, as though so defective in those cases, that without such helps it could not work a cure: professing, that for this very reason, he had forborn to make trial, and therefore could not tell, whether it would or not? The Reader may remember, what was said of *Valesius* before. But all this will not need, if we stick to *Trallianus* (who is conceived to have lived in *Theodosius* his time, not many ages after *Galen*) his answer, which is, that whatever his opinion hath been formerly, yet in his latter years, convinced by manifest and frequent experience, he did recant and acknowledge his error. *Galen* his words, as he doth exhibit them out of his book, Πϱὸς τὰς καθ᾽ Ὁμήρου ἰατρικὰς, in Greek are; *..................* &c. that is: *There be, I know, who think of Charms no better than of old womens tales. And so did I for a long time: but at last, by the evidence of those things that did clearly appear unto me, I am perswaded that they are efficacious. For in their case that are bitten by a Scorpion, I have found them useful. And and in their case who had bones that stuck in their throats, which they did presently cast out by the help of Incantation. And many noble atchievements in every kind of disease are wrought by it, when it doth not misse of*

K *its*

*its end.* Or if you will, with the Latine interpreter; *Ac multa præclara singula habent incantationes, cum institutum consequuntur.* Either way, *Galen* doth acknowledge that they are not always effectual: which to believe, or to maintain, were very absurd, and contrary to providence, and to the course of nature in general. But of that, enough hath been said before. Hereupon *Trallianus* doth conclude; *If then divine* Galen, *and most of the ancients with him,* &c. But where shall we find this in *Galen,* or where this book of *Galens?* In the Latine Edition indeed of his works, there is a book of that subject to be found, but not worthy *Galen*'s name, most are of opinion? However, though not extant at this time, nor mentioned by *Galen* in the *Catalogue* of his books, after which he might write many books, as we know St. *Austin* did some, which are not mentioned in his *Retractations*; yet it is not likely that *Trallianus,* whose love to the truth, made him not to spare his so much admired *Galen,* when he saw just cause, as himself in his fifth book (not to mention other places) doth abundantly declare; durst mention such a book, except such a one had been then extant in *Galen*'s name, or could be mistaken in his judgment concerning the Author, whom he had read so diligently, as by his writings doth appear. So that even *Valesius,* though he doth write against the opinion maintained by *Trallianus*; yet he doth, upon his authority, yield it, as unquestionable, that such a book was then extant, written by *Galen.* As he, so *Fererius,* who hath written a Chapter of that argument, and entituled it, as *Galen* had his *Treatise.*

NOW because in those times most *incantations,* used; not only by the *Jews,* but by *Gentiles* also; as by *Trallianus,* by *Lucian,* by *Origen,* and by others may appear, had the name of *Dominus Sabaoth,* as a chief ingredient; it is observable, that some godly Fathers, who

knew

*in things* NATURAL. 131

knew *Christians* had more right to that name, than either *Gentiles* or *Jews* of those times had; thought it no superstition, to commend unto them the nomination of *the Lord of Sabaoth* upon such occasions, not as an *inchantment*, but a lawful prayer. So doth *Cyrillus Alexandrinus*, in his book, *De Adoratione Spirituali, lib. 6.* whose words perchance some might interpret, as though he allowed those words to them that have faith, as a lawful *charm*. But what he writes in that very place against all kind of *inchantments*, as unlawful, and forbidden by God; may sufficiently acquit him from any such intention. But I cannot acquit *Origen*, neither is it much material, except I could acquit him of so many other pestilent errors, wherewith he stands charged in the Ecclesiastical story, and his books yet extant, though much purged by *Ruffinus*, the Latine interpreter, proclaim him guilty of. In his 20. *Homily*, upon *Josuah*, part of which, in Greek, is preserved in that *Philocalia*, collected out of his works; he doth very erroniously ascribe power to the very words and letters of ordinary *charms*; for which he doth appeal to common experience; and consequently would have the very letters, or words of the Scripture in any language, though not understood, if but read and pronounced, to be of great power and efficacy; which as it is against the very principles of Natural Philosophy, so against the determination of all sober *Philosophers*, *Physicians*, and *Divines*.

YET as there is nothing so uncouth or absurd, but shall meet with a Patron: so hath this opinion of the efficacy of bare *sounds and letters*, met with some, in our age: as *Thomas Bartholinus* for one. This *Thomas Bartholinus*, one of the King of *Denmarks* Physicians, the Author of many curious pieces; if he be not either too credulous sometimes, or too ambitious, to be the reporter of strange things; in his *Centuria, Historiarum Anatomi-*

K 2 *carum*

*carum rariorum*, upon the experience of some, to whom he doth give credit, doth maintain, that the *Epilepsie* may be cured by *charms*, and those charms upon a natural account of the causes not unlawful. His reason I will not stand to examine. I think they will not perswade very many, besides those, who think well enough of *charms* in general, whatever it be that makes them effectual; but would be glad to find a plausible pretence.

THIS mention of *Bartholinus*, puts me in mind of a strange story. I profess again seriously, as I have done before, this *Discourse* was never undertaken by me, to tell the Reader strange stories, though true; which might have made it much more both easie and voluminous. Yet the use that may be made of this, in point of *Credulity* or *Incredulity*; in case any such report, as very probably, may occur of any other place or Country; besides what inferences or experiments may be made upon it, for the publick good, if this be true, makes me take notice of it; and the rather, because having enquired of divers Travellers into those parts, whom I have had the opportunity to consult about it: I have not, as yet, met with any, that could give me any account. Now the story is this: In *Italy*, not above twelve leagues (they reckon there by *miles* ordinarily, but he saith, 12. *leucis*) near a Town or Village, vulgarly known, he saith, by the name of *Il Sasso*: (in Latin, *Bracciarum*) there is a Cave, commonly called *the Cave of Serpents*. Serpents at all times, it seems, but at some time of the year, more certainly, and solemnly, frequent it in great number. And then, if any troubled and afflicted with any ordinary disease, proceeding from a cold cause; as the *Palsie*, *Leprosie*, *Dropsie*, &c. come and lie down, immovable; which the better to do some take *Opium* beforehand; Serpents will come about him, and suck him, or lick him, till he be well. He tells

of

of more, but of one *Cardinal* among the rest, particularly, who being desperately ill, there recovered. Many other things he tells of it, which, it seems, with other company, he went of purpose to see. This upon the report of the Country people he more delivers of it, which sounds somewhat of a fable, that one of the Serpents, *Coronâ insignitus,* adorned with a kind of Crown, as the governor of the rest useth to come out of his hole first, and after diligent search, if he finds all things safe, gives notice unto the rest. This, if true, may give light to some other story, which, as I said before, made me the more willing to take notice of it.

BY this, I hope, yea and before this, as I have said before; but that I had some consideration of the good use, that might be made of what did offer it self over & above; but now again, by this, I hope, it will be granted by all, that do not profess wilful *incredulity,* and contradiction; that many things happen *supernaturally,* which are above the sphere and activity of the believed, and beloved *atomes,* and can be referred to no other cause, but the operations of *Demons,* or evil *Spirits*: which once secured; *Atheism* hath lost its greatest prop, and the mockers and scoffers of the time, the chiefest object of their confidence and boasting; which though not our immediate subject, yet of purpose, as before said, did we make choice of such instances of *Credulity* and *Incredulity,* that we might, *una fidelia* ( as they say ) *duos parietes*; and yet still according to my Title, in this *First Part,* have I kept within the bounds of *things Natural,* which by many, according to the *genius* of the times, are laid for a foundation of *Atheism*; or at least for the undermining of *Christianity*: which they that profess, & yet secretly endeavour to undermine, deserve to be accounted the worst of *Atheists.* I have now but a word or two concerning *Divination* and *Prodigies,* in general, because in all ages a main object of *Credulity* and

*Incre-*

*Incredulity*, to add; and then we shall see what *observations* more we can draw from the premised instances, and so conclude; which I begin to be weary of, as much as any Reader can be, this *first Part*.

*DIVINATION*, as it belongs unto God, more properly; (nay unto God *only*, if it be true *divination*; that is, such as hath no dependance from any natural cause, according to the course of nature, established by God in Heaven, or in Earth; but the will of God only) we have nothing to do with it here. Of other *divination*, common to men and Angels, (whether good or bad) but in a different degree, which is grounded upon the knowledge of natural causes, long observation and experience, and the like: First, *Humane*, so far as may be accounted for by natural causes, no man doth doubt of; though many things by men that have a natural sagacity, improved with long study and experience, may be done, or foretold upon grounds of *reason*, which by them that are not acquainted with such things, may be thought *incredible*; of which more afterwards. Secondly, *Dæmoniacal*, whether immediately by themselves, or by their instruments, which they that do not believe the existence of Devils and Spirits, are obliged to deny; is that which we are to consider of, so much as may concern us, to settle, or direct the belief of others, who may need it, and are content to hear reason. Further than that, we have no intention, or ingagement to meddle with it; which elsewhere we have done more largely, and concerning which, there be so many books already extant, as that it would be no small work to find any gleanings, worthy the acceptation of judicious men; as it would be very easie, (the work of most writers) out of which others have done, to compile whole volumes. Among us, of late writers, *Peucerus* is most known, who hath written a large volume *De Divinatione*. I wish he he had left out his *Divinity*, which fills a great part of the book; I should think better of it: though even so, the rest doth not give me that satisfaction, which I might have expected from a learned man. For, approved instances, or experiments, (as I may call them) he hath few or none; and what is it, the wit of man can find out in such an abstruse subject, but what is grounded (besides the authority of Scripture) upon experience? *Ragufeius*, a *Venetian*, *Theologus*, *Medicus* & *Philosophus*, as he is stiled, by himself, or by his friends; hath written two very learned Books, *De Divinatione*; but the greatest part is against *Judicial Astrology*, which he once professed himself, and got credit by it, he saith himself; but was so honest and conscientious, that notwithstanding the credit he got by it, he would be a *jugler* (his own word) no more; and to make amends to God and the World, for what he had been or done, thought himself bound in conscience, to write against it. I think I could reckon half a hundred, or more: but that is not my business.

THE several kinds of *Divination*, that have been used anciently, (and are yet most of them) and have got a proper appellation, as κοπινομαντεία, λιθανομαντεία, δακτυλομαντεία, and the like, are so many, that even to reckon them, would take some time. At the end of *Agrippa*, *De occulta Philosophia*, in that Edition I have, there is a prety full inventory of them. So in *Delrio*, *Pucerus*, *Wierius*; and many others. To these, if we add those, which by the relation of Travellers are proper almost to every Country or Nation, where Christ is not known; there being scarce any Country, for any other thing so wretched and barbarous, but hath attained to so much knowledge, (if we may call that knowledge, which doth commonly most abound, where brutish ignorance and savageness hath its reign) as to be masters of some kind of *Divination* or other. Of those many kinds that have anciently been used, and of those many that have been since devised, made known unto us by the relation of Travellers; I shall take notice of one or two particularly, and then proceed, with submission to better judgments, to a general conclusion concerning them all.

OF those anciently used, which I shall take notice of, the first ( because, where we have the relation of *Augerius* the Physitian, his haunted house promised ) shall be. ἰυχομαντεία, Ὀνυχομαντεία, or nail-*divination*, saith *Delrio* is, by anointing the nail of an impolluted boy, with some kind of oil, or soot; and using some conjuration of words; to see things at a far distance, and the event of things long before. But of an *impolluted boy*: why so? Let no man think the better of the *Devil* for that, or of this kind of Divination. It is *Porphyrius* his *observation*, or *admiration* rather, long ago, recorded by *Eusebius* in his own words; and since *Eusebius*, by St. *Augustine*, in Latin; his *admiration* I say, why such masters of uncleanness, in point of life and actions, should nevertheless, in their *mysteries*, stand so much for cleanness, and purity. *Porphyrius*, who might very well know, as one that had served them a long time, doth but propose the question by way of *admiration*; he doth not answer it: any Christian may, who is taught, that the *Devil* is the author of all *evil*, all *uncleanness*, and affects nothing more; yet is an *impostor*, withall, and would be thought an *Angel of light*; and to that end, doth amuse them that serve him, with some shews of *holiness*, in *rites* and *ceremonies* of his own institution, that he may be thought to love, what in truth, and sincerity of life, he doth abhor. And as he, so his servants, that promote his interest in the world by *sects* and *divisions*. What more rife in their mouths, and ordinary or external behaviour, than *holiness* and *purity*? I need to say no more; the rest is too well known. But this by the way only. Now to the *nail-Divi-*

*in things* NATURAL. 137

Divination; Delrio faith, he knew a *veteran Spaniard*, who did practife it, and inftances in fome particulars of his Divination: moreover obferves of the fame, that though he could ( he doth atteft it, it feems ) by *charms* and *incantations* cure the wounds of others; yet neither would cure his own, nor fuffer them to be cured by others, by the fame means. Some may miftake him, as though the man he fpeaks of, made fcruple, for fome hidden reafon, to have inchantments ufed upon himfelf, although he did not fcruple to ufe them upon others; which is not impoffible. But I rather believe his meaning is, though the man with *bare words*, as apprehended by many, but very erronioufly could cure other mens bodily difeafes; yet the wounds of his foul, whileft he continued in that bafe practice and fervice, *longe graviora*, ( that is wanting in *Delrio*, to make his expreffion full ) much more grievous, and much more to be dreaded; the proper cure whereof, are *words*, ( good advice and inftruction, according to that of *Horace*, *Sunt verba & voces*: that is, *charms*, and by *charms*. underftanding, *fermones Philofophicos*; as that which followeth doth evince ) he refufed, miferable wretch, either to admit, when offered, or to procure from others. What *Delrio* doth here atteft of one, *Filefacus*, *De Magia Idolul*. doth atteft of another, not upon his own knowledge, but upon the report of a man of quality, to him well known: *nobili & generofo*, are his words. But enough of this.

ANOTHER kind of Divination is, that they call ὑδρομαντεία, of which they reckon divers *fpecies*. One was, or is, to hang a ring by a thred, and to caft it, or to hold it over a boul of water, fo that it touch not the water. But this is nothing without the *charm*, that belongs unto it. After that, by the knocks of the ring upon one of the fides, which how many they fhall be, or how few, to fignifie fo and fo, is before agreed upon; the event ( God permitting, as always ) is declared. I have known fome-

somewhat, which in outward appearance may seem to have some affinity, though to another end: which is, to know the hour of the day. It was my luck once, at an Inne, in very good company, to see some trial of it. The ring did hit just so many times against one side of the glass, as the clocks did strike, or had struck hours, and then stood still. I saw it, when the ring was in the hands of some, that wondred at it, as much as I, and had never seen it done before. Yet I am sure, no *charm* was used, which is the main business; nor any of the company suspected. Yet the motion of the hand, in such a case, not easily discernable, might deceive them, that look, if the actor had any purpose to juggle: which, I am confident, was not the intention of any then present: not theirs especially, who wondred at it, and made trial themselves for better satisfaction; which was done then by some, who found it so too. But the surest trial would be, to hang the ring upon a little frame, made gallows-wise, and if then also, truly I should not stick to conclude, that there is somewhat in it more than *natural*; and should advise them that profess they had often tried it, both by day and by night, as some did to me since, with great protestation, that it never fail'd; earnestly advise them never more to meddle in it.

IN the life of St. *Hilarion*, written by St. *Jerome* mentioned before, we have a notable example of *Hydromancy supernatural*, but not *Diabolical*. The rites indeed, and ceremonies, *charming* excepted, were much alike; but the efficacy not from the *Devil*, but God. And probably, God might prompt that holy man to use the same rites ( but without their words ) that *Magicians* did, to convince them that ascribe much to them, as all *Magicians* do; that the efficacy was not from the outward visible rites and ceremonies themselves, which to that effect were but ridiculous; but from an *invisible* cause,

cause, or agent, whether good or bad; and withal the better to manifest his power, who could use their own weapons against themselves, that trusted to them; as we see he did in the case of *Balack* and *Balaam*; when *Balaam's inchantments* intended for a curse, were, by Gods power, turned into a blessing. Upon such extraordinary examples, we can ground no warrant for our imitation, no more than by *casting of rods upon the ground, or smiting of the dust of the earth*; we may lawfully attempt *to turn rods into Serpents*, or, *the dust* into *Lice*, because *Moses* did both; for which he had an express command from God, but we none. That *Hilarion* also had a command, or commission for what he did, if pious indeed, and holy, as represented unto us by St. *Jerome*, who might know better than we, I think we are bound to believe.

OF those kinds of *Divination* used at this day ( besides the Ancients ) which we have knowledge of, none, I think, either for the certainty, if reports be true, or for the manner, more notable, or considerable, than that which is described by *Leo Africanus* ( a man of no small credit among them, who are well versed in the History of the world ) highly esteemed, and chiefly practised in *Africa*, in *Fez* ( one of the Royal Cities of that part of the world ) especially. The particulars of it are there to be seen in the Latin translation of it, *lib.* 3. *p.* 131. as also in the English, in *Purchas his Pilgrimage*: ( a book of very good worth, with them that know the right use, and more valued abroad, than it is at home by many ) *second Tome, page* 796, &c. It is a very perplex and intricate way, and requires great learning: but if as many think, there be nothing of *Magick* in it, and that it never fails, which some, even Christians, have been bold to affirm, well worth the labour. *Leo Africanus* from the report of others, speaks of it very moderately;
he

he doth not affirm either. He profeſſeth, that being offered the learning of it, by ſome, well able to teach him, he durſt not meddle with it, becauſe it hath ſo much affinity with the black Art. What religion the man was of; when he wrote, I cannot gather certainly by this book of his: but a *Mahometan* I gueſs, though there be places, that favour of *Chriſtianity*; as in the deſcription of *Nilus*: if he did not himſelf alter thoſe places of purpoſe, in his *Italian* tranſlation of his original *Arabick*, after he was become a *Chriſtian*. *Erpennius*, whom I have reaſon to remember with honour, for the honour he did to me, when very young; but much more, for his noble performances, out of his purſe, ( being wealthy ) partly; and partly by his excellent knowledge and induſtry, to promote the knowledge ſo difficult before, of the *Arabick* tongue: he alſo is one of them, that did believe this art, or way of *Divination* infallible; though, and ſo we muſt excuſe it, he might ſpeak the more favourably of it, out of his love and reſpect to that noble tongue. For my part, I ſhall not ſcruple to conclude it, if not *divine*, for which there is no ground at all, than fallible, and more than probably, notwithſtanding all pretences to *nature, diabolical*. Certain enough, were it known *infallible*, there would be greater reſort to it from all parts of the world; and many more of all Nations would apply themſelves to the ſtudy of it, and that it doth ſo often prove true, as generally believed, is argument enough to me, becauſe not *Divine*, that it is *Diabolical*.

I WILL not trouble my ſelf, nor my Reader, with the relation of more kinds of *Divination*, uſed at this day, in ſeveral Countries, which all ſtories of *travels*, almoſt, into thoſe parts of the world, where *Chriſtianity* is not profeſſed, afford examples of, different from thoſe uſed in other Countries. Concerning all which

my

## *in things* NATURAL.

my opinion is, not that they are *infallible* any one of them, which I know cannot be: but that, really, by all, or moſt of them, where the Relator doth faithfully acquit himſelf, and doth not wilfully counterfeit and impoſe, or ignorantly miſtake, which may eaſily be avoided, where we have variety of *relations*, from ſeveral Authors, that doe not borrow one from another, to compare; but this caſe excepted, my opinion is, that really by all, or moſt kinds of theſe *divinations*, even thoſe that may ſeem moſt ridiculous, ſtrange things are foretold. Beſides printed *relations*, ſo many, in ſeveral languages, of men of all Countries, and profeſſions, in this our *Europe*: I have heard the depoſitions, or atteſtation of more than one intelligent man, and in their lives and converſations, and in their diſcourſe too, very ſober and ſerious, who proteſted to have been preſent, when ſuch and ſuch things, ſome in one place, ſome in another, were foretold, which hapned accordingly: But ſecondly, to believe that any of thoſe things, that really came to paſs, were foreſeen and foretold by vertue, or by any natural efficacy of thoſe rites and ceremonies, words, or actions, that were uſed, in, or by any of thoſe kindes of *Divination*, whereof ſome are apparently moſt horrible and abominable; others, as ſottiſh and ridiculous, were, I think, not much leſs ridiculous, or abominable. Neither ſhall I except *Judicial Aſtrology*; which though apparently, it be more myſterious, and deal in things more ſpecious and ſublime: yet, in very deed, is founded upon meer imaginary ſuppoſitions, and Poetical fictions, words and names, which have no ground at all in nature; as by them that have taken great pains in

the

the search of it, and have set out the vanity of it; and even by them, that have done their utmost, to uphold the credit of it, otherwise; but could never answer those things that are opposed; is acknowledged. Yet to say, that nothing, that hath strangely been foretold by profest *Astrologers*, according to the rules and maximes of their Art, such as they are; besides what may be supposed to have hapned by meer chance, as in the multitude of predictions, some things must, and do, were to contradict the experience of all ages, of all places; and to give men some ground, to doubt, whether there be any such thing as truth in the world.

AND what shall we say of the *Oracles* of the ancient times? That many of those things that went under that name, were meer jugling, and roguery, I grant it: but that they were nothing else, I think a man that hath read ancient Authors, and Histories, Greek and Latin, may as well doubt, whether ever really any such men as *Socrates*, or *Cæsar* and *Pompey*; ever any such place as *Delphos*, and *Dodona*, and *the like*; as to doubt of the accomplishment of many of those things, so foretold, as read in the Histories of those times. And to me it is a greater argument of Gods power and providence, that upon the *Incarnation* of his Son, the long promised and expected Oracle of the world, and the propagation of his Gospel, all those *Oracles*, attended before with so much solemnity; should in all places, to the great wonder and amazement of wisest Heathens, as by *Plutarch's* Treatise of that subject doth appear, did cease, or begin to cease in all places: than any matter of wonder, or offence, that God should give so much power to the *Devil*, (this always supposed, that his Providence in all answers, that were given, did over-rule, as himself pleased) in those times of darkness and ignorance. For though *Divination* doth yet, by Gods permission continue;

nue; yet all in that kind, is nothing in comparison of those ancient *Oracles*, in several places of the world; which all Nations almost of the then known world, did resort unto, with so much solemnity. However, even by the account the writers of those times have given us, it doth appear how much Gods power and providence did overrule, and restrain the power of the Devil, (as before was said) as himself pleased: which made so many answers to be so ambiguously given, that which way soever the matter fell out, the *Devil* or *Dæmon* (as the *Merlins* of our days have a *providence* to save their credit) might not be found a lyar. But of Oracles particularly, I have said more elsewhere, which I shall not need here to repeat.

NOW to return to *Divination* in general; it is observable, that many things appear to us under the notion of *Divination*, which to *Devils* and *Dæmons* are no such thing: and that partly through the priviledge of their nature, as pure *spirits*, by their creation; and partly, by their experience, much improved by time, in all kind of knowledge, of things *natural*; and in the affairs of the world, relating unto men; to whom the most understanding men compared, in point of natural knowledge or wisdom, are but as children; yea very babes, and *simpletons*, if we may so speak. For example, if (in some remote part of the world, we will suppose) it be asked, whether any English-ship be coming, or, when to be expected; and the answer according to the way of *Divination* by such rites and ceremonies, as are usual in the Country be, *three days*, or *three months*: if the Ship or Ships be upon the Sea; they that can, as the most learned that write of these things, are of opinion, in a moment, as it were, convey bodies some hundred of miles; how easie is it for them to know, though yet five or six days sailing distant, whether

ther any such be upon the Sea? Or if they say three *months*, and it prove so, what wonder, when even men, that are concern'd, and well acquainted with the course of those affairs, and see the preparations, though they cannot foresee many things which the *Devil* can, may probably conjecture, that within three, or six months, they may be at their journeys end, as it doth often happen? We might instance in a hundred things of the same nature: but this instance I have chosen, because some that I have conferr'd with, who had known in their travels such a thing done, more than once, did seem to make a great wonder of it. *Pausanius*, I remember, in his fourth book, doth tell us of one *Ophioneus*, famous in those days for *divination* among the *Græcians*; and his way; the more to be admired, because in shew, it had nothing that was extraordinary, and yet was very effectual. As he doth express it, it was this: πυνϑανόμενος τὰ γινόμενα ἑκάστοτε ἰδία τε, κὴ ἐν κοινῷ, προέλεγεν ὅτω τὰ μέλλοντα: that is: *He Would enquire what and how things had gone before, and so foretel both privately and publickly what should come to pass afterwards.* *Cicero* was famous for this kind of *Divination*, in his time, and seldom failed. The manners of it, and the grounds, he doth largely set out in an Epistle of his to *Cæcinna*, well worth the reading. What pity, that some in these days, who take upon them to be such *Diviners*, have not more of this kind of *divination*, at least, that they might not always so grosly mistake? Now this kind, though of all other kinds of *divination* (setting true *prophesying*, by divine inspiration, aside) most lawful, and commendable, in States-men especially; yet of all others, may be said, as I conceive, most proper unto the *Devil*, as he is a spirit of such standing, since his first creation. For being altogether grounded upon a good head-piece, and long experience; the disproportion between a man, and an

*Angel,*

*Angel* or Spirit, both in point of years and natural abilities; who doth not understand? Our conclusion then, as before, that there is not any kind of *divination* publickly practised, or commonly known, so strange or so ridiculous, but by the *Devil's* intervention, to whom, what rites or ceremonies are used, or whether some or none, but only to amuse, is altogether indifferent, is available sometimes: and yet none, as to mans judgment, so plausible, and so probable, but is *fallible*, and doth often deceive.

BUT that which in this matter of *Divination* most poseth my reason, which also posed *Aristotle* so much, that he could neither believe, nor yet absolutely deny, is, that there be men and women, but *women* especially, in whom resteth a *spirit* of *divination*, ( so expressed, *Acts* 16.16.) by which they foresee, and foretel strange things, and seldom miss. All Histories afford notable examples; so that even some that believe no *Spirits*, ( whether a God, or no, I know not ) yet acknowledg, There be such, that foretel ( they say ) very certainly, for the most part. They impute it to a proper temperament, an ἰδιωσμός: any thing, so neither *God* nor *Devil* be in it. What great occasion they had to fear him, should they grant him an existence, I know not. But one example, every where obvious, and well attested, ( for in this also, as in all things, there is frequent mistaking, and imposture ) I will instance in. *Innocentius* the Eighth, Pope of *Rome*, who sent a man into *England*, or *Scotland* rather, named *Adrianus*, famous for his singular wisdom, & judgment in matters of the world: which soon after, brought him unto *Henry* the Seventh, King of *England*, his favour; and his favour to the Bishoprick of *Bath and Wells*, in *Sommersetshire*. Returned to *Rome*, and in great imployment under *Alexander* the sixth; he was made a *Cardinal*; and after *Alexander*, flourished under more than one, but under Pope *Leo* the Tenth particularly. It was his

L                                                                                                 ill

ill luck, if not occasioned by any impiety, and unthankfulness to God, to grow acquainted with a woman, in whom such a *Spirit* was. Among many things, which she foretold, both publick and private, which in all points, and circumstances fell out accordingly; she also foretold, that one *Adrian* by name, born of mean parentage, preferred meerly by, and for his worth, should be *Pope* after *Leo*. This exactly agreeing with his case, and having had, he thought, sufficient proof of the truth of her predictions, he confidently applied it unto himself, and made no question, but he was the man, that should succeed Pope *Leo*. In this confidence, he began (such a bewitching thing is *Authority*, notwithstanding the sad examples every Age and Country, when too eagerly coveted, doth afford) to think the time long, before the Pope died; and, to hasten it, with some others, conspired against his life; and, though prevented, and pardoned, lived afterwards and ended his days miserably: or, if he had so much grace, as to think so, and to make a right use, more happily (because obscurely) and never heard of more, than before. But *Adrianus* is not our business. The womans prediction was verified by the event. For *Adrianus* the *sixth*, a man of mean parentage, of excellent worth, being then absent, was chosen: (of purpose, a man would think, for no such thing was intended, & scarce believed, when it was done) to verifie the prediction. But God forbid, we should so think seriously: but it fell out strangely, that cannot be denied. Now were it so, that this Spirit of *Divination* were found in men and women, such only, who by their life and conversation, did shew somewhat of either worth or godliness more than ordinary, (it is *Aristotle*'s objection) it would not be so strange, or *incredible*. But for the most part, if not always, (true *prophets* excepted) it falls out quite contrary. And

therefore

therefore by the law of God, such were to be put to death, *Lev.* 20. 27. And happy is that Kingdom, ( for there God hath promised a blessing ) where no such, who take upon them to *prophesie*, ( whether their predictions prove true or no ) are suffered to live. But *Credulity* and *Incredulity* is the thing we have to do with. What then shall we say? First, that *Aristotle*'s objection is very plausible, and worthy of *Aristotle*; and the same objection lieth against the *Salutators* of *Spain*, who for the most part, are ignorant people, of a leud conversation; and yet are believed generally, to do strange cures. *Francifcus à Victoria*, of whom, besides *Grotius*, divers Protestants speak with good respect, is so put to it in this case, that he doth not know what to pitch upon; as himself doth ingenuously acknowledge. Of four opinions, which he doth propose, he doth leave us free to chuse which we will: Either that they cheat, and impose: or that, what they do, they do it by the *Devil*: or perchance, by a special grace, for reasons best known unto God: or lastly, that it may be a secret of a proper natural temperament. So still we are left in uncertainty. But against manifest experience, besides the authority from the word of God, there is no arguing, as to matter of fact. It is not any part of our task, to examine the reason. But, were the nature and divisions, or kinds of *Spirits* better known unto us, than they are, or should be ambitious to know, whilest we live; it is likely we might say more to it, than now we can. I shall conclude, that, as I account great *Incredulity* not to believe that there be such predictions; so, to believe them, before the event have confirmed them; to enquire after them; to regard them, is little less, than *Apostacy* from God, and from the true faith. If true sometimes, yet false often; but always dangerous, if not pernicious to them that hunt after them.

L 2                           SAINT

SAINT *Augustin* in one of his books *contra Academicos*, under the name of *Licentius*, one of the *Collocutors*, in that *Dialogue*, doth tell us of one *Albicerius*, a notable *Diviner*, in his time, well known unto him in his younger years, ( an excusable curiosity, in that age, and profession ) long before he was a Christian. Three or four notable stories he hath of him; but first of all, or before that, what kind of man he was, for his life. A very rogue, as any was in *Carthage*, and such a whoremonger ( *innumera scorta*, faith St. *Augustin* ) as scarce any age hath known the like. The first story is, that, consulted about some silver Spoons, that were missing, by a messenger; he presently told the owner of the Spoons, the thief, and the place, where they were at present. I believe some of our *London-Prognosticators*, have done as much, or near, if publick fame ( though they may think it a credit ) do them no wrong. Another time, when St. *Augustin*, or some of his familiar acquaintances, went to him, to be satisfied about somewhat, which he doth not relate; he, not only satisfied them in that, to the utmost of their expectation, or desire; but moreover, acquainted them, that their boy, or servant, by the way, had stoln some money out of the bag of money, which he carried after them: even before he had set his eyes upon the said boy, or servant; and forced him to restore every penny, before the masters of it did know, what, or how much had been taken away. A third story is, of one *Flaccianus*, well known to St. *Augustin*, it seems, who being about to purchase a piece of ground, went to this *Diviner*, or *Cunning-man*, to see, what he could tell him about it : who had no sooner seen *Flaccianus*, but presently told him what he was come about, and named the ground, or Farm, as it was ordinarily called; which *Flaccianus* himself ( it seems, it was somewhat an uncouth hard name ) did not well know. But the

the fourth ſtory, made St. *Auguſtin*, ( a young man then ) under the name and perſon of the ſaid *Licentius*, even tremble for amazement, whileſt he did relate it. A condiſciple of his, or one that had been, hearing ſo much of the man, and either not believing, or, for further trial, and to know the utmoſt of his power, went to him, and boldly and importunately challenged him, to tell him what it was he had in his thoughts : who, put to it, as he was, told him, he did think of *Virgil*. Being further asked, what particular place of *Virgil*, the man, though otherwiſe, ſcarce able to read, pronounced aloud, boldly and ſecurely, the very verſe of the Poet, he had then in his mind. Who makes any queſtion, but he, that did this, ( no *man of God*, but a very rogue ) was really poſſeſt by the Devil ? And do we wonder at it ; or rather wonder, that any, men or women, that take upon them to do ſuch things, in a Chriſtian Commonweal, ſhould be ſuffered to live ? Or that any, that make uſe of ſuch, whether men or women, ſhould make any queſtion, ( if Chriſtians by profeſſion and education) but that, in ſo doing, they go to the Devil ? But ſome may wonder perchance, as St. *Auguſtin*, or his friend, did, at the firſt, ( for afterwards he made nothing of it ) that the Devil ſhould have ſuch power, which the *Scripture* doth ſeem to appropriate unto God, to know thoughts. But it is one thing, to have the thoughts of all men, in all places, at all times, open and naked, which belongs unto God only; &, by ſome ſubtilty or ſecret of nature, to know the thoughts of ſome men, at ſometimes, which the Devil can, it is certain, if God do not hinder : which men alſo, well acquainted with nature, by diligent obſervation of the eyes, and otherwiſe, may, in ſome part, attain unto. And why not this, as poſſible, as for men ( but women rather ) in the light, or day-time, at a good diſtance, to communicate, and to impart their thoughts,

freely

*Of Credulity and Incredulity,*

freely and fully, without any noise or voice, by the observation of the lips only, and other parts about the mouth? A secret of nature lately discovered; of which more in my Treatise of *Enthusiasm*, Chapter 4. of the second Edition, page 181, &c. I name the *second* Edition: because, not so much of it in the *first* to be found.

AFTER *Divination*, somewhat, because of the affinity, may be expected of *Prodigies*, of which, as of *Divination*, much hath been written, and argued to and fro; by divers: and very lately by one, by some whom I have heard much commended. I therefore shall say the less; neither indeed doth my subject engage me, to say much. As all other things in the world, not determinable by sense, those especially that relate to God, and his providence, have been liable to *superstition* and *credulity*; so this of *prodigies*, as much as any. The ancient *Romans* have been noted for their excess, in this kind; and their best Historian, *Titus Livius*, for inserting that, into the body of his History, which stood upon publick records, hath been censured as fabulous: for which nevertheless, he doth often excuse himself, and smartly doth censure the *credulity* of the people of those days. Yet I make no question, but by the contrivance of the *Divil*, in those days of ignorance and superstition, (as of *Oracles* was said before) for the increase of superstition, many things in that kind might happen, (besides what did by Gods order and appointment, which have not hapned so frequently since. But what excess soever they might justly be charged of, yet we must acknowledge, that the ground of it, *Quod omnium secundorum adversorumque causas in Deos* ( had he but said, *Deum* ) *verterent*: that is, in effect, *Because they believed a God, and a providence, the cause of all good and evil that hapneth unto men*; as the same *Livy* doth inform us; was commendable, which would make us (besides

sides other reasons ) think the better of *prodigies* in these days, wherein *Epicurism* and *Atheism* do so mightily prevail. And it cannot be denied, but they lived then, generally, according to their belief, frugally and vertuously. Witness those rare Examples, those times afforded, scarce to be matched in any other age. And, as this belief made them vertuous; so their vertue, conquerors of the best, and greatest part of the then known world. Whereas when all observation of prodigies ceased, which the same *Livy* saith did proceed, *ab eadem negligentia, quâ nihil Deos portendere vulgo nunc credunt* : ( a mild word *negligentia*, for *Atheism*, or *Epicurism* ) all manner of vices, pride, luxury, covetousness, and the like, crept in; which occasioned their Civil wars; and their Civil war, with these vices, the ruine of that glorious *Empire*. Were there no other thing in the world, to perswade me; yet the authority of two such men, as *Camerarius* and *Melanchton* ; so pious, so learned both, would make me not to reject all *prodigies*, whether publick or private. Yet it must be confessed, that where the opinion lights upon a man, who is naturally tender and fearful; and such was the nature of them both I have named, of *Melanchton* especially; it hardly escapes excess. But again, were there no other examples or instances of *prodigies* ( known to me ) than what hapned before the death of *Julius Cæsar*, the *Roman* Emperor ; and what before *Henry* the Fourth, late King of *France* ; who for their valour, and manner of death, may well be paralleled, being so well attested, as no rational man can make any question; I should think and acknowledge my self sufficiently convicted, that there be *prodigies*: presaging *prodigies*, I mean. And if in their case, why not in the case of many Princes, and others; such especially, who have been active men in the world, and made a great noise by their valourous or ventrous atchievements, and undertakings? Always provided, that there be like evidence and atteftation. I think I have read in *Julius Scaliger*, a man of fingular as learning, fo piety; fome where; ( I find it fo in my papers, but not the place quoted ) *Melior fuperftitio* ( fo it do not proceed to a breach of any particular command of Gods revealed word: fo I underftand it ) *nimiâ fobrietate, qua facile degenerat in Atheifmum*: that is, *Better is fuperftition, fometimes, than too much fobriety,* ( or *cautiloufnefs* ) *Which is apt foon to degenerate into Atheifm*. At another time, perchance, I fhould not think fo well of it: But now when Atheifm doth fo prevail, and true Piety, under the name of *fuperftition*, fubject to derifion; I think the advice is not amifs.

ANCIENT Heathens had an opinion, not unworthy the confideration, that no *predigie*, or bad *Omen*, could hurt them by the event, who did profefs not to regard them, or could elude them by a contrary interpretation. *Pliny's* words to this purpofe, are; *Exemplis apparere, oftentorum vires & in noftra poteftate effe, ac, prout quaque accepta fint, ita valere*. He doth add, *In Augurum certe difciplina*, &c. that is, *That by the difcipline of the Augures*, ( a fort of *Diviners* or *Soothfayers* among the *Romans* ) *it is very certain, that neither imprecations, or aufpicies* ( or prefages ) *did belong unto them,* ( to hurt them ) *who when they had any work in hand, did profefs and declare they did take no notice of either*: *Quo munere divina indulgentia, maius nullum eft*, faith he; that is, *Than Which, the Divine mercy hath not vouchfafed unto men a greater gift*, or *boon*. So *Pliny, lib*. 28. *cap*. 2. And in the next Chapter he doth mention fome particular rites and ceremonies, which they ufed, to elude, or avert mifchiefs, when threatned by fome ill *prefage*, or inaufpicious accident. Of which St. *Auguftin* doth treat, and reckon many, in his fecond *de Doct. Chriftiana*, Chap. 20. I

make

*in things* NATURAL. 153

make no great wonder, if many of those superstitious rites and ceremonies by both *Pliny* and St. *Augustin* mentioned, were thought efficacious to elude, or avert; when the observation of *prodigies* was so transcendent, that every thing almost, that did not happen every day, was looked upon as a *prodigie*. It was not hard to avert, or elude ( as they interpreted it ) what probably, as founded upon such groundless fears, and imaginations, would never have hapned: though probable too, that meer fear and imagination, though no better grounded, might be the cause sometimes, that some things hapned really, which otherwise had never been. But however, because *Pliny*, no very superstitious man, who elsewhere hath not faith enough to believe, that God cares for the world, or takes any notice of mens actions, whether good or bad: because he doth here, we see, so magnifie the power of faith, and therein the goodness of God, that would so provide it, and appoint it: and that, besides *Pliny*, there be others, that attest the same, or much to the same purpose: as afterwards in due place may be shewed: we may consider, besides Christian *faith*, whether there be not some kind of natural *faith*, such as *natural*, meer *natural* men are, and always have been capable of; which with God, by his own order, and appointment, is, and always hath been more or less meritorious, or efficacious for the averting of some temporal evils; and a good pledge, or forerunner of that true faith ( in Christ ) by which we hope, not only to be rescued from that misery, which, as the wretched posterity of a sinful *protoplast*, we are born unto; but also ( I expect no otherwise, but that the *wits* will laugh at our simplicity ) purchase Heaven it self, and Immortality. But of this, more elsewhere, which I will not here transcribe.

WITH this of *Pliny* the elder, doth well agree the resolution of *Pliny* the latter, and as well with
Christi-

*Chriſtianity*; and therefore not unworthy our obſervation. A friend of his, who was to plead a cauſe, within one or two days after, had a dream, which much troubled him, and threatned, as he did interpret it, ſome kind of miſcarrying. Whereupon he doth addreſs himſelf to *Pliny*, that he would procure him a further day. *Pliny* firſt doth propoſe unto him, what in ſuch a caſe himſelf had done, preferring that excellent rule or *maxim* of *Homer*'s: Εἰς ἰωνὸς ἄεισ᾽ ἀμύνεδαι περὶ πάτρης· ( That is, in effect; *That a good cauſe ought to be regarded more than any ſigns or prodigies whatſoever*) before terrifying dreams and viſions, when he was to defend the cauſe of an innocent friend, againſt potent enemies: Wherein, notwithſtanding his terrifying *preſages* or *prodigies*, he proſpered. He did ſo, and hoped his friend might alſo. But if that would not ſatisfie him, his next advice is, *Quod dubitas ne feceris*: which he calls *Conſultiſſimi cujuſque præceptum*, the precept or advice of all that are wiſe and prudent: *Not to do that whereof you doubt*: which, I think doth very well agree with that of the Apoſtle; *And he that doubteth is damned if he eat, becauſe he eateth not of faith*: *For whatſoever is not of faith, is ſin*. But laſtly, I make great difference of *prodigies*, that concern private men only; and thoſe which concern *Princes*, and whole *common Weals*. I do not think theſe ſo eaſie to be avoided, as thoſe.

I HAVE done with *prodigies*: I now proceed to that I have to obſerve upon the inſtances, or the chiefeſt of them, that have been produced, which may be uſeful, as I conceive, in all, or moſt other caſes of *Credulity* or *Incredulity*. And here, firſt of all, I propoſe this rule of *Credulity* or *Incredulity* in general, in St. *Auguſtin*'s words; *Multa* ( St. *Auguſtin* hath it, *Nonnulla* only; but I think it will bear *multa* very well ) *credibilia, ſunt falſa*; *ſicut incredibilia multa, ſunt vera*. Or in *Minu-*

*Minutius Fœlix* his words, more pithily: *In incredibili, verum; & in credibili, mendacium*: that is in English, That many things, which seem incredible, are true: and many things false, which are very credible, or likely true. Which is no more, if so much, than what *Aristotle* long before in that known Axiom of his taught; that, *fal,a quædam*, &c. *that some things that are false, have more appearance of truth, than some things that are true.* It is no argument to me, that a thing is true, because it is possible; no, nor because probable: nay, it is certain, that many lyes and falshoods are founded upon this very thing, *probability.* Though civility may oblige, not to contradict, where we see no impossibility; yet discretion will, to doubt, and to suspend assent, till we see good ground of *belief.* I know the wisest man may mistake sometimes; many are credulous; and many love to tell what themselves have forged, or what they have from others, though themselves perchance do not believe it. I am no *Sceptick* or *Pyrrhonick*; and whether ever any such were, really, is a question: which to be, in my apprehension, is little less, than of a rational creature born, to turn into a *senseless* brute. And it doth much derogate from Gods goodness, to think that he should give us *reason*, the best of gifts, for no other use, than always to doubt; which is worse, than to have no *reason* at all. Yet this I must say, which I think most true: their profession was, if ever any such, to doubt *of all things*: the best way, never to be a *Sceptick*, is, not to be too quick of belief, and to doubt *of many things.* Take it from St. *Augustin*; that it may have more authority, best in his own words, but because very worthy to be known unto all, that would be wise, I will put them into English. They are out of his book *De Magistro*, which in a *Socratical* way, that is by way of *Dialogues*, doth comprehend divers curious speculations

tions concerning the end, or use of speech. St. *Augustin*, one of the two speakers, taking upon him to be the *Magister*; and *Adeodatus* the other speaker, made to be the *disciple*. This *Adeodatus*, after much arguing to and fro, having often been compelled by force of argument, to confess that *true*, which he thought *false*; and on the contrary, that *false*, which he thought otherwise of before; being grown, at the last, more cautious, what he denied, or assented unto; he is commended for it by St. *Augustin*, in these words: *I am well pleased with your doubting, as it is a sign to me of a mind* (or *disposition*) *not inclinable to rashness, than which* [such a disposition] *nothing doth more conduce to setledness or tranquillity of mind. For how can we avoid trouble of mind, when those things which through too great facility of assent,* ( or Credulity ) *we had yielded as true, by opposite arguments begin to totter, and at last are extorted from us against our wills? So that, as it is but reasonable to yield assent unto those things which we have throughly considered, and perfectly understand: so to embrace that we know not, as though we knew it, and understood it, is no less dangerous. For the danger is, that when we have been often beaten off from those things which we conceived once most firm and solid; We fall at last into such a hatred, or jealous suspition of reason, that we shall not think fit or safe, to yield assent unto any truth, though never so perspicuous and apparent.* So St. *Augustin* there. Though he speak properly of *belief* and *unbelief* in matters of opinions, determinable by *reason* only; and we of *belief* and *unbelief* in matters of fact, only, determinable, not by *reason*, but by *experience*: yet his words are very applicable to our purpose; one great ground of *Incredulity*, and that which doth most justifie it to the world, is, *groundless Credulity*.

BUT on the other side, to go on where we began, with St. *Augustin*'s rule; besides what is against the *faith*,

or

or doth imply manifest *contradiction*; to me, I confess, nothing is *incredible*. I see so many things with mine eyes; and many more I read of, in them that have collected, and set out Nature's Wonders, in several kinds; all *miraculous* to me, because though I see the thing plainly and undeniably, yet I comprehend not the reason; and those that have attempted to find it, I speak it of many *natural* things, as the Load-stone, and the like, are either ridiculously come off, as *Pomponatius*, and the like; or have still left the matter in great obscurity, and their *reasons* liable to many objections: and again, I see or believe upon good attestation, so many strange effects of the power (with God's permission) of *Devils* and *Spirits*; so many (to sight, and for any reason that we can give) *miraculous operations*; that I know not what it is, besides what I have before mentioned, without good and mature consideration, that I can think *incredible*, or *impossible*. Yet I know that the *Devils* power, allow him to the utmost of what can rationally be allowed to a created *Spirit*, is limited, and that he cannot do many things. What those things are that he cannot, is disputed, and argued by many, to whom I willingly subscribe. But he can so imitate and counterfeit, that we shall find it a very hard task, to distinguish between the *reality* of that which he cannot, and the *resemblance*, which he doth offer unto our eyes. He cannot create *substances*: he cannot create men, or women, nor the least *creature*, I believe, that hath its Beeing by *generation*: but he may cast before our eyes such shapes of those things, which he cannot create; or so work upon our phancy, that it shall create them unto us so *vigorously*, so *seemingly*, that he may attain his ends by those counterfeits, as effectually, perchance, as if all were in good earnest,

earnest, what it appears to our deluded eyes. So that the most satisfactory limitation I can find or think of, of his power, is, that he can do no more, than what God doth permit, who hath reserved to himself the Sovereignty of the worlds government, and will not suffer them that trust to him, and depend of him, in the least degree, to suffer by him more, than what may be for his own glory, and their further good, if they patiently submit, and their faith and confidence hold to the last. Whereîn I am so confident, and so much confirmed, even by those strange effects of the Devils power, which I have read and believe,• that it never yet entred into my heart to fear any thing of him more, than his *temptations*, against which Christ hath taught me daily to pray. But of this more, by and by. Upon these grounds, *Miranda natura*, *Nature's wonders* first; for which no satisfactory reason can be found; collected, as many, or most, hitherto known by divers; but, if diligently sought, daily to be multiplied: and secondly, the power of the *Devil*, which though not so great now, as it was before Christ, yet great enough still, to cause admiration; I know not well, I say, what to account *incredible*. Could one man, trusting to the strength of his wit, and the efficacy of his art, not without some ground ( as some learned professors of the art have taken upon them to maintain, which I meddle not with ) speak so proudly, εἰς μὲ ςῖ, ᾗ κινήσω τὴν γῆν: *find me but a place where I may stand conveniently*, ( at a convenient distance from the earth it self, I suppose his meaning was ) *and I will move the whole earth*: and could the same man do things in the sight of many, which were then generally thought *imp.ssible*, and now to many more *incredible?* and how shall we limit the power of *Spirits*, in knowledge and experience so far exceeding that of mens, when God doth permit? Yet for all this, I do not deny, but it is

limited,

## *in things* NATURAL. 159

limitted, as I said before, because it is both against faith, and against reason to believe, that God will permit them to do many things, though not so easie, precisely to determine, what those things are; and much harder to discern what is real, and what is counterfeit, among the works of so skilful juglers. Not easily to *believe* then, what otherwise is acknowledged very *possible*; nor yet absolutely to reject as *incredible*, what to ordinary sense, and reason may seem impossible, but to consider how attested, and not to dispute against clear evidence; that's our first *rule*, or *observation*.

OUR second shall be; In the relation of strange things, whether *natural* or *supernatural*, to know the temper of the *relator*, if it can be known: and what interest he had, or might probably be supposed to have had, in the relation, to have it believed. Again, whether he profess to have seen it himself, or take it upon the credit of others: and whether a man by his profession, in a capacity probable, to judge of the truth of those things, to which he doth bear witness. Every one of these particulars would require a particular *consideration*, but that I would not be too long, or tedious. To make application of this to those witnesses, or the chiefest, I have produced and made use of: I can give no account of their temper by their life, or actions; they were not, nor could be known unto me, that way. But he was not altogether out, who said, *Loquere ut te videam*: though subject to many exceptions, I know; yet ordinarily, a man may give some guess at a mans temper in point of seriousness, or lightness, by his writings. *Cardan* was a learned man, and one that was well acquainted with the world; of great experience, I make no question. But he was a man *ventosi ingenii*, *self-conceited* beyond measure, and as covetous of popular applause: never spake man more truly, than he that first past that censure

censure on him. Any man of ordinary judgment may quickly perceive it by his writings. A man, that did affect to tell strange things, that cause wonder, that he might be wondred at, and admired by them, that did believe him. And indeed he doth tell more strange things of himself, and his father, and some other relations of his, than a man shall likely meet with any where else. But he was not only *ventosus*, as censured by others, but also *mendacissimus*, a notable lyar, as acknowledged, and proved by his great friend *Nodæus*; and by his confession of himself, according to his *horoscope*, *Nugax*, *religionis contemptor*, *maledicus*, *impurus*, *calumniator*, &c. all which the same *Nodæus* doth acknowledge most true of him.

SOME man may wonder, (this by the way) what made *Nodæus*, who otherwise doth most ridiculously exalt him, to acknowledge so much truth: but there was a reason. *Cardanus* and *Nodæus* were not of one Religion, in point of *Spirits*; of whom, though *Cardanus* tells many strange stories, which I believe (from such a convicted lyar) are false; yet among so many, it is possible some might be true. But whether false or true, *Nodæus*, as all, or most that are of that perswasion, admirers of *Epicurus*, &c. could not indure to hear of them. In that particular, he doth cast dirt upon him, and makes him the vilest man, that ever was: In others, if you will believe him, *Cardanus* was an incomparable man. This in another age, might have been thought a contradiction; and *Nodæus* himself censured for a man of no judgment at all, if not worse. But he knew what times he wrote in, and how men stood affected. Neither did his judgment herein deceive him; which in a more sober age, if God will be so merciful, may cause no small wonder. Well, *Cardan*, for one, was a learned man, of great experience: but I say, by *Nodæus* his leave,

leave, this *mendaciffimus* doth spoil all. I think they that trust him, deserve to be deceived; and I doubt many stand not upon that so much, so they may be thought some body, because they read *Cardan*.

I KNOW not any I have made use of, but, so far as may be guessed by their writings, were sober and serious men: and so accounted by those (known unto me) who mention them in their writings. They were all, or most of them, learned Physicians, and therefore best able to judge of those things, which they wrote of, and attested. How it should advantage either the credit of their Art and profession, (which to preserve, made *Galen* so unwilling a long time, as before observed, before he would acknowledge the efficacy of *charms* and *incantations*) or their particular profit, in their practice, to acknowledge, and of their own accord publish and proclaim the efficacy of *supernatural means for cures, &c.* (such as we have made choice of too for instances) no man, I think can imagine: how it might impair it, is very apparent. The best reward of their ingenuity from the greater number, or those *sapientissimi*, in *Seneca*, they could expect, is, to be accounted either *lyars* or *idiots*. Lastly, *Remigius* excepted, of whom some question may be made; because he saith, *vidi hominem*, *he saw the man*; he doth not say, he saw the *thing*: (which yet may be true enough, for any thing he saith) all the rest expresly profess, to have seen with *their eyes*, what they relate. *Vair* indeed doth not mention *his eyes*, but he hath those *circumstances*, which he doth attest, which, as I say there, amount to a *vidimus*, or, *occular attestation*.

BUT then, thirdly, *Seneca* saith, *oculis nihil fallacius*: and doth give some instances. His instances are

M                                                   true,

true, yet I cannot allow of his inference. We muſt truſt to our eyes, in moſt things; to our ears, and other ſenſes, elſe we ſhall not know what to truſt to. However, it is very true in ſome caſes, our eyes, our ears, and other ſenſes may deceive us; and that relation may be ſuſpected, which is grounded upon two eyes, or ears only; though the witneſs be granted an honeſt diſcerning man. I could mention many things that have hapned unto my ſelf in that kind: but one thing, that hath made moſt impreſſion, I ſhall make bold to relate. It is not many years; but it was ſome time before our *happy reſtoration*: My Son (the only I have or then had) and I had rid ſome twenty or thirty miles that day, and came to the houſe of a worthy Gentlewoman, of ſome relation, by marriage; where I had been often kindly entertained. In the night, about midnight I then gueſſed, my ſaid Son, and I lying together, and both faſt aſleep; I was ſuddenly awakened by the report of a Gun or Piſtolet, as I then thought, diſcharged under the bed. It ſhook the bed, I am ſure. Being ſomewhat terrified, I awakened my bed-fellow; asked him, whether he had heard nothing; told him what I had heard, and felt. He was ſcarce awake, when a ſecond blow was heard, and the bed, as before: which did put him in ſuch a fright, that I forgat mine own, and wholly applied my ſelf to put him out of it, and to keep him in his right wits. Thus buſie, it was not long before a third blow, and ſtill the bed as before. I would have riſen, but that he did ſo cloſely embrace me, that I durſt not leave him, neither was he willing to let me go. It was an hour at leaſt after that third and laſt blow, before I could get him to ſleep; and before day, I alſo fell aſleep. In the morning, being up before me, I bid him look under the bed, which he did, but not ſo carefully, as one poſſeſt with other apprehenſions about the cauſe,

as

as he might have done. I charged him not to speak to any, until my self had first acquainted the Miſtreſs of the houſe, whom I knew, an underſtanding diſcreet Gentle-woman. It was about dinner-time before ſhe came down to the Parlour, and then as ſoberly as I could, none being preſent, but two of her daughters, vertu-ous Gentlewomen; I firſt prepared her, not much to wonder, or to be troubled. So I acquainted her. I perceived by her countenance, it did trouble her, and as we were diſcourſing, ſhe looking upon me, as expect-ing ſomewhat from me, that might prevent further jea-louſie or ſuſpition; I hapned to tell her, that I had ſome thought in the morning, that it might be the cords of the bed: She preſently, and with a joyful countenance, ſaid, It is ſo certainly; for the bed was lately corded with new cords, which were ſo ſtretched, that the man told us, he was afraid they would break, if not then, yet ſoon after, when the bed ſhould be uſed. She had no ſooner ſaid it, but ſends one of her daughters up to look, and it was ſo indeed: the cords were broken in three ſeveral places. What others, to whom the like, or ſomewhat like had hapned before, or otherwiſe bet-ter experienced in ſuch things, might have thought of it, I know not: I have no thought to make a wonder of it, now I know the cauſe: But I ſuppoſe it might have hap-ned to ſome other, as it did to me, till I knew the cauſe, to be terrified; and ſo terrified, that had I gone away before I had been ſatisfied, I ſhould not have been con-ſcious to my ſelf of a lye, if I had reported, that the houſe was haunted. I could never have believed, that ſuch cords could have made ſuch a loud noiſe; beſides the ſhaking of the bed, which added much to my won-dring, until I knew the certainty. I could not have be-lieved, I ſay: though I have conſidered ſince, that even a ſmall thread, haſtily broken, maketh no ſmall noiſe;

and besides, that a Pistolet could not be discharged, but there would have been a smoak, and smell. But whatever some might have thought, it is enough that it might have hapned unto some others, as to me, to prove that our senses may deceive us sometimes, and that it is not always enough to say, I have seen it, or I have heard it. But when a thing doth happen in the clear light of the Sun, and in clear sight ( for at a distance many eyes may be deceived; and a *panick fear*, in the time of war, may make a whole camp upon some very slight mistake or suspicion run away: but that is another case) but clear light, and clear sight, of many sober, and not pre-occupied with any passion, if then many eyes be deceived; it is very likely, and so I grant, it doth often happen; it is by the art and intervention of the *Devil*, that they are so. Now in those relations I have made use of, some things were done very publickly, before many; not any, but had more witnesses than one or two, and therefore more likely to be true.

FOURTHLY, At *the mouth of two or three Witnesses shall every word or matter be established*: we know who saith it; and, if there be no just exception against the witnesses, is most agreeable to the practice of men, in all places. I have cleared my witnesses from all exceptions; and they are more than one or two that witnesse the same thing, though not the same thing numerically, yet the same thing in effect; to wit, the truth of *supernatural operations*, by *Devils* and *Spirits*; which they, who upon such proofs and attestations will not believe, may justly be charged with *obstinate*, and if we consider the ill consequence of such unbelief, *pernicious incredulity*.

LASTLY, somewhat hath been said of it before, but it cannot be too often repeated: Let no man that doth aspire to the knowledge of *truth*, discredit the truth

or

or reality of any business that is controverted, because the thing is liable to abuse and imposture. It is a very popular way indeed, and with vulgar judgments, of great force: but it is the way to deny all *truth*, and to overthrow all government, and whatsoever is most holy among men. For what is it, if well look'd into, that is not liable to abuse, and imposture? To insist upon somewhat that is obvious, and what every man may judge of: No wise man doth doubt, but that there is such an art, as *Physick* or *Medicine*; acknowledged in the Scriptures, both of the Old and New Testament: magnified in the Civil Law: besides the testimonies of private men, of all professions, every where obvious. And for my part, though all the world should be of another belief, yet I should think my self, who more than once (with Gods blessing) have been saved by it, bound with gratitude to acknowledge the efficacy and excellency of it. Yet if a man were disposed to argue against it, as needless, or pernitious, how easily might he find arguments? As first, because divers Nations have done without Physicians, as well as with them: the *Romans*, for a long time; the *Babylonians*, whose custom was, as witnessed by *Herodotus*, to keep records of diseases and cures; and to expose their sick to the view of all men: not to insist in other Nations, which have been specified by others. And then, the Sects and Factions of Physicians, that have been at all times: their different judgments of the causes of diseases; and different courses in curing; not only different, but even contrary: as every man knows, that hath but looked into their books. And then, if we consider the number of *Empericks*, bold illiterate, ungrounded men, that go under that name; and the *credulity*, or coverousness of many, who to save somewhat, will trust them-

themselves into any hands, rather than be at the charge to send for, or go to an allowed, and well-grounded Physician; it is a great question, (or perchance, no question, but many more, certainly) whether more are not kill'd by such usurpers, and counterfeits, than are saved (under God) by true learned Physicians, where they most abound. But all this may easily be answered, and Physick vindicated; but with this acknowledgment, that the best things that are, may be abused: and so those things, that in their nature have the truth and reality of existence as certainly, as those that are seen and discerned by the eye, may be counterfeited and falsified, and are liable to the mistakes of men that are ignorant, and the illusion of juglers and impostors.

FOR a further direction to them that may want it, in this matter of witnesses to make faith to strange relations; I will take notice of some objections that are made, or may be made. As first, what can be more creditable, than what doth stand upon publick records? may some body say. So did all those *prodigies* Livy doth relate. Must we then think our selves in reason bound to believe them, all, or one half of them? No: it is a mistake. That which stood upon record, was, that such and such (if more, than one: of many *prodigies*, but one) did inform that such and such a thing had hapned; who delivered it upon their honest word, (not *oath*, that I can find; except it were upon some extraordinary occasion) that it was true. This was the superstition of the *Romans*, of those victorious times, that they thought nothing, that did relate to the service of their Gods, must be neglected: and so a record of it was made, *nunciatum esse*, that it was *reported*, not *verum esse*, that it was *true*. Yet we find in the same *Livy*, that oftentimes, upon just suspicion; that which was related, did pass some kind of examination; and if found defective, not

not allowed. But what shall we say to *Plutarch*'s relation, who not upon his own credit only, and yet he acknowledged a grave, and serious Author; but upon the credit of many then living, in his *Treatise* of the *Soul*; not now extant; but so much of it is preserved in *Eusebius*; doth seriously relate, of one very well known unto him, and his familiar friend, as I take it; who died, he said, and his Soul after three hours, remanded to his body; because it was upon a mistake of the messenger, that he was deprived of life by such a sickness, when another man was intended and sent for. After which restauration to life, he lived many years, and was then alive, *Plutarch* saith, when he wrote this of him. This relation, I must confess, did somewhat trouble me, when I first read in *Eusebius*; and the rather, because *Eusebius* doth barely relate it, and excepts against nothing, which some might interpret as an assent, but is not; there was no need, if what he aimed at, be considered. But however so barely related, did trouble me for a time. But afterwards, upon better consideration, I thought and still think that both *Plutarch* and his friend, might be very honest men, and speak no more than what they believed to be very true; and yet we not bound at all to believe them. For first of all, this departing of his soul was in a καταφορᾷ, *Plutarch* saith; that is a kind of *unnatural deep sleep*, which by them that are not much acquainted with the proper terms of Physick, and differences of every disease, might easily be mistaken for an ἔκστασις; which Physicians define, *Soporem gravem, quo qui tenentur,* &c. that is, *A kind of sleep, which they that labour of, sleep profoundly, and dream; and afterwards, when awakened, what they did dream, they think to be true, and relate it unto others for very truth.* Or, as *Sennertus* elsewhere; *They lie as though they were dead, and frequently, after they are awakened,* k̶ned, m..ke report what ſtrange things they have heard and ſeen.

NO wonder then, if the man in ſuch a diſtemper, ſaw ſtrange viſions, and it is probable, he had read of ſome ſuch thing, that had hapned, or commonly reported to have hapned unto ſome others; whereof the learned *Annotator*, in the laſt *Paris* Edition will give a further account to them that deſire it. But this granted; it follows in *Plutarch*, that the other, who by right ſhould have died, (for there was a miſtake of men, or ſouls, as was ſaid before) upon the return of *Antillus* his ſoul, (that was his name) when he heard what had hapned to *Antillus*, and what report he had made of his viſions; that is, that his ſoul ſhould be returned indeed; but the others, firſt intended, would be ſent for; he fell ſick, and died in very deed. Truly I think according to the belief of the vulgar of thoſe days, it were a wonder, a great wonder, if he had not. For he was not only told, what this revived (as was thought) *Antillus* had reported of him, as revealed unto him in that other world; but people (ſo goes the ſtory) were daily and hourly at his door, to ſee the event, which was enough to ſtartle any man, that had not a very great courage, and knew nothing to the contrary, but that what was reported of *Antillus* his death, his miraculous reviving, and what *Antillus* himſelf had ſince reported, as revealed unto him, where he had been, was very true; enough I ſay, to ſtartle him into an alienation of mind, or a ſudden death: whereof there be many examples of men, who ſurprized with a ſudden great fear, though without any other hurt, or danger, have fallen into ſome ſickneſs, which hath ended in death. He therefore, who upon this, or like relation of *Plutarch*, ſhould cenſure him for a *fabulous* writer, would do him wrong, and bewray either malignity or

igno-

ignorance. Yet many *fables* we may find in *Plutarch*, which being delivered by him, not credited, nor to that end they should be credited, but according to the *Mythologie* of those times, which was no small part of their learning, and is yet to all men, for the understanding of ancient books, without which no true learning can be purchased; for such fables, and the like, delivered upon certain suppositions; it were very ridiculous, and injurious also, to account him fabulous.

BUT because this is a profitable point, to prevent rash judgment, which commonly proceeds from ignorance, or want of judgment, or ingenuity, the worst of the three; among them that have lately written of *Dæmons* and *Spirits*, and their instruments, men and women, *Witches* and *Sorcerers*: *Bodinus* and *Remigius* are most known, I think, and read. Learned men both; and who I think, had no intention at all to impose upon their Readers, but wrote as themselves believed. Yet for all this, I do not think my self bound to believe every thing that they believed, and thought truth: neither could I, for the reasons before alledged, ground upon any of their stories, but as the authorities, and circumstances of the story, well pondered, shall induce me. Though learned, yet men; and as men, liable to errors and mistakes; and in some things, perhance, more credulous, than I should be. What either of them might think of the efficacy of *Washing of the hands*; of *Salt*; and of a *Vine-stick*; of the *crowing of the Cock*, and the like; I make no question, but they had some plausible grounds, & the confessions of divers *Witches* (first deluded by the Devil, that they might delude others, and by degrees, draw them to other more superstitious observations for it; besides what is objected to *Bodinus* particularly by the censors of his book, if true. Many men who have got some such thing by the end, that actually prove false, or it may be justly suspected fictitious; they think they have enough to prove it a man, and to blast his labours, though otherwise never so worthy, or profitable; which, as I said before, is an argument of great either weaknefs, or malice. I know it is the manner of many, *incredulous* men especially; when they are pressed with any authority, and cannot otherwise evade. A very learned man, in his books, *De Origine Idololat.* ( or rather, *De Theologia Gentili*, &c. a far more proper Title, except he had followed it otherwise: which gave me encouragement to write of the same subject, *De orig. Idololat.* long ago, though never yet printed ) doth pass a harsh judgment against *Bodinus*, as for some other things; so particularly, for his severity, or rather, as he makes it, rash and injurious partiality, in admitting all kind of witnesses against suspected Witches: and to draw out compassion more forcibly, he stiles them *imbecillem sexum*. I will not take upon me to excuse *Bodin* in all things. Yet had he as well considered the atrocity of the crime, than which none can be either more injurious to the Divine Majesty, or more pernicious to the community of men; he might as well have censured his severity in this case, an excess of zeal for God and men ; as he doth censure it, and aggravate it, want of equity and mercy. And sure I am, that a very learned man too, and of great fame in the world; out of meer indignation, and zeal to God, seeing *Witches* and *Sorcerers* so indulgently dealt in *France*, ( where *Bodinus* lived ) did write, as himself professeth, that learned Treatise; *De Idololatria Magica*, which is extant.

BUT in very deed no man can deny, but in this case of *Witches*, and persons *bewitched*, great judgment and circumspection, and all little enough, ought to be used. I remember when I lived in *Sommerfetshire*, very young then; I heard, at my first coming into those parts, of one that was much pitied, ( a Gardiner by his profession, on, and a very honest man every body said) as strangely bewitched: who also, as I was told, had appeared before the Judges, at the *Assizes*, more than once, in some of his fits. It was said, as I remember, that one or two, if not more, had been condemned, and suffered about it. I was also told of divers of the Clergy, who being desired, had been with him, to comfort him. Yet at last, some years after, this very man proved to be the *Witch*, ( a Witch or Sorcerer himself ) and was at *Bridgwater* Goal, I being then in the Country: where he carried himself, by common report, as a desperate Atheist, and seemed to slight the proceedings of Justice against him, being confident he should escape. The very night before execution, ( intended ) though kept with great care, and well fettered, I believe; yet being left alone some part of the night, or his Keeper sleeping, he got away by casting of himself down through a high hole, or window in the wall; and it was said ( my habitation was not very far from the place ) that a great heap, or pile of Fagots, which lay far enough in the yard from the place, were removed, and placed under the wall, for his escape. But the man being diligently pursued, after a day or two, was found in a Barn; and for all his confidence ( upon the *Devils* promise, I suppose ) that he should *escape*, was speedily executed. Thus the *Devil* deals with his vassals. He doth keep his word to them, ( worse than the *Devil* they then, who promise, and take no care to perform ) and yet they are not much the better for it, but in this, the utmost of miseries; that their confidence doth hinder their repentance: It is bad to have to do with him. I have given a true account of the business, if neither my memory, nor my information have deceived me. I wish we had yearly, an account of all memorable things, that happen in this kind, in all parts of *England*. I doubt not, if performed

by

by such as are creditable, and judicious; but good use might be made of it.

BUT again, when strange things are pretended, and creditable witnesses produced; yet it is the part of an intelligent reader, or auditor, before he gives full assent, to consider the nature of the thing, and all the circumstances of it. For some things are of that nature, though never so well attested, a man would think, that are yet possible to be mistaken; either because they cannot be so throughly examined and searched, as some other things: or because, not accompanied with convincing circumstances, that make it clear unto all men, not set upon contradiction, that there is somewhat *supernatural*, or besides the course of ordinary nature, in the case. I will instance in a notable example. In the year of our Lord, 1593. a rumor was spread, far and near, concerning a *Silesian* boy, about seven years of age, who had, they said, *a golden tooth* growing in his mouth. It was two years after, time enough a man would think to find out the truth, before the story was published in Print; and then too, by no mean man, but by *Jacobus Horstius*, a learned Physician. Soon after ( I follow the account *Sennertus* gives of it ) he was seconded by one *Martinus Rulandus*, a Physician too, of good account. These, it seems, made no question of the truth. But two years after that, one *Ingolsterus* opposed him; *Rulandus* I mean; and the same year, *Rulandus* replied in his own defence. The substance of their reasoning to and fro, is to be found in *Libavius* his *Singularia*, ( one of the first books that stirred me up to apply my *self*, when very young, to the study of *nature*, so far as at spare hours I might compass ) *Tome II*. with his own conjectures all along, rational, and well worth the

the reading. It is incredible what strange apprehensions some men had, concerning this prodigious *tooth*; extending their *prognosticks* of it, as far as the *Turkish* Empire, and his war with the Christians. But in the end, it proved but a cheat. How discovered, is nothing to my purpose. But I would have the Reader to consider, though I cannot excuse the *credulity* of men in it, which may be a warning to others, not to believe every thing, that is believed, and well attested, till they have well pondered all circumstances; yet to consider, I say, that it was very possible for men to be mistaken, where they could not have such full inspection; except the tooth had been out, as is easie in many other, whether pretended, or real wonders. Besides, there was no convincing circumstance, but such rather, as might induce a man, to suspect a fraud. For the Parents were poor, and reaped great profit, by shewing this tooth, in this way of shewing it, such as it was. But if a man of good credit and judgment, should tell me he hath seen a maid in the presence of divers others, *sow,* and *write* (exquisitely both) with her tongue; which I think a greater wonder, than to do it with the *feet*, as of more than one I have read: or seen a man, whose arms were so cut off, that nothing but short stumps were left, handle (pardon the word: if I should say, *manage*, I know no great difference) a sword, charge and discharge a musquet, and the like; though the matter seems to me very strange, and almost *incredible*; yet I cannot suspect any fraud or mistake, if my Author be true, and sober; as I am sure I have good authors for both, which no judicious man can *rationally* suspect, or question; *Nicolaus Tulpius*, of *Amsterdam*, for the maid; and *Ambrose Parcus*, for the man; who also relates, that the said man made a trade to rob and kill upon the ways, and for it was condemned to death. BUT

BUT to return to our miraculous *Tooth*: Though the cheat was then discovered, and the discovery published by more than one; yet the noise of the miracle had spread so far before that; and in the minds of many had made such deep impression, that the credit of it continued long after; and for ought I know, doth yet, among some, to this day. Sure I am, that a Jesuit, who not many years ago, with no small diligence, and yet much brevity, hath given us an account of three parts of the world, (I have seen no more) doth mention it, as a thing very real. Except he should intend it of another boy; because it is in the description of *Hungary*, that he hath it; whereas ours was in *Silesia*. But I rather think it is his mistake, or the mistake of some, whom he hath followed. If so, then we must say, that the miracle by time, hath well improved: For he doth not only tell of a boy with a *golden tooth*, but also *of nine tendrels, and natural leaves, of pure gold*: which might (upon good attestation of eye-witnesses) be thought the more probable, if, as some are of opinion, gold grew in Mines, altogether as a tree; and gold mines be nothing, but sundry trees of gold. His words are; *Schemnitium — civitas alia, ubi dives fodina aurea, quin etiam ex vitibus claviculi, & folia ex puro auro aliquando enata; puereque succrevit dens aureus.* I could have named a man of these times, (an English writer) also, who doth mention it as a true story. But for his love to ancient learning, and the pains he hath taken to vindicate it against the attempts of some others; I will reserve his name to some better occasion.

BUT in all those stories, either of *supernatural cures*, or *incantation of Serpents*, I have told; things were acted publickly, or in the sight of many; or accompanied with such circumstances, as make the case indubitable, and out of all possibility of a mistake. Except a man will say,

*in things* NATURAL. 175

say, that some of those things, were indeed represented to the eyes, whether of more, or fewer, so that they did verily believe they saw such and such things; which yet were not so, truly and really, as apprehended. This indeed doth happen sometimes, but never ( *in clear light,* &c. as before limited ) but by diabolical art, and illusion: so that as to the proving of *supernatural* operations, it comes to one. Yet this I will say: if in the *incantations* of Serpents, one or two only, of that kind, had been charmed at once; I might have suspected, that by art, and industry, they might have been taught that obedience, if not to run into the fire, yet to suffer themselves to be handled, and the like; because I know of dogs, and Horses, and Elephants, ( besides what I have seen my self ) and even of *Serpents*, what hath been written by some, both ancient and late.

 TO instance yet in another particular of *ungrounded* I cannot say; for I think the most cautelous, might have been deceived; but deluded *credulity*, whereof I think I can give a better account, than yet hath been given, for ought I know, by any in Print, though more than one, I know have taken notice of the *cheat*; so I call it, though the authors of it aimed at somewhat better, they will say, or some for them, perchance. In the year of the Lord 1550. *Henry* the second, King of *France*, being then *Bononia*; that is, ( for there be three Towns, if not more, one in *Italy*, another in *Germany*, and a third in *France*, of that name ) *Bologne*, in *France*; which having been taken a year or two before, by the *English*, was then restored; a Letter was written by one *Pinellus*, a *French* Physician, who was then, it seems, at Court with the King, to a friend of his, of the same profession, one *Mizaldus*. I have not met with the whole Letter any where, which therefore I here exhibit.

*Job.*

Joh. Pipinus, Anto. Mizaldo, suo S. P. D.

GAUDEO mihi oblatam esse occasionem, charissime Antoni, qua rem novam, & plane admirabilem, tibi nunciare fit datam. Nuper ex India Orientali Regi nostro allatum hic vidimus lapidem, lumine & fulgore mirabiliter corruscantem, quique totus veluti ardens & incensus incredibili lucis splendore præfulget micatque. Is jactis quoque versus radiis, ambientem circumquaque aerem luce nullis fere oculis tolerabili, latissime complet. Est etiam terræ impatientissimus: si cooperire coneris, sua sponte & vi, facto impetu, confestim evolat in sublime. Contineri vero includive loco ullo angusto, nulla potest hominum arte: sed ampla liberaque loca duntaxat amare videtur. Summa in eo puritas, summus nitor: nulla sorde, aut labe coinquinatur. Figuræ species nulla ei certa; sed inconstans & momento commutabilis: cumque sit aspectu longe pulcherrimus, contractari sese tamen non sinit; & si diutius adnitaris, vel obstinatius agas, incommodum adfert: sicuti multi suo non levi malo, me præsente, sunt experti: quod siquid ex eo fortassis enixius conando adimitur aut detrahitur, nam durus admodum non est; fit (dicta mirum) nihilo minor. Addit insuper, is hospes, qui illum attulit, homo uti apparet, Barbarus; hujus virtutem ac vim esse ad quam plurime cùm utilem, tum præcipue, Regibus imprimis, necessariam: sed quam revelaturus non sit, nisi pretio ingenti prius accepto. Reliqua ex me præsente audies cùm primùm Rex ad vos redierit. Superest at te, & si quos isthic habes viros eruditos diligentissimè orem, ex Plinio, Alberto, Marbodeo, aliisque, qui de lapidibus aliquid scriptum reliquerunt, solicite disquiratis, quisnam sit hujusmodi lapillus, aut quod illi nomen (si modo fuerit, antiquis cognitus) præscribi vere possit. Nam in eo peranxiè, nec minus infeliciter ab aulicis nostris eruditis, hactenus laboratum, quibus si

palmam

*palmam in ea cognitione præripere possim, mecum feliciffime
actum iri exiftimarem. Incredibilis enim, & Regi imprimis, & toti denique procerum aulicorum turba ea de re
commota eft expectatio. Vale.*

*Bonóniæ, Pridie Afcenfionis Chrifti,* M.D.L.

I HAVE fet down the whole Epiftle, as it was written, becaufe, as before faid, I have not met with it whole elfewhere ; and pity it were, that what fo many years, to fo many, hath been the ground of fo much trouble and inquiry, fhould not be fully known. And now for their fakes that underftand not the *Latin,* I will fet it down in *Englifh* too.

Joh. Pipinus, *to* Ant. Mizaldus, *his loving friend, health, and greeting.*

I AM glad, deareft Anthony, *that this opportunity hath offered it felf of a new, and wonderful relation. We have lately feen a ftone, which was brought to our King, out of the* Eaft-Indies, *fhining with admirable light and brightnefs, as if it were all on fire ; fuch is the fplendor and flafhing of it, filling the air round about with rays, which no eye can bear. It is very impatient of earth, and if you go about to cover it, it makes its way by force, and flieth up on high. No art of man can conclude it, or contain it in a narrow room ; naturally affecting wide and free places. It is of perfect purity and cleannefs, and cannot be foiled with any fpot or foulnefs. The fhape of it is not certain, but inconftant, and in a moment changeable : and though it be of a beautiful afpect, yet cannot endure to be touched ; and if you think to ufe any force, it is not without fome inconvenience, as fome, in my prefence, have found to their coft. And if with much endeavour, you happen to take any part, or parcel from it,*

(*for*

*Of Credulity and Incredulity,*

(*for it is not very hard*) *it is not* (*O wonderful*) *the less for it. To all this, the same man that brought it, a meer Barbarian to sight, doth add, that the vertue of it, as it is useful for many things; so chiefly to Kings, very necessary: but not to be revealed, without a good summe of money first payed. Nothing now remains, but earnestly to entreat you, and other learned men where you are, that you will make diligent search in* Pliny, Albertus, Marbodeus, *and others, that have written of stones, what this stone is, and in case it were known to the Ancients, what is the true name of it. For in this is the industry of our Courtiers, who pretend to any learning, now occupied; wherein if I could prevent them, I should think my self very happy. For it is incredible, how much the King himself, and the whole Court, long to be satisfied. Farewel.*

From *Bononia*, Afcenſion Eur. 1550.

WHERE *Mizaldus* was, when the Letter came to him, I know not certainly: but I guefs at *Paris*. Hereupon, the fame of this rare *ſtone* was fpread far and near; and all curious men, Philoſophers, and Naturalifts, invited to fpend their judgments. *Thuanus*, many years after, enters it into his *Hiſtory*, as a thing worthy of eternal memory: *Dum Rex Bononiæ eſſet, allatus ad eum ex India Orientali*, &c. concluding thus: *Hæc, ut in literis Johan. Pipini, oculati rei teſtis*, &c. making no queſtion at all of the truth, but whether ſuch a ſtone ever known to the Ancients or no, leaving that to the further enquiry of *Philoſophers* and *Naturaliſts*. No ſuch thing is now to be found in *Thuanus*, after the matter was once come out, and he knew it was a cheat. Yet, ſo long did the fame of this pretious *ſtone* continue, that in the year 1622. when that admirable Treaſury of choice rarities, called *Muſæum Veconenſe*, (which I value

value the more, becaufe of the fobriety, and piety of the fetters out of it, as by the difputation at the end, doth appear) it was yet current in thofe parts, and great endeavours were ufed, for the procuring of it, if to be purchafed at any rate. So we find it there, and moreover, how men verfed in thofe things, differed in their opinions: fome accounting it a *natural*, other a *magical* ftone, and the like. Whether *Fernelius* was the firft, (as Dr. *Harvy* doth inform us) who placed the *Oedipus*, and unfolded the riddle, I know not: I rather fufpect, becaufe I find it explained in the copy of the Letter I have, which I take to be ancient, that it came from them, or theirs, that were the firft contrivers of it. Now truly, had any man but fufpected, that it was poffible, (concerning which we fhall have a more proper place and full enquiry in our fecond part) that any learned ingenuous man would be fo difingenuous, and fo idle, as meerly for the pleafure of the trouble, and puzle of others, to bufie himfelf to contrive a cheat: I think a lefs man than *Oedipus*, might have unfolded the riddle, for any great intricacy of it. I am confident, that nothing but a ftrong prefumption and confidence, that *Pinellus* was too grave and too ferious, to take fuch a perfon upon him, made it a riddle fo long. It might have been obferved, that though the Author fet down the time and place, when, and whether this ftrange *ftone* was brought, and alfo make bold with the Kings name, either upon a confidence, thofe whom he did abufe, would not foon have the opportunity to ask him; or becaufe he had obtained fo much favour of the King, upon fome plaufible pretence, that he was content to be named: yet it might have been obferved, that in fome other things, he fpeaks not fo particularly, as might have been expected. He doth intimate indeed, that many they were, befides the King, that had feen it, and wondred

wondred at it: but names none particularly, as *Josephus* doth, ( by their relations and offices, which doth amount to a naming ) and *Laurentius*, in their stories: this last especially, very particularly; which takes away all possibility of either fiction or mistake. And if any man think that the very strangeness, or *incrediblenessi* of the story, was enough to make a wise man suspitious; should we take a survey of those strange things, secrets of nature, time hath discovered, in several ages of the world, somewhat might be found perchance, though since, because better known, not so much regarded, that might deserve as much *admiration*. To pass by, what either *Pliny* upon the report of others, more ancient, or since him, *Albertus Magnus*, the wonder of his age, and many ages after, for natural knowledge, have written of some stones; which though written by such, yet I believe no further, than I see cause; that is, than is approved true, by good experience, which is repugnant, I am sure, to many of their traditions: I will only instance in the effects of *quicksilver*, known and tried, vulgarly enough, but *accurately* collected, and set out by *Acosta*, in his *Natural History of the Indies*, lib. 4. cap. 10. and 11. and by *Levinus. Lemnius, De occult. Nat. Mir. lib.* 2. *cap.* 35. we shall find some particulars of this imaginary stone, truly verified of *quicksilver*, and divers others not less admirable, with equal truth attested of it. But let us see: I think with little alteration, as strange a riddle as this, might have been contrived: as thus, *A very resplendent stone,* ( or if you will, without any sophistication; *A liquor, that wets not* ) *of no certain form, not tractable, Without danger: and if you divide it in never so many parts, or parcels; of it self, it will come, or affect to come into an entire body again: and which is most admirable, though it be the heaviest thing in the world, yet with fire, it will vanish into*

*smoak,*

*smoak*, *the lightest thing in the world: and though vanish, yet not consume; for sooner or later, it will come to a body again, without any loss or diminution*. All this, to which more may be added, according to the description of the two forenamed Authors: the word *stone*, which I am sure is more proper of *quickfilver*, as it is a *mineral*, than of *fire* only added. Not to mention *Gabriell Fallopius*, who, of all I have seen, hath written of it, the vertues and properties, most accurately, in his book, *De Metallis & fossilibus, cap.* 11. *&* 36.

AND who could tell, had the relation been true, but that this stone might have proved a *Magical* stone? Who hath not heard of those *Astrological* (according to the vulgar opinion, and their usual graveure; though the efficacy, by many ascribed to the Stars and Planets; by more, and the more solid, to the *Devil* only) *stones and gems*, called by the *Grecians*, ϛοιχεῖα, and by the *Arabs*, *Talismata*; the use and superstition whereof though we abhor, yet the operations, attested by so many, how can we *rationally* deny? Let *Gyges* his ring, though not thought so by all that write of it, pass for a fable; yet learned *Camerarius*, I am sure, doth write of a ring of his time, for which he had the attestation of some, whom himself did believe very creditable, much more miraculous, than that of *Gyges*, because this made the wearer only *invisible*; when he would, and gave him light in darkness, at pleasure; but the other represented things future, and a-far off, which of the two I account the greater wonder.

THIS, I thought not amiss, to prevent the insulting of those *sapientissimi*, or *Wondrous wise men*, *Seneca* speaks of, who when they hear, how many both learned and wise, were gulled by this *cheat*; will be ready to applaud themselves, and say, what fools were they, that they could not see, that it *was a lye: an arrant lye: an impoſſible thing.* So that, if learned men, and honeſt men by common reputation; meerly for the pleaſure of deceiving, and puzling, (which hath too much of the humor of the *Devil,* to be believed of real honeſt men) will conſpire to turn *juglers;* I know no fence againſt it, but abſolute *Incredulity,* in ſuch caſes: which is a remedy as bad, or worſe than the diſeaſe; the danger of being cheated. But if, as by *Fernelius* is alledged, the end of the project was, to make men more ſenſible of their folly, who admire nothing generally, but what is ſeldom ſeen; whereas, in very truth, thoſe things, that are ordinary and daily, if looked upon with a Philoſophical eye, deſerve as much *admiration;* and ſtill ask for new ſigns from Heaven, when all that is about us, if rightly underſtood; what we daily handle and ſee; what we eat, drink and wear; are *clear ſigns and evidences* of the infinite power and wiſdom of the *Creator;* this, indeed, is a uſeful and pleaſant ſpeculation, which many Philoſophers and others, have largely inſiſted upon; and the *fire,* I grant, (as well obſerved by *Avicen,* whom *Fernelius* doth cite) is a very pregnant example; yet, ſome other way might have been found, I believe, as by a convenient *parable,* ſome prety *fable,* or ſo; which might have wrought upon the vulgar as well, as this crude lye.

---

I AM at an end of my firſt part, as to matter of *Credulity* or *Incredulity,* in things *Natural,* taken in that general ſenſe, before ſpoken of, and this will be our biggeſt *Part.* Now as a *Corollary* to it, not unbeſeeming my profeſſion, I will take the Ninty Firſt *Pſalm* of *David,* or ſome words of it, into conſideration, which will afford us ſome uſeful conſiderations, not improper,

or

*in things* NATURAL. 183

or impertinent to the subject we have handled. The subject of the *Psalm*, is, the security of a godly man, who liveth under the protection of *Almighty God*, in times of greatest dangers. But whether intended by the Author of it, to set out the security of all godly men, in general; and to all that are such, equally appliable: or penned upon some particular occasions, and more particularly appliable to some, than to others, may be a question. Some superstitious *Jews*, from whom it is thought by some, that the custom, or invention of such *rings*, did first proceed, as the fashion is of such that deal in unlawful arts, to seek protection from the *Scripture*, by violent applications; have made bold to interpret this security here promised to the godly, of those *magical* rings, made under such and such constellations, which have been, a little before spoken of. So I learn from that great Master of all good learning, *Josephus Scaliger*, in some Epistles of his, set out in his *Posthuma*. It is a great chance, if a bold *Chymick* will not say as much of the mysteries of his art. But wishing them sounder brains, or better consciences; whether the *Psalm*, according to the first, either occasion of it, or intention of the Pen-man, be generally appliable or no; we need not be very solicitous, since the substance of it, the security of the Godly, *&c.* is by other places of Scripture, affirmed and asserted; though not so *emphaticaly*, yet plainly enough, to make good all herein contained. *Du Muis*, late professor of the Hebrew tongue, in *Paris*; who hath learnedly vindicated the integrity of the Hebrew Text, against *Morinus*, is so taken with the elegancy of the stile, in the Original Hebrew, and the sublimity of the conceptions, that he thinks no *Latin*, or *Greek* piece, worthy to be compared with it. I shall not contest with him about that; neither is this a place: but it is observable, that even Heathen Poets have exercised

their

their wits upon this subject, the security of a pious, upright man: which to set out emphatically, they have used some expressions as high, as any in the *Psalm*. Witness *Horace* his, *Integer vitæ scelerisque purus : Non egit Mauri jaculis, neque arcu,* &c. Yet I never heard, that any body in those days, did quarrel with them for it, though it was then, as it is now, a common observation, that honest upright men, were subject (besides oppression, to which their integrity under a tyrannical government doth more particularly expose them) to all publick calamities, or irregularities of Heaven, or Earth, as Plagues, and Famines, or the like; as other men. If thereof we take the words of the *Psalmist*, as applicable to all godly men in general, which I think is the truest sense, and first intention; they will not bear a *literal construction*; neither, in that sense, are they reconcileable with *Jeremie*'s, and divers other holy mens complaints; even *Davids*, among others, in the 37. and 73. *Psalms*, concerning the prosperity of wicked men in this world, and afflictions of the Godly. And though, as in all ages of the world, so now, there may be many, who are ready (in their secret thoughts, at least) to quarrel with God Almighty for it, and tell him, in the language of these days, *That he was bound in his Justice,* to have ordered it otherwise; yet my opinion is, except God to allay the complaints of insolent wretched men, would new mould the world; and retract or annul the *mysteries* of our redemption by such a *Saviour*; (which to fancy, were both ridiculous, and damnable) it was, and is expedient, if not *necessary*, (a word not very fit to be used, when we speak of Gods counsels) it should be as it is. For, what shall we say? That in times of publick calamities, as *Pestilence, Inundations,* and the like; Godly men should be exempted, and *they* only perish, that have not the fear of God before their eyes;

known

known unto themselves and others, for such, by their lives and conversations? *They only*, but, *not all*, that are such, for then the world would soon be destitute of inhabitants; that is apparent. Well, *they only*: but if not all; would not this give ground to them, that escape, to think themselves, though nothing less perchance; righteous, and godly, and in the favour of God? And so harden them in their wicked courses, as justified by God himself, in their preservation? Certainly, besides profest or secret *Atheism* and infidelity; there is not, among them that profess to believe; there is not, I say, any greater cause of miscarrying, than *presumption*; so prone we are, if we keep not a very strict watch, and make it our daily business, over our actions, to think better of our selves, than we are, or God doth think, and know. What then would it be, if we had this further inducement of *presumption* of our goodness, and Gods favour, that when others perished, we escaped? But again, would it not, if none but such perished, give ground to them that are really godly, and upright in their lives and conversations; even to them, to think better of themselves than they are; and as men out of danger, to grow proud and secure; highly conceited of themselves; despisers of others, ( witness the late *Saints*, as they did call themselves ) than which no greater misery can befal a godly man. And then, how can it stand with that grand mystery of our *faith*, that we must be saved by *faith*; if this present world apparently were a place of reward to good and evil? Or a place, where good and evil are discriminated and discerned, by such apparent, as I may call it, partiality? How can St. *Paul*'s inference be justified and verified, that the prosperity of wicked men

in

in this world, is a sure evidence unto us, of a day of *Judgment*, becaufe we know, which even ordinary reafon doth prompt, if we believe there is a God; that God is juft?

HAD thefe things been well confidered of, and much more, though not able to give an account of, we may think our felves in duty bound to believe, fome both ancient and late, might have written more warily, than they have done. Of the Ancients, I could name fome that write fufpitioufly, but none that I remember, more peremptorily, than *Lactantius*: a profeft Rhetoritian, and an elegant writer, but a raw Chriftian; who maintaineth, that it is not poffible, that either at Sea by tempeft, or at Land by war, (or Peftilence, he intended alfo certainly, though he doth not exprefs it) any *juft man* fhould perifh; but that either God, for his fake, will preferve the reft, or when all the reft perifh, that are not what he is, he alone fhall be preferved. So he the more excufable, becaufe, as I faid before, but a raw Chriftian. I am much deceived, if among the Proteftant *Commentators* on the *Pfalms*, fome one might not be found, who doth maintain the very fame opinion. *Bodinus*, I am fure, whether a Proteftant, or a Papift, faith little lefs, concerning the power of *Magicians* and *Witches*; when he faith, that they cannot delude, or blind the eyes (an ordinary thing with them) of them, that fear God; to reprefent things unto them as true and real, which are not fo, but in appearance only: which if true, we may upon the fame ground conclude, they have no power at all upon their bodies, to annoy them: which indeed, without Gods permiffion, we know they have not; but that is not to the purpofe, for neither have they upon the bodies of others, till God permit, and give them leave; fo that, in that, there is no difference. But to believe that none are *poffeffed*, or
other-

otherwise annoyed by the *Devil*, but wicked men, is a very uncharitable, and erroneous opinion: easily confuted by the *Scriptures*: besides what hath been said before, of Godly men, being subject to publick calamities, as well as other men. They that desire further satisfaction in this point, may, if they please, and be able, read St. *Chrysostome* his large discourse, in three several books, to one of his time, that was possest, and had already been so, when he wrote, for the space of three years; whom he accounted, and so describeth, as an exemplary man, for his holy life and conversation.

THERE was a tradition anciently, so ancient, that *Gregory Nazianzen*, and *Prudentius* were, and many more since, have been deceived by it; that S. *Cyprian* had been a great *Magician*, before he was converted to the Christian faith: The occasion of his conversion some say, was, that being passionately in love of a chast Christian Virgin, and out of all hopes to speed any other way; he had recourse to his Master, the *Devil*, that by his means he might obtain his desire. I find it in *Vair*, that the Devil should presently reply unto him, that against them that did truly and sincerely worship *Jesus Christ*, no power or art he had could prevail: at which *Cyprian* being surprised with great astonishment, resolved presently to become a *Christian*. But this part of the story, I do not find either in *Prudentius* or *Nazianzen*; but in *Prudentius* only this, that whilest he was of that profession, among other things, he made use of Magick, to compass his luftful desires; and in *Nazianzen* thus, that the *Devil* having done what he could to work upon the Virgin, in vain; at last ( he hath done so, upon like occasions, more than once, as later stories bear witness ) did acknowledge so much to *Cyprian*, and put him out of all hopes of obtaining his desire: at which *Cyprian* was so troubled, that he made bold to revile the

*Devil*,

*Devil*, ( there be too many that will revile God himſelf, when they miſs of their ends ) who in revenge, entered into him, and grievouſly tormented him; which forced him to apply himſelf to Chriſt for help, which having found, that ſo he became a *Chriſtian*. The beſt is, if this be not true of our St. *Cyprian*, whoſe learned and pious works are extant; it may be ſure, and probably is very true, of another, ſomewhat later *Cyprian*, who died a Martyr too; ſo that it is probably, but a miſtake of the name.

BUT if *Vair* were miſtaken in his account, as to the particular we are upon, grounded upon St. *Cyprian*'s authority, to prove that a good Chriſtian is exempted from the ſtroak and ſmart of the *Devil*'s perſecution, in general, and perſonal poſſeſſion, particularly: yet it may be ſupplied, partly out of *Celſus*, in *Origen*; and partly out of *Origen* himſelf. Out of *Celſus*, in *Origen*, *lib*. 6. *pag*. 312. where *Celſus* doth declare, that he had learned from an *Ægyptian Muſician*, ( μουσικός ſo Printed, and ſo tranſlated, *Muſicum*, by the Latin interpreter: But I propoſe it to the conſideration of them, that are more at leiſure, whether μάγῳ, be not the more likely word; there being ſo much affinity between *Magus* and *Ægyptius*, in thoſe times, at leaſt, that the bare word, *Ægyptius*, as *Baronius*, *Anno Ch*. 327. *Par*. 17. doth well obſerve, is ſometime taken for *Magus*: And beſides, why ſhould *Celſus* regard what was ſaid, or affirmed by a *Muſician*, in this particular, being altogether out of his element and profeſſion ) that *Magick* could not hurt them that were *Philoſophers*; that is, as the word is often taken, moral vertuous men; but only thoſe that were ἀπαίδευτοι, *undiſciplined men*; ᾗ διαφθείραντες τὰ ἤθη· *corrupt in their lives and converſations*. Out of *Origen* himſelf, who there doth very peremptorily deliver it, as a thing approved by good experience, that

that none that served God according to the prescript of Christ, and lived according to his Gospel, and diligently applied themselves night and day, to those prayers that were prescribed ( by which I understand *the Morning and Evening Service* of the Church ) could receive any harm by *Magick*, or by *Devils*. All this if taken precisely, and limited to this present world and life, except it be restrained to some particular times, and occasions, is, I think, spoken with more confidence, than truth.

YET I will not deny, but that probably, pious upright men, whom the consciousness of their piety and probity, hath not ( as it often doth happen ) made them secure, and presumptuous, or proud, and arrogant, and despisers of others; are not so subject to this kind of trouble, as wicked leud people. Neither will I be afraid to say, though ridiculous, I know, to the *wits*, and *wise* of these times ; that it may be true enough, which by some *Witches* hath been acknowledged to *Remigius*, that they had not the same power to execute their malicious designs upon those, even little children, who daily and duly said their prayers, as they had upon others. But withal, I would have that remembred and thought upon, which out of *Pliny*, where we treat of *Prodigies*, was observed before, of a natural kind of faith, and the efficacy of it, which may in part satisfie, why some, sometimes, though not so religious otherwise, may be less obnoxious to the attempts of *Devils* and *Witches*, than some others, though more innocent and deserving, for want of this kind of faith, ( which, in some things, may supply the want of a more perfect, or Christian faith ) are.

NOW for them that are scandalized, that the *Devil* ( with Gods permission ) should have such power

power over men, as well the good, as the bad: firſt of all, let them remember, that even St. *Paul*, that choſen veſſel, ſo great and gracious with God, was not exempted from the common condition of other Godly men; and what Gods anſwer was, when St. *Paul* addreſſed himſelf to him, for relief, and releaſe: and leaving to God, the ſecrets of his *will*, and his *providence*; let us conſider, what is, or may be manifeſt of it unto all men, to prove that there is a *providence*, which doth take care of the world, and all men in general: firſt, in reſtraining the power of the *Devil*, ſo that he that as an *Angel*, by nature, is able to do ſo much, can do nothing at all, without his permiſſion. In what caſe do we think the world, this *ſublunary world*, (though but a very little and inconſiderable point or piece, a man would think, in compariſon of the higher world, which he hath nothing to do with) this ſublunary world, I ſay, would be, if the government of it were left unto him; who nevertheleſs for the great power he hath in it, is ſtiled in the Scripture κοσμοκράτωρ, or *Governour of the world*: For what he doth to ſome, who partly ſeek unto him themſelves; or for ſome hidden reaſon, beſides their ſins, by Gods permiſſion, become obnoxious unto him; he would do unto all, who doubts it, even to the deſtruction of all, (his great ambition) were not his power reſtrained. And it is obſervable, that he hath moſt power, where God is leaſt known, and ignorance and brutiſhneſs moſt reign; as in the moſt *Northern* parts of the world, as by many is obſerved. But again: O the goodneſs, and mercy of God towards men! that though the *Devil* have ſuch power in the Earth, that all the treaſures of the Earth, may in ſome reſpect, be ſaid to be in his hands, and at his diſpoſing; yet he hath no power, or very little, to gratifie them, who by covenant, tacit or expreſs, have entred themſelves into his

ſervice;

service; which if he had, for one sworn vassal, or servant that he hath, (such is the madness of most men, left to themselves, because they do not seek unto God) he would have a hundred, if not a thousand. But again, what miserable ends they make commonly, that have served him most faithfully, (an account whereof is given by more than one ) and how basely, he doth usually forsake them in time of greatest need; leaves them comfortless, desperate and despairing; yea sometimes, betrayeth them himself, and seems to rejoyce *openly*, (which we know, though he doth not shew it, he doth always *secretly*) and to insult at their calamities. How many have been torn in pieces, by himself: or unmercifully snatched, and carried away, God knows whether? Others, with many curses, stoned by the people; others some other way, not natural; helpless and hopeless ended their miserable life? So have many of Gods servants too, as to bodily pains and torments; ( some *Atheistical* wretch perchance, will be ready to reply ) as those the Apostle, in his Epistle to the *Hebrews* speaketh of, who died cruel deaths: yea, cruel as to the world, we grant it, but not comfortless, even in greatest pains; and honourable after their deaths.

BUT lastly, is there not a providence, yea a miraculous providence, though little understood, and therefore less thought of, in this, that the Devil by the priviledge of his nature being endowed with such power, and bearing such hatred to mankind; yet cannot do one half, yea one quarter of the hurt, he doth unto men, were it not for the help of men, as imployed, and set on by men. A great and incomprehensible *mystery*, to the wisest that write of it, that their power should be so limited; but an effect, certainly, of Gods love, and respect towards men.

FOR these things therefore that are manifest, it well
becomes

becomes all good Christians to praise God, and to acknowledge his good Providence towards men; and for those things we can find no satisfaction from *reason*, to submit unto him with humility; which is so great a proof of true Religion, and Christianity, that for this very thing we may believe many things are not revealed, for a trial of our submission and humility in this kind.

NOW to return to our *Psalm*: It argued a noble mind in *Plato*, and doth relish of some kind of inspiration, (I did think so, where I treat of it more largely, in the *Annotations* upon the *Psalms*, before mentioned; upon the 37. *Psalm*) who would have in his Commonweal, all happiness, by law, so annexed to goodness, and righteousness; that it should not be lawful for any man, young or old, in any discourse, publick or private, to speak otherwise. And some pregnant arguments he hath, to prove it so, that such only are truly and really the happy men of the world, who are upright honest men. But however, what opinion soever men might have of his arguments; it should not be lawful for any man to speak otherwise, hoping that in time such language in all places, and companies, would breed in young people, an honourable esteem of vertue and probity; and so dispose them the better to the pursuit of it. Which, though some men may slight and deride, as they are ready to do every thing, that doth not fit their own fancy, yet to men of better judgment, and experience, may appear very considerable. And who can doubt, but that, when children, and young people, never hear the dead spoken of, (such as died in wars, especially, for their Country) but in the phrase of μακάριται or *happy men*, which in those days, was the proper expression for *a dead man*: it did much conduce to breed in people a contempt of death, without which there can be no true generosity? Whereas now, the common phrase of,

*poor*

*poor Man! poor Father! poor Mother!* and the like; ( which I could never hear without some kind of secret abhorrency, that Christians should come so short of Heathens wisdom ) what can it breed in children, and weaker people, but a fear and detestation of death?

COULD I be perswaded, as many anciently, and some of late have been of opinion, that *Plato* was acquainted with the Scriptures of the Old Testament; I should make no doubt, but when he Commented that Law, he had in his thoughts the words of *Ecclesiastes*, which to me, in times of greatest desolation, when violence and oppression were at their height, always proved a very comfortable cordial; *Though a sinner do evil a hundred times, and his days be prolonged, yet surely I know, that it shall be well with them that fear God; which fear before him: But it shall not be well with the wicked, neither shall he prolong his days, which are as a shadow, because he feareth not before God*, Eccles. 8. 12. What is the effect of all this, *Though he prolong; yet he shall not prolong*, &c. but this; that though wicked men, in, and by length of days, and other worldly prosperity, may seem to ordinary reason and judgment, to be happy; yet really, they are not so, but in their very happiness ( as supposed ) miserable, and unhappy: a kind of contrariety, but not to faith. And what is it *Plato* would have, but this very thing; and that it should not be lawful to speak otherwise? But as to *Solomon*'s words, let me add by the way: I conceive some wrong is done unto them, by breaking the coherence with the foregoing verse, by a new *Paragraph*. For having in the eleventh verse, pointed at one main ground of wickedness, and *Atheism*; which is, the not speedy execution of Justice, in this world; and Gods suffering of wicked men, to thrive by their wickedness, ( for, *God is known by the Judgement he executeth:*

saith

saith the *Psalmist*) he doth oppose this noble confession, or profession of his faith, to vulgar judgments; which would be more clear, if, as often, supplied with a *But*: *But I, though a sinner,* &c. *Theognis,* nay *Homer,* have said the same, in effect: but I will not digress so far.

NOW to apply this to our *Psalm*: It is the opinion of some learned men, that this *Psalm* was penned of purpose for a *formula,* or pattern of praying, in time of danger. And indeed, I account it a most excellent, and Divine form of prayer, to that end; provided that we take St. *Paul's* exposition along with it, which is, not to think our selves secured by those words, that we shall not suffer any of those things, private or publick, which are naturally incidental unto all men, as men; but to secure us, that if we put our trust in God, and have a lively apprehension of his *Goodness, Power,* and *Mercy,* the end of our sufferings shall be comfortable, and glorious. St. *Paul's* words are: *Who shall separate us,* &c. from verse 35. to the end of the Chapter. Certainly, if in all these, *more than conquerors*; then in all these *happy,* (as *Plato* would have it) truly, and really; though not always, nor all equally, so sensible, of our happiness. Neither I think did the Prophet *Habakkuk,* by those words, *Yet we will rejoyce in the Lord: We will joy in the God of our salvation,* Hab. 3. 18. promise himself much *joy,* in a time of publick famine; such a time *Jeremy* speaketh of, when he saith, *His eyes did fail with tears,* &c. *because the children and sucklings swoon in the streets,* &c. or altogether presume, when others round about him died for want of bread; God would miraculously feed and preserve him: but only this, that no calamity can be so great, and grievous, but if we trust in God, and patiently submit, we may find comfort in this confidence; That (to use St. *Paul's* expression) *the sufferings of this present time, are not worthy to compared with*

*with the glory that shall be revealed in us,* Rom. 8. 18.

I HAVE said what I intended upon this *Psalm*: More perchance might be expected by some, concerning the several kinds, or orders of Spirits, which, by some, are supposed to be alluded unto, by the *Psalmist* in those words; *Thou shalt not be afraid for the terror by night, nor for the arrow that flieth by day, nor for the pestilence that walketh in darkness, nor for the destruction that wasteth at noon-day,* Verse 5. and 6. That there be different kinds or orders of Spirits, all evil, and enemies to mankind, I easily yield, though not so ready perchance, to subscribe to every thing that *Psellus*, that learned *Platonist* ( whether so sound Christian in all things, I cannot tell ) hath written of them. And besides them, there may be, perchance, some other substances or *Spirits*, ( so called, because not discernable by bodily eyes, in their own nature; but whether *immortal*, or no, I do not know ) which have no quarrel at all to mankind, nor any particular interest in the affairs of men, but as they are casually provoked or molested; and sometimes, invited, and allured perchance, as some are of opinion. But all this, more than God by his Word hath been pleased to teach, and reveal, is to me but *perchance*, and, *it may be,* nothing that I know, or believe, with any certainty. And for my part, such speculations and enquiries, if pursued with much ambition and eagerness; and without some special occasion, incident to any mans office or duty; I hold to be much more curious, if not dangerous, than profitable, or convenient, as elsewhere I have had occasion more largely to declare my self. As for those words of the *Psalmist*, there be, *Delrio*, and others, that will give a further account, if it be desired. My purpose did not engage me, and I am very willing to let it alone.

# OF
# CREDULITY
## AND
# INCREDULITY
## IN
## Things CIVIL.

---

*The Second Part.*

---

ERE I shall desire the Reader, in the first place, to take notice, that though we distinguish between things *Natural* and *Civil*; by *Natural*, understanding properly such things, as are the work of Nature, immediately, without the concurrence, or intervention of man's will or counsel: and by *Civil*, those which owe their production to the will or counsel of man: yet, in many things, *Nature*, and *the Will of man* do cooperate, so that the same thing may in different respects, be reducible

cible to either of the two, *Nature*, or *the will of man.* For example, some things that are done by Art, or commonly ascribed unto Art, and of the same kind, apparently, as artificial things : yet, in truth, the effects of Nature, more than Art. So many actions of men, which flow originally from the natural temper, or present constitution of the body; or from some other natural cause, moving and inciting, but not constraining; except the present temper, or distemper have so far prevailed, as to force. Besides, the very *will* of man may, in some respects, be reduced to nature; and all actions that proceed from it, in some respects, I say, not unfitly, be termed natural. For in very deed, God excepted, ( whom nevertheless the *Stoicks* termed ζῶν ) there is nothing but in some sense, is *natural* : even Monsters, the greatest that are, and most wondred at; as *Aristotle* hath long ago taught us. If therefore in this *Second Part*, we insist upon any thing, that might as well have been spoken of in the *first*, that the Reader might not rashly censure, or condemn, as though we had forgotten *our text*, or ignorantly confounded matters ; this warning, I thought, would not be amiss.

BUT now I must meet with another objection, which may be as considerable, if not more. *Of Credulity and Incredulity, in things Civil* : what need of this, in this age; among us, in *England*, at least ? If ever there were a time, when those verses of the Poet,

*Omnia jam fient, fieri quæ posse negantur ;*
*Et nihil est, de quo, non sit habenda fides :*
In *English*, more to our purpose, thus :
*All wondring, cease : such things our Age, our eyes*
*( have seen ;*
*Nothing now incredibl' which incredibl' hath been :*

If

*in things* CIVIL.

If ever a time, I say, when appliable, and true, in this our *England*, at least: surely this is the time. Have we not seen a most godly religious Prince, and King; not by one single Rogue, as two late Kings of *France*, one after another; but by his own Subjects, in multitude, pretending, not to *Christianity* only, in general, but to the *Protestant Religion*, (or *Reformation* rather) upon pretences of Justice and Religion, massacred in cold blood, upon a Scaffold, erected in triumph before his own House, or ordinary place of abode; with the applause and *Hallelujahs*, not of the said multitude only, but of some others also, whom by their birth and education, no man would have thought capable of such savageness and immanity? Have we seen this, and wonder to hear, that there was, or is yet, any such people, or Nation, who when their Parents, Fathers and Mothers, are grown old and crazy, knock them on the head, or some other way, hasten their death, and feast themselves, their Wives and Children, with their flesh? Or if we be told (of which more afterwards perchance) of a certain People in the North, men and women, who for some time of the year, of creatures that are naturally rational, and *made after the Image of God*; turn into very Wolves; of all wild Beasts, the most cruel and ravening: can we wonder at it, and think it *incredible*? But again, we have read with wonder, (if we believe it; though, truly, some later stories, well attested, may incline us, not to think it *incredible*) of a *Remus* and *Romulus*, two Brothers, preserved by the milk and nursery of a She-Wolf; and with no less wondring, but more certainty, of a Prophet, fed by *Ravens*, in a Cave. Should we well ponder that connexion, and concatenation of providences, which attended our present *Gracious Sovereign*; and among others, by what hands he was led, lodged, and fed in a Tree, whilest his enemies

mies round about did hunt and purfue him ; to preferve him to as miraculous ( becaufe without bloud, and by thofe hands, in part, that had been active in his Father's ruine ) a *Reftoration* : we need not make fuch a wonder of either, to think the one ( that of the two Brothers ) *incredible* ; or the other, of the Prophet, not *credible*, but as we have Scripture authority for it.

BUT thirdly : the burning of Cities ; by enemies, efpecially, and chances of war, to them that have read ftories, cannot be very wonderful. Yet, fuch is the nature of man ; who would have believed, that he fhould live, to fee the burning of *London* ? Efpecially, when not by any publick Enemy? But that which makes it moft wonderful, is, that though, to our great horror and amazement, we fee it is done ; yet how, and by whom, we do not yet certainly know : though, if reports be true, it was known and talked of by more than one, fome days before it hapned. And, who knows, had not our *Gracious Sovereign*, and his *Royal Brother*, both by perfonal attendance, and by wife contrivances, appeared fo zealous, as they did, for the quenching of it ; whether any part of either *London* or *Weftminfter* had been to be feen, at this day ? All thefe, fome as *mercies*, other as *judgments* ; ( not to mention the late dreadful *Plague*, the like whereof, for the continuance, and number of the dead, hath not been known in *England* ) great wonders, as I fuppofe ; and fuch, as to, if not immediate, yet more remote pofterity may feem *incredible*. But the greateft wonder, not to be uttered without deepeft fighs and groans, is yet behind. Such *mercies*, fuch *judgments*, were enough to have made diffolute Heathens, if not *Chriftians*, ( without fome preaching alfo ) yet moral honeft men, religious, in their kind, and fenfible of a Deity. And, behold ! they have made of Chriftians, in outward profeffion, real Atheifts, in their opinions ;

nions; and worfe than Atheifts, for all manner of licentioufnefs, in their lives. *Epicurus,* who generally, in former ages, among all accounted fober and wife, Heathens and Chriftians, learned and unlearned, for his life; but more for his impious doctrine, and outragious oppofition of whatfoever pretended to God, or godlinefs, was a name of horror and deteftation; is now become the *Saint,* of many Chriftians.

BUT left this by fome, may be thought to be fpoken more *Rhetorically*, and in oppofition to the times, than truly and confcionably: it will not be amifs, nor impertinent to our prefent theme and task, to paufe a-while upon this fubject, and to confider, how this man (which in former ages, among fober wife men, that had any fenfe of piety, would have been thought fo prodigious, and *incredible*) came of late years, among other late *difcoveries* of the age, by fome accounted none of the leaft, to be fo well thought of amongft us. But I began this, of the wonders of our age, in an *objection*: let me firft anfwer it, left I forget it. It is very true, that this age beyond former ages, hath brought forth fuch things, which they that have feen and believe, may, in a manner, think nothing *incredible*. But firft, all men are not of one temper. And then, what we have *feen*, pofterity muft believe, upon relation: and there will be a time, when what we know, to be true, becaufe we have feen it, to many, may feem fo ftrange, that they will, if not deny, yet doubt the truth of it. In a word therefore, whatever our luck may be, it is our defire, that more than one age, or fome that are not yet born, may reap the benefit of what we write. Now to *Epicurus.*

FIRST,

FIRST, for his life, of which more afterwards. But we will suppose him, for a time, to have been a sober temperate man: or rather, his life to have been, sober and temperate, externally. For it is a true observation, both of Philosophers and Divines, that not the outward actions barely, is that that can denominate a man truly sober and temperate, or just and righteous, and the like; but the opinions ( τὰ δόγματα ) from which those actions do proceed. So neverthelefs, that we, who do not see the hearts of others, judge charitably of all men, by their actions, which we see; except themselves reveal their hearts, and make open profession of their opinions. *Epicurus* his opinion, did very much engage him to a sober temperate life; who, as he did acknowledge no humane felicity ( I know what I say, and shall make it good, before I have done ) present, or future, but in *bodily pleasure*; so, knew well enough, and to that end, hath many specious profitable *memento's* and advices to others of his crew; that the right and sober management of such pleasures, was the way to enjoy them long, and to make them more pleasing, at the very time. Besides, I would ask, if the Devil have a design to infect men, with some impious execrable doctrine; will he chuse ( if he have choice ) an open riotous leud man, to be his instrument, or a sober man, in shew at least, if he can have him? Which makes me remember, what I find in the Margents of a *Lucretius*, which once belonged to a very learned and judicious man. Over against those words, at the beginning of the fourth book, *Deus ille fuit*, *Deus, inclute Memmi*, &c. he writes; *Epicurus, Deus judicio Lucretii: meo, Diaboli* ὑποκριτής *nequissimus*: that is, Epicurus, *in* Lucretius *his judgment, a God: in my judgment, a wicked Proctor, or Minister of the Devil.* Let us therefore, in the first place, look into his opinions out of his own writings,

*in things* CIVIL. 203

tings, whereof no queſtion can be made. Firſt, that the world ( Heaven and Earth ) came to what it is, not by any Providence, but by a caſual jumbling of *atomes*, ( I need not comment upon that : ſome men I believe would be well pleaſed, to have them in childrens Catechiſms inſtead of ſomewhat elſe, that doth not ſo well pleaſe them ) that Sun and Moon, were not intended, either for light, or for any other uſe, for the benefit of men ; nor the eyes made to ſee, or the ear to hear, or the feet for motion ; but all by chance, without any fore-caſt of providence. This is horrible : and there is more of it. But by the way, that the Sun and Moon were but juſt ſo big, and every Star, as they appeared unto us, and our eyes. There is no impiety in this, perchance, ſome will ſay : but I pray, hath not this man well deſerved, that his *Philoſophy* ſhould be inquired into, with ſo much care, and diligence? But we go on : That, what men call right and wrong, juſtice and injuſtice, vertue and vice, were but fancies, and empty ſounds ; nothing, truly real, and worthy our purſuit, but what was pleaſant and delightful, which alſo was profitable. Is not this impious ? can any thing be more ? Was he a man, or a monſter, a Devil that could harbour ſuch thoughts, and take ſuch pains to ſeduce others, to the ſame perſwaſion ? But I know it will be ſaid : Did not the ſame man explain himſelf, that by *pleaſure*, he did underſtand chiefly, a vertuous life, without which there could be no true pleaſure? And again, Doth not the ſame, though he acknowledged no Divine Providence, yet acknowledge and profeſs to believe, that there is a God ; and that he thought it very convenient, that God, (whether one or more ) *for the excellency of his nature*, ſhould be reverenced and worſhipped by men ? But I beſeech you, can any man be ſo fooliſh, ſo ſottiſh himſelf ; or ſo far preſume upon the ignorance and ſimplicity of others,

as

as to plead this for *Epicurus* in good earnest? What is before objected to him, is written, and maintained by him, very positively, without any exception, or qualification, in divers of his writings: as shall be more fully declared afterwards. But *Epicurus* knew, what had hapned to other professed Atheists before him: it did concern him no less than his life, not to deny positively, the being of a God, or Gods. But what Gods I pray, did he acknowledge? How doth he describe them? *Homunculis similes, lineamentis duntaxat extremis, non habitu solido*, &c. that is, *Like men and no men: having all the members of a mans body, but not the use of any: in the shape and outward appearance, but not substance of a body.* So *Cicero* out of him, who, though he liked not his Philosophy, yet did much favour his person, and never, or seldom speaks of him, but very tenderly; not so much for his sake, I believe, as for theirs, some of his best friends, that were of that Sect. Neither could he mistake him, or misreport him, than whom no man of those times was better versed in the writings of Greek Philosophers. *Seneca* also, who did study to the utmost of his power, to acquit *Epicurus*, and to advance the credit of his sentences; not without some respect to himself, probably, ( whereof more afterwards ) yet when he speaks of his God, what a creature doth he make of it? *Epicurus*, saith he, *did disarm his God, as from all manner of weapons, so from all kind of power too: and that no man might have any cause to fear him, he hath thrown him far out of the world:* ( *Extra mundum*: for which some Editions, *metum*: others, *motum*: which *Lipsius* would have, *metam*: but *mundum*, the right certainly: confirmed by what followeth; *In medio intervallo hujus & alterius cœli, desertus, sine animali, sine homine, sine re, ruinas mundorum*, &c. as also by the same expression, in another place, *Alius illos*

*illos extra mundum suum projicit* ) *out of the world*, both *Terrestrial* and *Celestial*, as he doth explain himself afterwards: *Nulla illi, nec tribuendi, nec nocendi materia est: Non exaudiens vota, nec nostri curiosus*, &c. *De benef.* 4. *cap.* 18. Any man that reads that whole passage, may easily see, that *Seneca* doth but make himself sport with *Epicurus* his God, and thereby doth give us to understand plainly enough, what *Epicurus* his true intention was, by making such a God. And yet, strange, though that whole fourth book of *Seneca* be written against *Epicurus* his brutish opinion, that no man *should be kind, or loving to any other, but for his own sake*; *and that, the only end of all friendship among men*; and that he speak very roundly of his, and their sensuality, that were of that Sect, in some places, as in the second, and thirteenth Chapters particularly: yet some of his late Patrons are so shameless, as to produce some words out of this book, as spoken in good earnest by *Seneca*, to commend him, and his admirable piety; than which nothing can be more senseless and impudent, and more contrary to the drift of the whole book. And so, when he would seem to explain himself sometimes, that by *pleasure*, he did chiefly intend such, as did proceed from a vertuous life; what sober man that hath read his other writings, or such passages out of them, in best Authors, whereof no question can be made, where he doth so punctually, so expresly deliver himself, and argue the case, but must think, except he had formally recanted, and disowned those writings, that he did but basely, and impudently abuse the world, by such palliating glosses and explications? Might not he fear here also, that they ( we call them *Heathens*: I wish there were no worse *Christians* ) who were once ready, as *Seneca* doth somewhere record, to tear an Actor, upon the Stage, in pieces, for

extolling

extolling the happiness of *wealth* or *money*, so much, as to make it, *Summum humani generis bonum* : that is, *The thing wherein mans happiness doth chiefly consist* ; would meet with him, some time or other, in the streets, for setting up pleasure, and voluptuousness, as the only *good*, the only *God*, unto men? And such an enemy to God and Providence was this wicked man, that in his writings now extant, when his *atomes* could not help him, and he doth acknowledge himself at a stand, and doth beg of others, that they would study and find somewhat, that hath any shew of probability, to help him out; yet he makes it always his condition, that they would not fly to God and a Providence; he had no patience to hear of that. And so much for the Doctrine of the new *Saint* : Now for his Life.

WHAT was laid to his charge, whilest he lived, even by some of his own disciples, who professed they left him meerly for the leudness of his conversation ; and by others after his death : *Diog. Laertius*, who hath written his life, doth, in part, at the very beginning of it, declare. But then he tells you, they were all lyes; and that such and such Epistles, and other writings, evidences of his wicked life, were but fictitious writings : and this, *Gassendus* his friend, the great reviver and abettor of *Epicurism*, in this unhappy age, doth take for a very sufficient refutation. But I pray you, what was *Diog. Laertius*, that his authority, so many ages after *Epicurus* his death; when all the world almost, had consented in their judgments against him; should be opposed to the authority of so many worthy men, of all professions, Philosophers, Historians, Mathematicians, Poets, of his, and some precedent ages? Of which numbers some were so far from being *Stoicks*, that they wrote against them. Was he not, himself, this *Diogenes*, not to speak of his defects otherwise, which have been observed by
learned

learned men; a profeſſed *Epicuræan*? 'Οικόθεν μάρτυς· not therefore, among indifferent impartial men, in reaſon, to be admitted as a witneſs; or if admitted to ſpeak, yet not ſo to be truſted, as *Gaſſendus* doth him, in every thing, though there be never ſo many witneſſes, of far better worth and credit, to the contrary. And yet we may obſerve, how *Gaſſendus* doth ſtretch his words ſometimes, to make them ſerve his turn, beyond all reaſon and equity. For example: Where *Laertius*, after that he hath related the accuſations of many, of ſeveral heads, or crimes, againſt *Epicurus*; he concludes, μεμνήσθω δ' ούτοι. This *Gaſſendus* ( page 140. 163. ) would have to belong to all, that went before; whereas it will appear ( to ſay nothing of the ούτοι, which may be here a pregnant word, oppoſed to ἐκεῖνοι, that is, thoſe before ſpoken of; including a tacit conceſſion ) that it belongs to the laſt accuſation only, ( though that alſo, moſt true, by the atteſtation of more ancient and conſiderable witneſſes, than ten ſuch as *Laertius*: as *Cicero*, *Plutarch*, &c. ) whereby *Epicurus* is cenſured as one, that deſpiſed all men, but himſelf; even thoſe to whom he did owe what he was, and whoſe writings he had uſurped, and ſubſtituted for his own. To which *Laertius* doth oppoſe many things, to prove his φιλανθρωπίαν πρὸς πάντας: his *Parents*, his *Friends*, his *Diſciples*, his *Country*; and then goes on to the refutation of other crimes. And indeed, how could *Laertius* ſay, that all the former accuſations were falſe, when ſome were taken out of his own books, and writings, acknowledged by *Laertius*, and whereof no queſtion was ever made, but that that they were his? As for example, that he ſhould write in his book, περὶ τέλους, ( or, *of mans felicity* ) 'Ου γὰρ ἔγωγε ἔχω τί νοήσω τ' ἀγαθὸν, &c. that is, *For what to call good, if you take away the pleaſure of taſte, and of the ear, and thoſe pleaſures, which ariſe from beauty, and carnal copulation, I*

*know*

*know not.* Which words to be *Epicurus's*, is attested by divers Ancients, (whose attestation we shall not need, because not denied by *Laertius*) but especially by *Cicero*, very particularly; first in his *II. De finibus*, where he translates him thus; *Qui testificatur, ne intelligere quidem se posse quid sit, aut ubi sit ullum bonum, præter illud quod cibo & potione, & aurium delectatione, & obscænâ voluptate capiatur*: but more fully in his third *Tusculan*, where he hath a long Comment upon the words, taken out of that book of *Epicurus, De summo bono*: of which *Cicero* saith, that it doth fully comprehend their *discipline* or *doctrine*; and is full, he saith, of such sayings, in commendation of voluptuousness, and carnal pleasures. Durst *Cicero* oppose these things, to his *Epicuræan* friends, who were many, and of the best he had, had there been any ground at all, in those days, of suspition for that, which *Gassendus* would have us to believe, that those were spurious writings, or interpolated, and corrupted by the *Stoicks*, *Epicurus* his enemies? If we take that liberty, we shall not know what to say of any man, what he believed or maintained, by his writings: What *Plato*, what *Aristotle*, what any Fathers or Hereticks; if it will serve to say, those writings are spurious, or adulterated and corrupted. But observe, I pray, how earnestly, how ingenuously *Cicero* doth express himself, and appeal to the consciences (if they had any) of those men: *Num fingo, num mentior? cupio ref.* &c. *Do I feign* or *forge? Do I lye? I rather wish I could be confuted. For what do I labour, but that the truth ( O Christians hear this ) in every controversie may prevail*, or, *be understood, and come to light*. Here *Gassendus* should have fixed, could he have found or devised any thing, to help his friend out of the mire. But such convincing passages, not to be eluded by any art, or sophistication of wit, he wisely passeth over: but with all
possible

possible diligence ransacks all kind of Authors, to see what he can find, that may with the help of his sophistry, and false dealing, have a shew of somewhat, to make that beastly swine, to appear in the shape of a rational man. Were it my business now, or could I stand so long upon it, without trespassing too much either against my Readers patience, or my present weakness of body, as to examine all his allegations, I am very confident, there is scarce any thing considerable in his whole book, but would be found, either impertinent, or false: as if it had been the priviledge of that cause, (as indeed it is the *necessity*, because not otherwise pleadable) and for which he hoped no man would blame him. I should say so too, could any *necessity* oblige an honest man to undertake so wicked a cause. However, that I may give a taste to the Reader, I will take one of the most considerable Chapters in the whole book, the seventh of the third book, where he doth examine *Plutarch's* authority, or testimony concerning *Epicurus*: a Chapter, one of the most considerable, I say, because of that high *Elogium* which he doth give unto *Plutarch*, *Nullum authorem omni memoria extare, quem cum viro illo eximio comparandum existimem;* That no age (without exception) *hath born any Author, Whom he can, for true worth, compare with him.* I have a very great opinion of *Plutarch* too; and if instead of so many foolish *Romances*, *Stage-plays*, and the like; such a serious Author, who hath variety enough to please every palate, were read; it is not likely, that the Gentry and Nobility could degenerate so much every where, as they are generally reported. But except he were read in his own tongue; (which to do, were he the only Greek Author, now extant, I think three or four years study to learn that tongue, would not be

P   mispent)

mif-fpent) I wifh he were better tranflated. But I muft except the *French* tranflation of the *Lives*, which is excellent. Such an opinion I have of *Plutarch*; yet I fhould hardly go fo far, as *Gaffendus* doth. Now let us fee how he doth deal with this worthy man, and how with his Reader. That *Plutarch* doth generally (always I might fay) fpeak of *Epicurus*, as an infamous and fenfelefs man, that is not denied. Such a lover of reafon, and vertue, could not but heartily compaffionate the phrenzy of fo many men, who in all ages have been glad to find a patron of their fenfuality. Though divers books he wrote againft him, are not now extant; yet there be enough to fatisfie any man, what he thought of *Epicurus*, and his doctrine. This could not but grievoufly pinch *Gaffendus*, and deeply wound the caufe that he had undertaken. But what if he can fhew from *Plutarch* himfelf, that he rather followed the *common opinion*, in what he wrote of *Epicurus*, than his own judgment, or the *truth*? I muft needs fay, that in my judgment he had done much, and more than any ten or twenty Chapters of his book, if well examined, will amount unto: though very ftrange, if not *incredible*, that fo grave a man, fo ferious, would not only occafionally fpeak of him, as others did, generally, whether right or wrong: but would write books of him, and againft him, of purpofe, which nothing did oblige him to do; only to countenance a publick falfe fame. But let us hear. *Plutarch*, faith he, *in one place after he hath mentioned what thofe crimes are, which made* Epicurus *and his followers infamous to the vulgar, to wit, want of friends,* (that is, to admit of no friendfhip among men, but fuch as is grounded upon prefent profit, or gain, and *felfifhnefs,* if I may fo fpeak; which to have been *Epicurus* his opinion, *Laertius* himfelf doth not deny) *an idle life, Atheifm, voluptuoufnefs, neglect of all things:*

(but

*in things* CIVIL. 211

(but pleasures, or sensuality) well, what then? *Then,* saith he, *Plutarch* doth object to himself; *but these things unjustly, perchance*; (are objected or laid to their charge) *to which he doth answer; yea, but it is not truth, but opinion that we look after.* And so concludes, that *Plutarch* by his own confession in those things he did write of *Epicurus,* was ἐπιδίξως not φιλαλήθης: *a follower, or lover of opinion, and not of truth.* And if *Plutarch,* so grave, so serious; why not we, as elsewhere he doth argue, believe it of others also? Is not this enough, think we, to make *Epicurus* victorious, in despight of all testimonies, and evidences? For if *Plutarch,* who was no *Stoick,* (the common exception, as if all *Stoicks* had been *Epicurus* his sworn enemies, which is most false) nor friend to *Stoicks,* he hath written against them it is well known: But if *Plutarch* also, was carried with the general fame, though he knew the contrary to be true: what may we expect from others, though very numerous, yet, with *Gassendus,* not of equal credit and authority, as *Plutarch*; according to that judgement which he made before of him? But now look upon *Plutarch,* and we shall see (for he was too learned and diligent, that we should think it a mistake) what conscience this man made, of lying for *Epicurus.* Among other books that *Plutarch* did write against *Epicurus,* one is Ὅτι οὐδὲ ζῆν ἰδέως ἔστιν, κατ' Ἐπίκουρον: that is, *That in following* Epicurus *and his doctrine,* (though *pleasure,* the only thing that he did seek) *a man cannot live with pleasure.* This to prove, he doth use many arguments, and doth alledge divers passages out of *Epicurus* his own writings. All this while, nothing, as doubting, or following the common *opinion,* but very positively and peremptorily. At last, two or three parts of the book already spent, still pursuing his purpose, that according to *Epicurus,* men cannot live with pleasure; he proceeds

P 2

ceeds to another proof, or argument, which is this: *Epicurus* did believe, that from a good report, or name, (δόξης) some pleasure was to be reaped. Himself, as *Plutarch* out of his own writings doth prove; a vainglorious man, if ever man was, and covetous of praise and reputation. But *so it is*, saith *Plutarch*, that ἀφιλίη, ἀπεριξία, ἀδοξοτης, ἀυπαθειαι, &c. *that Atheism, voluptuousness*, &c. *which things all men,* ( I defire the Reader to obferve ) *but they that profefs it, afcribe to that Sect, are things generally odious, and infamous, in the higheft degree;* whence it muſt of neceſſity follow, that from this confideration alſo, *Epicurus* doth not go the right way to *pleaſure*. This to make yet ſtronger, and to prevent all ſubterfuges or evaſions, *Plutarch,* as from one of them, doth anſwer: *O but theſe things are laid to our charge wrongfully* : (the baſeſt of the world generally, would be accounted honeſt, if they knew how ) *what is that to the purpoſe*, replieth *Plutarch, whether true or no?* The queſtion is not now, whether deſervedly, or undeſervedly ; whether truly or falſly ; but what *reputation,* (δόξαν ) you have in the world. For who doth not ſee, that if a man, ( which was proved before of *Epicurus,* and his adherents ) place happineſs, or part of happineſs, in a *good name* ; and become, whether juſtly or unjuſtly, *infamous* ; he doth thereby undoubtedly loſe ſome part of his happineſs. Therefore faith *Plutarch,* arguing from their own ſuppoſitions and opinions ; τὴν δόξαν, ἐ τὴν ἀλήθειαν σκοποῦσιν: *reputation,* and not *truth,* or *true deſert, is the thing we here enquire into.* And indeed had *Plutarch* upon this their anſwer, gone about, by good proofs and evidences ( which elſewhere he doth plentifully ) to make good, that what was laid to their charge, *Atheism,* &c. was very true, and real, as it was generally believed ; he had, in that, wronged his cauſe, and made an unſeaſonable digreſſion ; ſince, it was nothing

*in things* CIVIL. 213

thing at all to the queſtion propoſed, what man *Epicurus* had been really, or what his followers were, or had been; but what *fame* ( δόξα ) they had in the world. And could *Gaſſendus*, grounding upon the ambiguity of the word δόξ·, and concealing the occaſion, and the coherence, ( a notorious kind of jugling, and falſification ) could *Gaſſendus*, I ſay, from theſe words infer that, as *Plutarch*'s acknowledgment, that what he had written of *Epicurus*, was all in compliance to *opinion*, ( δόξη ) and not according to *truth?* Or did not *Gaſſendus* more probably rely ſo much upon the favour of the times, and thoſe that did ſet him on work, that he thought any argument that had but any ſlender appearance of truth or probability; if but favouring Atheiſm, and ſenſuality, would paſs currently enough, and get him fame and good will, to boot?

BUT we have not done. *Plutarch* in the ſame book, a little before, doth mention that famous *Letter* ( mentioned by ſo many ) of *Epicurus*, when upon his death-bed: by which he makes himſelf a notable ſtout man, who in ſuch extremities of bodily pains, ( as he doth expreſs ) could enjoy himſelf with ſuch peace and tranquillity of mind. In which peace and tranquillity to preſerve him, that which, by his own words and acknowledgment, as ſet out by *Plutarch*, did moſt conduce; was, ἡ μνήμη τῶν ὑποκελαυσμένων πρότερον ἡδονῶν: that is, *the remembrance of thoſe* ( according to the propriety of the words, *fleſhly* ) *pleaſures, he had formerly enjoyed.* This *Plutarch* thinks very ſtrange, and almoſt *incredible*: ( wicked varlet! as though he intended with his laſt bloud, to ſeal the truth of his abominable doctrine ) But here *Gaſſendus* doth inſult: *At hic Plutarchus*, &c. *But* Plutarch, *to the end that he might more effectually traduce* Epicurus, *hath depraved and changed the words*, &c. who can excuſe *Plutarch*, if guilty of ſo great a crime: or *Gaſſendus*, if it prove an arrant falſehood,

P 3 and

and calumny? The queſtion is, whether *Epicurus* wrote, ἢ μνήμη τῶ ἐπαλλαυσμένων πρότερον ἡδιῶν, as before exhibited, and tranſlated: or ἢ μνήμη τῆς γεγονότων ἡμῖν διαλεγισμῶν· that is, *The remembrance of our former diſcourſes and reaſonings*: as exhibited by *Diog.* Laertius, and tranſlated by *Cicero*, *II. De finibus*; *memoria rationum inventorumque noſtrorum*. And this, *Gaſſendus* thinks is enough (himſelf, I doubt, did not think ſo: he had read *Cicero* better than ſo) to prove *Plutarch* a falſary. I muſt acknowledge, that *Cicero's* tranſlation is a great evidence, for that reading, exhibited by *Laertius*. But had *Gaſſendus* looked further into *Cicero*, or rather ingenuouſly told us, all that he knew, *Una eademque manus, vulnus opemque*: he would have told us, that as the reading exhibited by *Laertius*, is found in *Cicero*; ſo, that exhibited by *Plutarch*, in the ſame *Cicero*, more than once, I am ſure; as particularly, *V. Tuſcul. Sed una ſe dicit recordatione acquieſcere præteritarum voluptatum*: and again in the ſame book, from whence that other reading is produced, more punctually, and emphatically; *ſed vobis* (ſpeaking to men of that Sect) *voluptatum perceptarum recordatio beatam vitam facit, & quidem corpore* (according to the proper ſignification of the word, ἀπόλαυσις) *perceptarum*. And this enough, I think, to acquit *Plutarch* from all ſuſpicion of any falſification: what can be ſaid for *Gaſſendus*, to acquit him of falſe and injurious dealing, except this, that it was for ſo good an end, as to promote *Atheiſm* or *Epicuriſm*, I profeſs I know not. Well, it muſt needs be, that either in *Cicero's* time both thoſe readings were in the Text of that Letter, (which may be thought the more probable, becauſe *Cicero* in the ſame book, or place, takes notice of both) or, that there were two different Copies of that one *Letter*, and that *Cicero* made uſe of either reading, as he ſaw occaſion. This is certain: to which I will add, as

*in things* CIVIL. 215

as to me not improbable, though I will not affirm it, that some of *Epicurus* his friends, or disciples, when that letter came first abroad, being much ashamed of those words, exhibited by *Plutarch*, did make that alteration, of the reading exhibited by *Laertius*: which probably, that reading I mean, never came to *Plutarch* his knowledge. But see the force of conscience, sometimes, let a man resolve against it never so much. After *Gassendus* had charged *Plutarch* with two such foul crimes, the one, of conforming himself to the opinions of the vulgar, to take away an honest and worthy mans good name, against his own conscience: the other, of adulterating writings, of purpose, that he might have some ground to calumniate: ( what could be said more, of the arrantest rogue of the world ) yet at last, a sudden qualm takes him; ( *Ne Plutarchum accusare videar* ) *lest I may be thought to accuse* Plutarch, saith he, and so doth end: whether pricked in his conscience, because he knew he had accused him falsly, as I rather believe: or ashamed of his own inconstancy, that he had commended one so highly, whom afterwards he had charged with the greatest baseness and dishonesty, that can be laid to any mans charge; for either, or for both, let the Reader judge: but a fit man ( observe we that, by the way ) to make a *Saint*, of a *rogue*; that could make a *rogue* ( to serve his turn ) of such *an incomparable person*, according to his own testimony, in the beginning of the Chapters. ⁕ And as he hath dealt with *Plutarch*, in this, just so, in effect, by false glosses and interpretations, doth he deal with *Galen*, in the next Chapter. *Galen*, no *Stoick*, but a true lover of *vertue* and *sound reason*; and upon that score, a mortal enemy of *Epicurus* his phrensies, and leud doctrine: and let me add, one, ( and so *Plutarch*, and *Cicero* ) who was better able to judge, what was falsly adscribed to *Epicurus*, what

P 4 not;

not; than a hundred such, as *Diogenes Laertius* ever was.

WELL, but was not *Epicurus* however, a valiant man, who in such pains, as he was then in, could write so couragiously, as in this, and in some other Epistles of his, written at the same time, he doth? I answer briefly: It is no wonder at all, that a very wicked man, should die in his wickedness, very resolute and undaunted. There be many examples in all Histories: and some reasons might be given, were it our businefs here, why it is so. But secondly, we are not bound to believe whatsoever he saith of himself, that he was in such pain, when he wrote those Letters; whom we know to have been a most vain, self-conceited wretch, as covetous of praise, as ever man was; so far as may be learned by his own writings. A vanity ( such is the force of it in some men ) for which men have endured great torments, wilfully; and have undergone strange deaths. I could say more, but this is more than I needed. But I may not omit, that this Letter of *Epicurus* is mentioned by *Seneca* also, more than once: as particularly, *Epist.* 9?. which I think *Gaffendus* would not have omitted, had he been pleased with *Seneca*'s words and judgment about it. For *Seneca* there, as a *Stoick*, arguing that bodily pleasure, or *indolency*, was not a thing considerable at all, to true vertue: *These things may seem incredible*, saith he: *but is it not as much incredible, that any man in extremity of bodily pain, should say*, I am happy. *And yet this very word* ( or speech ) *hath been heard in the shop or wardrobe* ( officina ) *of pleasure.* I am at my last and happiest day, *saith* Epicurus, *when on the one side, great difficulty of making of water, on the other, the uncurable dolour of an ulcerated belly, did torment him. How then should these things we have said, seem incredible to them, that apply themselves to the study and practice of vertue; when even among them, who are lead altogether by pleasure, they are found?*

*in things* CIVIL. 217

*found?* Even *those degenerate, low* ( or, *base* ) *minded men, cay say, we see, that a wise man in greatest pains, greatest miseries, can be happy. And is not this incredible, yea much more incredible, than any thing we have said of true vertue? But I cannot conceive, how true vertue being once cast down from its true height, or eminency,* ( of being able, of it self, to make men happy, without the accessories of fortune, bodily pleasure, *&c.* ) *can keep it self from sinking to the very bottom :* ( of scorn and contempt ) So *Seneca* of *Epicurus*, and his doctrine, in that place. What, elsewhere, somewhat shall be said of that too, by and by.

I HAVE done with my Chapter, and if any be so much at leisure, to follow this example, in all the rest; I durst promise them, if judicious, and diligent, no worse success in all the rest. But it may be, though I chose this, as the most considerable Chapter, yet some will think St. *Gregory Nazianzen* his authority much more considerable, even in this, than *Plutarch's*; whose testimony, and his only, of all the Fathers, or Ecclesiastical writers, as I remember; *Gassendus* doth produce to prove *Epicurus* his innocency, and chast life : *De vita, &c. lib. 7. cap. 4. Quem merito*, saith he, *innumera obloquentium turba præferendum censeas.* Well, be it so. What saith this godly Father? The summ is : (it is in *Verse*) that Epicurus *did maintain pleasure to be the chiefest good of man ; but lest he should be understood to speak this of base bodily pleasure* ( so *Gassendus* his translation : but the words rather imply; *lest he should be thought to commend pleasure unto others, because of the pleasure himself had taken ;* or *b cause himself had indulged unto pleasure* : which makes a very different sense ; for it doth not acquit *Epicurus*, of making bodily pleasure the end or happiness of man ; but this only, that himself forbare such pleasures, of purpose, to acquire the more authority to his doctrine ) *himself lived* ( it is falsly printed, 'Εξω in my book, for 'Εζη ) *chastly and soberly, helping his doctrine by his practice.* So *Nazianzen*. And

this

this may seem somewhat. But had *Gassendus* dealt ingenuously with his Reader, besides the true sense which he hath concealed; he would have told him, that *Nazianzen* in that piece, and place, doth profess to relate, Σμωίρατα, *things that were ordinarily reported* of ancient Philosophers, not engaging himself for the truth. He saith indeed, Ου γδ ἀπιστῶν: that is, *That he would not deny them,* or be *incredulous* ; for that *it is possible to find examples of temperance and sobriety, even among Heathens.* That he must be understood *tenderly,* not of perfect belief, doth clearly appear even by the examples which he doth relate. For after *Epicurus*, the next he doth mention, is, *Polemon*, of whom, among other things, he doth relate (from *publick fame*, as all the rest) that a publick whore, being sent for by a young gallant; as she was come to the door, by the sight only of *Polemon*'s picture, was turned back. *Nazianzen* doth call it, Θαῦμα, *a Wonder,* or *miracle*; which I think we may read, and suspend our belief, without any breach of that respect, which we owe to that holy Father. But *Gassendus* might have told us withal, what the same *Nazianzen,* elsewhere, not in Verse, but in Prose, doth object unto the same *Epicurus* ; ἀθεΐαν, *Atheism*: ἀτόμως, his *atomes*: that is, the denying of a *Providence*: and ἐφιλίσοφον ἡδονήν, the *commendation,* if not *pursuit* (which is more likely ) *of a voluptuous life,* ( or pleasure ) *unworthy the name* ( or *profession* ) *of a Philosopher*: Naz. Orat. 33.

BY this may appear, how *Gassendus* may be trusted, in this cause. Yet we deny not, but *Epicurus,* what ever his life was, hath many fine sayings, which might make *Seneca* to judge, at least, to speak the more favourably of his life; and the rather, because it was, in part, his own case. I have a better opinion of *Seneca*, than to compare him with such a leud man. Yet it cannot be

denied,

denied, that he alſo gave too much occaſion to the world to upbraid him, that he did not live, as he ſpake, and taught others. Which troubled him not a little, as may appear by that paſſionate Apology that he makes for himſelf, and all Philoſophers in general, to whom the ſame was objected, in ſome of his books. Yet for all that, though ſome men can diſtinguiſh between doing, and ſaying; who may be more ſcandalized, where they obſerve ſuch contrariety between ſpeeches and actions, than edified; yet generally it hath always been the propriety of the multitude, to be led more by words, than by deeds; by appearance, than reality: which made that grave Hiſtorian, *Polybius*, to pronounce the generality of men, much inferior to bruits, in point of forecaſt and judgment. And to this, we may aſcribe *factions*, and *rebellions*, and *ſchiſms*, and almoſt all the evils, by which the publick peace and tranquillity of either Church or Eſtates is diſturbed, and infeſted. And ſo in *Epicurus* his caſe: *Atque his* ( fine ſentences of *Epicurus*, and his Mates *) capiuntur imperiti; & propter hujuſmodi ſententias iſtorum hominum eſt multitudo*: *Cicero*'s true judgment, and obſervation in a place.

NEITHER is it impoſſible, or improbable, that *Epicurus* and others of his company, either by fits, through meer mutability of mind, which is obſerved, of many: or of certain deliberation and purpoſe, after great debauches and ſurfeitings of pleaſures; did betake themſelves to more than ordinary temperance, and frugality, for a-while: not out of any love to *vertue*, which he doth abſolutely deny in his writings, to have any real being, or exiſtence; but that they might return to their *wallowing*, more freſh and vigorous: and ( as before ſaid ) that they might hold out the longer. So that, as his writings ( obſerved by ſome Ancients ) were full of contradictions, ſo might *Epicurus* his life be: and thence

thence proceed that variety of judgments concerning it, which *Gaſſendus*, but very partially, hath set out. To this purpose *Lactantius* his words *De Div. Inst. lib.* 3. c. 17 having first proved the effect of them, by sundry particulars of *Epicurus* his doctrine, are very pertinent: *Hic homo astutus, ex variis diverſiſq; moribus, circulum colligit, & dum ſtudet placere omnibus, majore diſcordia ſecum ipſe pugnavit, quam inter ſe univerſi*: that is, Epicurus, *being crafty, out of ſeveral and different manners*, or *diſpoſitions of men, he did gather unto himſelf* (the Congregational way, as I take it, *a number*, or *company* and *whileſt he doth endeavour to pleaſe all men, he did diſſent from himſelf, no leſs, or more, than his promiſcuous company did from one another*.

THERE is a Letter of one of his whores, yet extant, which doth set out his abominable lechery, and jealouſie withal, even in his old age. What ſaith our Author to that? That certainly, if *Laertius* had seen it, he would have said of that also, that it was a counterfeit Letter. So, he takes it for granted, that whatſoever *Laertius* the *Epicurean*, hath said, or might have said, as he doth surmiſe, to defend *Epicurus*, must be true: and indeed, deny him that, and all his book doth come to nothing. But to do him no wrong; he saith moreover, that that whore was dead, before *Epicurus* died. What is this to the purpoſe? Might not ſhe write, as ſhe doth of him, and yet die before him? But ſhe makes *Epicurus* eighty years old when ſhe wrote; and he was not so old, (true, or not, I do not enquire at this time: I need not) when he died. As though it were not ordinary, in such exprobrations of unnatural lust, to make a man somewhat elder, than naturally, and in exactneſs of computation, he is? But the ſtyle of the Letter is affected, and studied. The more likely, to be hers. For ſhe was *Epicurus*, not his whore only, (one of them) but also disciple; and mentioned by others,

*in things* CIVIL. 221

others, as a piece of a Philosopher. Let any man read it: it is a prety long Letter. If he find so much affectation in the whole Letter, as may be found in three or four lines of *Epicurus*, acknowledged to be his; I must acknowledge, that my judgment in such things, is very small. However, this Letter, though acknowledged for a true Letter, by two learned men, who have written upon *Diogenes Laertius*; yet, were it the worst thing that can be objected to *Epicurus*, I should not speak of him, with so much confidence, as I do; because I do not remember any thing of it in *Cicero*, nor any other Ancient; which to me, is a greater argument to suspect it, than any thing that *Gassendus* doth object against it. But though I remember nothing of this particular Letter, in any ancient Author; however, he that shall read what *Plutarch* ( that *incomparable man*, as *Gassendus* doth style him ) out of *Epicurus* his own books, doth record of ways devised and commended by *Epicurus*, to prolong and maintain lust and leachery ( that is, *happiness*, in their sense ) in old age, when nature is spent; he will either believe, this Letter, probably, a true Letter; or that they, that made that strumpet of *Epicurus* as she doth, did *Epicurus* no great wrong. *Plut.* Ὅτι οὐδὲ ζῆν ἔστι κατ᾽. &c. as before: not very far from the beginning: *Edit. Gr. in 8. pag.* 2008.

BUT that which, in my judgment, is, beyond all exaggeration of words, wicked and impious, is, that not content to clear *Epicurus* ( so well as he could ) from the imputation of an *Atheist*; he doth endeavour to make him a very religious man; yea so religious, as I doubt few Christians, were it true, as it is most false, can be compared unto him. For, saith he, ordinary men serve God, either for fear, or for a reward, which is *a servile worship*. But *Epicurus* did not fear God;

## Of Credulity and Incredulity;

God; that is, believe that God could, or would do him any hurt; nor yet expect any reward at his hands: if therefore he did neverthelefs honour, and worfhip God, meerly for the *excellency of his nature*; (as he would have us to believe) it doth follow, that his fervice did proceed from *meer filial Love and affection*, which is the trueft and nobleft worfhip. But before we fpeak of the *impiety*, let us obferve a little, the *abfurdity* and *incongruity* of this affertion. Was not *Epicurus* the man, who peremptorily maintained, that a wife man loved no body, but himfelf; did nothing, but for his own fake, his own profit, and intereft? What more frequent than that, in his writings? Infomuch, that he would not allow of any love or friendfhip, between man and man, but fuch as was, διὰ τὰς χρείας, as *Laertius* hath it; that is, *fuch as is grounded upon meer profit and utility*. How probable then, nay poffible, that he fhould love God, for his bare conceited excellency; who profeffed to love nothing, and fo taught others, but for his *profit*? *He that loveth not his brother, whom he hath feen, how fhould he love God, whom he hath not feen*? He that could not believe, that God could be fo good, as to take any care of men, becaufe men could not do any thing for God, by way of requital: (witnefs *Lucretius*, that perfect *Epicurean*, and fuch an admirer of his doctrine; *Quid enim immortalibus atque beatis, Gratia noftra queat largirier emolumenti, Ut tantum noftra caufa gerere aggrediantur*) could he be fo good and ingenuous himfelf, as to honour, love, and ferve God for nothing? This therefore was a great over-fight, in a learned man; a great *folœcifm*, as I may call it, or *incongruity*. And whereas he doth quote fome words of *Seneca*, and is very proud of them, (and well he might, in fo uncouth, hidious, and paradoxical an opinion) as though *Seneca* had been of the fame opinion; let the whole paffage be read,

read, and if the contrary do not appear, that what *Seneca* faith of *Epicurus* his *piety* or *voluntary worship*, he speaks it ironically, in derision both of his God, and his pretended worship; I shall acknowledge my self very much deceived: who not only think so of the place, but am also very confident, that *Gassendus* thought no otherwise of it himself; whatever he was willing his well-affected Reader to the cause should think of it. But, *absurdity*, be it so or no, I make nothing of that, in comparison of the *impiety*. For besides many pregnant testimonies of the Old Testament, where, among other things, we shall find, that, *that which doth not profit*, is the *periphrasis* of an *Idol*; ( and so *Epicurus* his God, not a God, but an Idol upon that account ) how shall we excuse St. *Paul*, who every where, almost, layeth it for a ground of his exhortations to Godliness and Piety; that, *Religion is profitable? For therefore we both labour and suffer*, &c. *For as much as you know, that your labour is not in vain*; and, *for the hope that is layed up for you in Heaven*, &c. and, *looking for the blessed hope*, &c. and, *the end of your faith, the salvation of your souls*: and, *for he had a respect unto the recompence of the reward.* And yet more positively: *He that cometh to God, must believe, that he is; and that he is a rewarder*, &c. and how Christ himself? *What doth it profit*, &c. *for your reward is great in Heaven*: and the like. And what is it, that the *Deists*, as they call themselves; such *Deists* as *Epicurus* was; who pretend that they believe a God, and that they worship him, not for any fear, or hope of reward, which they exclaim against, as *servile worship*; ( witness their wicked *Catechism* in Verse, set out, and refuted by *Mersenius* ) but for his *goodness*, ( in that he suffers men to live as they will, and do what they will, and takes no notice ) and for *the excellency of his nature*: what is it, I say, that they more uphold themselves with,

or

or intice others more effectually by, than this wicked and abominable; but, to weak carnal men, very plausible plea and pretence?

THAT *Gassendus* himself was an Atheist, really, I would be loath to say; I hope not. He hath written against some of *Epicurus* his opinions. But in discharge of my duty to God, and religion, I shall say, and my conscience doth oblige me; that had he had the advice of all the Atheists that ever were: had he advised with Hell it self, he could not have lighted upon a more destructive way, to all religion and piety; to all goodness and vertue, than this, of *Epicurus* his *filial fear*, or *love of God*. For what inference will carnal men, ( in such an age, as this, especially ) will, or can make of it, but this? that they may *believe*, as *Epicurus* believed; *no God*, I will not say, ( though it be true enough ) but, *no providence, no conscience, no difference of good or evil*, ( in nature ) *of what is just, or what is not*: I might add, and live as *Epicurus* lived; but I will only say, *believe as* Epicurus *believed*; and yet flatter and comfort themselves, that they are *religious*, nay more *religious* than many, nay most Christians, accounted religious, are? Was there ever a more wicked and pernicious device? The Reader will excuse me, if in all this discourse, I have dealt with *Gassendus* somewhat roundly, more than I would have done with a man of his learning, and whom I believe to have been a civil man; besides a particular respect I have to him, for laying open the vanity and falsity of *Des Cartes*, and his Philosophy, some part of it at least: which I think was a very good work, and may prove very useful, when once that malignant humor of innovating, which doth now so greatly prevail, will wax more cold and remiss. I wish he had not had so much of that ἐπιθυμία, in him, as *Galen* calls it, ἣ δόξαν ἔχειν ἐν ἀνθρώποις, which I believe was the chief thing,

that

that did put him upon this *Unchristian project*, of magnifying *Epicurus*. Wherein, how much he went against his conscience, we need not appeal to God, who is the only καρδιογνώστης: any man may quickly find it by his book, who shall but look into it: any man I say, that hath not, according to the current of the times, more affection for *Epicurus*, than the truth. But what if any man shall reply for *Gassendus*, that all this may be, and yet *Gassendus* not so much in fault; who doth in the same book openly profess, that whatsoever he had said, or should say for *Epicurus*, was but, *Exercitationis gratia*? *Absit alia mente id præstem, quam exercitationis gratia*: his own words: that is, *God forbid I should do it to any other intention, but by way of exercise, or exercitation only*. And why not as free for him, to praise *Epicurus*, as others have done the *quartan Ague*, the *Gout*, an *Asse*, a *Louse*, and that Monster of men, as described by *Homer*, *Thersytes*? Had he rested there, it had been better and more justifiable. Upon the same grounds, for ought I know, a man ( though I should not commend it ) might write the praises of the *Devil*. For many things might be spoken, of the *excellency of his nature*, as he is a Spirit, a good Spirit, by his first creation: then, his improvement, by his experience, since that time: his wonderful feats and projects, from time to time, to bring himself into credit among men: and if a man would say, that out of his love to men, he tempted our first Parents, that he might be the occasion of a further good unto them, in Christ, and by Christ; and therefore to be honoured, and worshipped by men: were it but for the conceit, ( and in very deed, somewhat I think to that purpose hath been said by some ancient Hereticks ) and novelty of the opinion, there would be some, I make no question, but would embrace it. But *Gassendus* goes on, on, and when he comes to that, as indeed he was bound, or he had had no thanks; that he did it *bona fide*, though *ready to recant, when better informed*; yet, this *bona fide* doth spoil all. But whatever himself thought, or knew; what amends can he make to such, who (some, *good Christians*, I make no question, and *learned* enough, perchance, to have found out his jugling, had they but suspected him) upon his credit, without any farther disquisition, have espoused his cause, and think it no disparagement to Christianity, (if Christians indeed) to speak with honour, and respect of that monster of men, and spiteful enemy of God, and all Godliness.

I HAVE been somewhat long upon this subject of *Epicurus*: somewhat longer perchance, than some would have wished. But I shall not apologize. I have not forgotten that *Credulity and Incredulity*, *in Civil affairs*, which doth include the judgments, as well as actions of men, is my subject. And truly, of all things of that nature this age hath produced; this of *Epicurus* seems to me, and I believe to many others, the most prodigious, and *incredible*. Not, that any one man, for some particular end, or meerly to shew his wit, (which I know hath been done by more than one) should attempt such a thing: but that so many, professing Christianity, should entertain the attempt with so ready an assent, and applause: an argument to me, with many others, of the inclination of the age. God avert the event.

SINCE this written, I bethought my self, that *Gassendus* happily, in those large Comments and *Animadversions* upon *Epicurus* his *Philosophy*, (if we may so call it, which deserveth better to be called, *dotage and madness*) set out some years after, in three *Tomes*; might retract some of those notorious *mistakes*, if any man can think them so. I have searched, but I find, that instead of of *retracting*, he doth *repeat*, and endeavour to confirm: and that, especially, by the addition of two testimonies, which I shall take notice of. The first of St. *Jeromes*, out of his second book against *Jovinian*, *Chap.* 8. where he doth say, with this Preface, *Quod mirandum sit*, a *thing to be wondred at*, because *assertor voluptatis*, an *assertor*, or *patron of pleasure*, (*bodily*, certainly, else it had been no wonder) *that* Epicurus *did fill his book with the commendations of a spare diet*. That *Epicurus* did it, all the wonder is, that the man should be so inconstant to himself, if in so doing, he doth make any mention of vertue, or seems to have any regard unto it, it being sure enough, that in this, he doth but abuse the credulity of his Readers. But if he commend a sober life in general, and highly extol it, before a riotous and leud: this he might well enough, without any repugnancy to his doctrine, in placing the happiness of man, in bodily pleasures. Though the practice of it, a rare thing, in men of that profession; yet the commendation of it, might as well become a professed *Epicurœan*, as any other. Besides, it should be considered, that St. *Jerome* his purpose, there, being to collect out of all profane Authors, whatsoever he had read in any of them, tending to the commendation of a spare diet; which he doth very copiously, as a very learned man, and excellently versed in all ancient Authors; any man may see, that he doth relate many things, as in such a case is ordinary; which it is not probable, that he believed, or did expect his Readers should, (I could instance in many particulars) but only to serve his present subject, upon a supposition nevertheless, that many things, though not so probable, yet might be true; the truth whereof he doth not stand to examine, which every Reader, as he should find himself concerned, might do, better at leisure. Not therefore to add any credit to *Epicurus*, but more forcibly

bly to fhame them, that lived riotoufly, or difcom‑
mend a fpare diet, or fpake flightly of it; is that paffage
of *Epicurus* produced by St. *Jerome*. And let me add,
that *Gaffendus* doth make that quotation, by adding fome
of St. *Jerome*'s words to it, as may eafily appear, fome‑
what longer, than in it felf it is, or can well be: but I
make no great matter of it.

HIS other long quotation, is out of *Porphyrius* his
excellent book ( περὶ ἀποχῆς ) of *abflinence*, &c. *Porphyri‑
us*, a Magician, it is well known; and as great an ene‑
my to Chriftianity, as ever it had any: yet *Porphyrius*,
of *abflinence*, &c. an excellent book, as I think ever was
written of that argument. I wifh we had the old tran‑
flation of it more common, than it is; out of which
many corrupt places in the Author, might be corrected,
at leaft, underftood. Well, *Porphyrius* in that book,
juft as St. *Jerome* upon the fame occafion, and to the
fame purpofe: A wonder, faith he, *that even they that
make pleafure to be the end, the* Epicuræans; *even they*,
&c. It is a long paffage, and it will appear, if well ex‑
amined, that here alfo *Gaffendus* doth afcribe fomewhat
to the *Epicureans*, which doth in *Porphyrius* his Text,
belong unto them. And which is worfe, fo unlucky
fhall I fay, or fo bold, is *Gaffendus*, ( fuch confidence
he had in himfelf, when he faw how currently every
thing did pafs, that he had written in that wicked caufe)
that he doth deprave as excellent a paffage, in the Text
of that long quotation, as any is extant in any Heathen
writer; I will not fay, becaufe it hath too much Chrifti‑
anity; nor yet can I fay, becaufe it is very obfcure; but
truly, ( as he doth in *Epicurus* his life, many ) through
unadvifed rafhnefs, and temerity. The Author there
doth fay, very pioufly, if fincerely, whoever he was,
that we fhould not *firft provide for the World*, ( and he
gives an excellent reafon for it, afterwards ) *and then
make*

*make Philosophy*, ( ωςοσκην· the very word used by Christ, upon the same occasion, if the Greek be authentick, ωςοπιωται ) *an addition*, or an *accessory*: ( according to that of the Poet: *O Cives, Cives, quærenda pecunia primo est; Virtus post nummos* ) *but first provide* ( by good instruction, I suppose, and Philosophy ) *for a generous confidence*, ( in God ) *and then content our selves with what every day doth afford*. This, *Gassendus*, by correcting ( or corrupting rather ) the ἐμὲ ( which is in the Gospel also, or the effect of it: well expressed in the English: *But seek ye first*, &c. ) into ἐμὲ, turns it quite into another sense. I shall not proceed to any further examination. But if any body will make it his business, he will, without much trouble, find matter enough.

CIVIL affairs and actions, the proper object of *Credulity* and *Incredulity*, which we propose to our selves in this *Part*, come to be known to us, either by our own experience, or by the relation of others; private, as Friends and Travellers, or publick, as the Historians of present, or past ages. Our aim is, by some instances and *observations*, ( it is an ordinary thing for men to forget their *Text*; this often repetition, may help to prevent it ) to direct them that may want such help, in point of *Credulity* and *Incredulity*. Wherein, our first *observation*, for a caution to some, how they take upon them to judge, before they be throughly versed in the world, shall be that old saying with little alteration, appliable to many occasions: *Homine imperito nunquam quicquam injustius: Qui nisi quod ipse fecit, nihil rectum putat*: we say, *Qui nisi quod ipse credit* ( or *vidit*, if you will ) *nihil verum putat*. It is a sad thing, to converse with men, who neither by their own experience, nor by the relation of others, Historians and Travellers, are acquainted with the world. How they will stare, and startle at things, as *impossible* and *incredible*, which they that are better acquainted with it, know to be very true, or judge, by what they have known in like cases, to be very *possible* and *credible*. It were great wisdom in such, who are so happy as to know their defects, though they suspend their belief, yet to be very wary, how they contradict, or oppose; and as much wisdom in men, that are better acquainted with the world, when they meet with such, to be very sparing of their stories, which have any thing of strangeness; nor yet to be very peremptory, or forward to contest, lest that, besides the offence, that unseasonable pertinaciousness may give, they wrong their own reputation, and be accounted lyars, or wonder-mongers, though unjustly. Others there be, who because they have seen *somewhat* themselves, or are not altogether unacquainted with Histories, or the travels of others; ground upon that *somewhat*, so much, that they will not believe, or acknowledge to be true, whatsoever is beyond their knowledge, or hear-say: when God knows, a man had need to be almost as old as the Devil, before he can take upon him to know, or peremptorily to determine, what the world doth afford. Though not born, yet I have lived a long time in *England*, a very small portion of the world, for extent of ground: sometimes in one place, sometimes (but necessitated partly by the late troubles) in another: always studious to observe, or to learn from others, what every place afforded, worthy the knowledge; besides what might be learned by printed books, without much pains. Yet to this day, I think my self but a stranger in it, daily meeting with many things, that I never heard of before. But I have often admired at the confidence of some Travellers, who if they have been but six moneths abroad, (it may be, less) say *France*, or *Italy*, they think and talk of it, as though they knew it

as

as perfectly, as the Country, or Parish, where they were born, and bred a great part of their life. Nay, some be so simple and ignorant, that whatsoever they have observed in an Inne, or single house, as they passed by; they will tell you confidently, that so and so, such is the fashion in *France* or *Italy*; when it may be, that they that have lived in either Country all their lives long, never met or heard of any such thing. Doth not every Country, as *England* particularly, consist of several Shires and Provinces or *Counties*; and hath not every *County*, their particular rites and customs, not only different, but even contrary? He therefore that shall ascribe the particular customs of any one *County*, as *Yorkshire*, or *Devonshire*, to *England* in general; doth he not expose himself to the just censure and indignation of those, that shall believe him, when they shall come to know their error, and make themselves ridiculous to others, that have better knowledge of the Countrie? Hence proceed variety of reports and relations, even in printed books, which may be true perchance, of such a place, at such a time, particularly; but generally, for want of wit and more experience, delivered, are most false, and happily, ridiculous. In a great fight, ordinarily, men think their relations very creditable, that can say, if honest civil men; they were at it. Whereas it is very possible, (and I have known such a thing, in my time more than once) that one man, of the same fight shall report a flight, and the other (both, present and actors) a victory, and both truly enough; but not so wisely, because what they have seen in one part of the Army, they rashly, or ignorantly apply unto the whole: and perchance call that a *victory*, (so, for the time, perchance) which before the day be over, may be the occasion of a *total rout*. It is the observation of learned *Cambden*: *Ita in pugnarum ratione, qui rebus gerendis ad-*

Q 4 *fuerunt,*

*fuerunt*, &c. Englished by Bishop *Carleton* : *Thus it is in Battel, they who are present, and actors, report not always the same thing, each reporting what himself observed.* This is very appliable to the relations of Travellers, concerning the same places, or Countries. A man therefore had need to consider well, (if truth be his end, and aim) whom he doth believe in such things, or how he speaks himself, upon the credit of others; honest men, perchance, and such as have no intention to deceive; but, of what judgment, what experience, yea, and moderation; that also must be taken into consideration, or we may miss our end. I add *moderation*, because some men, naturally *passionate*, are so swayed by their interest, whether of profit or meer affection; that they think they speak truth sometimes, when they speak that, which to others, of the same judgment, as to the cause, but without *passion*; doth appear notoriously false. These things observed, many seeming contradictions in Histories may be reconciled, and we the better prepared, when we read or hear strange things, to judge and discern, what, upon grounds of probability, we may believe, and what not. I rather say so, than what *credible* or *incredible* : because (as in the *First Part* hath been declared) I allow not of many things, besides what is against the faith, as absolutely *incredible*, because what is really *impossible*, is beyond our skill, absolutely to determine.

WHAT may be required of an Historian, in general, to deserve credit, many have treated of it. Of late writers, among others, that offer now themselves to my remembrance; *Bodinus* in his *Methodus Historiæ*, (a book well deserving to be read) and by *Melchior Canus*, sufficiently known, in his *Common Places*, are two. But I have nothing to do with History, or Historians here in general, but only as

they

*in things* CIVIL.

they relate strange things, which in their own nature may be thought, by some, *incredible*. Of which nature, every man knows, *Herodotus*, the Greek Historian, (so much admired, for the sweetness of his style, and the ancientest Historian now extant) in the judgment of many, to be. Insomuch, that of all Historians, whereof any account is made, he hath got the name, of a fabulous writer. Indeed, he had not the luck to write of things of his own time, or Country, for the most part, as *Thucydides* did: except it be, in the last books: and what is worse, not of things, which many others, now extant, have written of: so that most things must be believed, upon his credit, if we see cause; or may be rejected, as fabulous, or *incredible*, if we think fit, because not confirmed by any other. But they do him great wrong, that ascribe all that he tells of that nature, generally accounted fabulous, or *incredible*, as though he were the Author, or inventer of such things; or did deliver them unto us, for things which himself believed, or did expect that others should. For, for the first, there is no probability, that he, who to satisfie himself of the truth of those things, which he had heard, would take such pains, to travel into *Ægypt*, yea all *Ægypt*, in person, with so much diligence, as himself tells us in many places; and not *Ægypt* only, but some other more remote places, as *Syria*, *Palestina*, and the like, would make so bad use of his travels, (though some have done it, I must confess, *Thovetus*, of late, for one) as to abuse his Readers with stories of his own devising, when his own travels could furnish him with such admirable relations, whereof no question could be then made, or now can, rationally; whereof more afterwards. And that he did not deliver most of those other strange things, as things that he did himself, or would have others, absolutely to believe;

himself

himself doth profefs fo often, and fometimes doth openly teftifie his own disbelief, that none can lay that to his charge, but they, that have not read him. Now, if St. *Jerome* was in the right, when he determined, ( more than once, if *Melchior Canus*, doth him no wrong ) that, *Lex vera hiftoria eft*, &c. *One Law of a true Hiftorian, is, to write thofe things that are generally believed, though not really true* : in this *Herodotus* hath not offended, as, in thofe very words almoft, or equivalent, he doth exprefs himfelf : fo that St. *Jerome* ( whether in the wrong or right ) may not improbably be thought, to have taken it out of *Herodotus*. In matters of *Oracles* and *Predictions*, I muft confefs, he is very copious; fo that they, who do not know what the condition of thofe times was, may think many of his relations, more like the dreams and fancies of fome doting old women, than the reports of a fober Hiftorian. But thofe were the *Enthufiaftick* times, as *Plutarch*, and others call them; when not only publick States, but even private perfons, fenfible of any religion, in all actions almoft, of any confequence, were governed by *Oracles* and *Divinations*, more, than by any humane judgment or direction : which though fubject to much impofture, whereof *Herodotus* doth give divers inftances; yet, generally, thought and approved fo beneficial, that the moft grave and fober, as *Plutarch* for one, long after that humor of men ( or *power of darknefs*, fhall I fay ) was well over, did acknowledge, that the State of *Greece* was much advanced, or advantaged by them : as elfewhere hath been more particularly declared.

NOW, before I come to any particular inftances of his ftrange, and generally accounted fabulous relations; I muft not conceal, that a very learned man, by whofe labours the common-weal of learning hath been benefited as much, as by any's, that I know, hath written a book,

## in things CIVIL. 235

book, entituled, *Apologie, pour Herodote* : to prove, that no actions of men, mentioned by *Herodotus*, are so strange and *incredible* ; but have been equalled, if not exceeded, by some of later times. But it doth appear too plain, that under this title, his only aim was, to inveigh against some men, who indeed have given too much occasion, it cannot be denied ; but, against them, whether more, or less deserving it ; not, to justifie or vindicate *Herodotus*, which the accumulation of so many strange tales, whereof a great part grounded upon bare report, he knew, well enough, could not do. Some other title therefore, might have become that book better ; or indeed that book, another man better, than him, that had been the Author of so many noble and serious atchievements, for the benefit of learning. Now before I look upon *Herodotus* as the most considerable Historian we have, ( both for his antiquity, and for that conformity of sundry relations and customs, with those of the Scriptures of the Old Testament, observed by some, in part, but in part only, that I know of ) I will take some of his strangest stories into consideration ; for the truth whereof, after such a revolution of ages, though I cannot, no rational man will expect, that I should undertake : yet if we obtain so much, that they are not *incredible* ; it may not only dispose many to think better of that Noble Historian, than they have done ; but also make them more wary, how they pass their judgments hereafter, in the like cases.

ONE of the first strange relations in *Herodotus*, ( himself calls it a *miracle* ) is the story of *Arion*, the Musician, his deliverance ; who, when forced by covetous Mariners, to cast himself into the Sea, was saved by a *Dolphin*, who, delighted with his musick, offered himself, and carried him upon his back, to land. Few Children, I think, but have heard of it, at some time or other; but not many men, that think of it otherwise, than of a meer fable. Which if granted, yet *Herodotus* is in no fault, who tells us, without interposing of his own judgment, what was then said, when he lived, and averred for truth, by the people of two several Towns, *Corinthus* and *Lesbos*. Had he omitted it, he had been too blame certainly; and, since *Herodotus*, no Chronologer, (I think, or few) have omitted it. Neither was it then a relation of the old times, as we may say, and out of memory; such, as without good attestation of some, that lived at the same time, or shortly after, may rationally be suspected, even for the antiquity: but, as yet, of fresh memory, when *Herodotus* lived: 100. or say 200. years, because Chronologers do not precisely agree in their computation, was the utmost interval of time. But what ever any other may think of it, there is so much to be said, if not for the truth, yet probability of it; that I must suspect their *ignorance*, or condemn their *incredulity*, that peremptorily censure it as fabulous. But, this I mean, of the substance of the story, that such a man, *Arion*, a *Musician*, was saved by a *Dolphin*, who carried him upon his back to land. Besides others, that are not so well attested; *Pliny* the elder, in his *Natural History*, hath two stories; the one of *Augustus* his time, (not far from his own, who wrote in *Vespasian* the Father, his reign) of a Schoolboy, who grew so familiar with a Dolphin, and the Dolphin so much at his command, that no Horse can be more to any Master by Land, than he was to this Boy, by Sea; and this for many years, in the sight of all the Country; which makes the matter indubitable. At last, it so fell out, that the Boy fell sick, and died. After which the *Dolphin* also, after he had several times shewed himself about the shore, as he was wont, and no Boy appeared, he also for very grief, as all men thought, died, and was no more seen. *Pliny* doth name three eminent men,

*in things* CIVIL. 237

men, who had written the ſtory at large, in *Auguſtus*
his time, when the thing hapned. And beſides them,
*Appion*, or *Apion* rather, ſirnamed *Grammaticus*,
( but I know not why, except we take the word in a
very general ſenſe : for he dealeth altogether in *Hiſtory*, for which he got the name of *Polyhiſtor*, alſo )
who alſo lived about the ſame time, or ſoon after,
under *Tiberius*, did write it : whoſe teſtimony, beſides ſome others to the ſame purpoſe ; and very
words, are to be found in *Aulus Gellius* ; who alſo
hath the relation of *Arion*, out of *Herodotus*, at
large. Where perchance ſome body, not much verſed in the Latin tongue ; as once by ſome ignorant
Monks, learned *Eraſmus* was charged, he had turned the Goſpel into a *fable*, for uſing the word *fabula*, or *confabulari* in his tranſlation ; may ſtumble
at the word *fabula*, which by beſt Latin Authors,
is often uſed for *a true ſtory*. I think it will be
granted, no man can reaſonably doubt of a thing, ſo very well atteſted : But if any do, *Pliny*, his ſecond ſtory,
if he be not ſet upon contradiction, will certainly ſatisfie
him. For I think, next to ocular evidence, nothing
can be more certain. It is a ſtory of his own time, ( *in-
tra hos annos* ) of another Boy, in *Africo littore*, *Hipponis
Diarryti* : ( for there was two *Hippo*'s, in *Africa* : *Hippo
Regius*, or *Regia* ; which S:. *Auguſtin* was Biſhop of ; and
*Hippo Paluſtris*, or Διππῶτος, as *Pliny* himſelf, elſewhere,
doth teach) who uſing to ſwim with others in the Lake, or
*æſtuarium*, ſubject to Tydes, and very convenient for that
purpoſe ; a *Dolphin*, after ſome wooing by careſſes and
geſticulations, ſuch as nature afforded him ; got his good
opinion & will ; ſo that he durſt venture himſelf upon his
back, in the Lake ; & out of the Lake, into the main ; & out
of it, back again, as far as the ſhore, yea, and beyond the
ſhore. For, as if they had ſtrived, who ſhould ſhew
more

more confidence, the *Dolphin* would follow his beloved, even to the land, and suffer himself to be touched, and careffed, by others alfo, men and boys, that had the confidence; fo long as he was able, which was not long, to fubfift upon dry land. And this lafted not days or moneths only, but years: one year, at leaft, as I gather, though not expreffed, by the tenor of the ftory. Infomuch, as the noife of this miracle (as generally apprehended) being fpread far and near; there was daily a great concourfe of all kind of people, from all places. The Governor of the place under the *Romans*, moved, or ftruck with a kind of religious horror, at the fight; and among fo many Gods, they worfhipped in thofe days, apprehending, probably, fome kind of Deity in that Dolphin, attempted to do him divine honour, according to the religion then in ufe, by pouring fome kind of odoriferous confection, or ointment upon him; which the poor Dolphin annoyed with the fcent, and otherwife too, probably: (*Sopitus*, Pliny faith, if he do not mean it metaphorically) refented as an injury, or affront, and abfented himfelf, *per aliquot menfes*, faith *Pliny*. But at laft, appeared again, and by degrees, became as loving, and familiar, as before. This lafted till the inhabitants round about, to whom the *miracle* was now no *miracle*, by reafon of its frequency; overcharged with the frequency of guefts, which flocked thither from all parts, to be fpectators of this ftrange fight, to them that had never feen it before; cruelly, but fecretly, confpired againft him, and (what will not men do, to fave their money) killed him. I have this from *Pliny*, the elder, the Author of the *Natural Hiftory*: but confirmed and enlarged with fundry particulars, by *Pliny* the Second, (*Epift. lib. 9. ep. 33.*) who makes no mention at all of his Uncle, but had it from others, of whofe fidelity, in the relation, he bids us, us, as he was himself, to be confident. And indeed, what we may believe, besides what we have seen, with our own eyes; if we believe not this, I do not know. *Pausanias*, who lived under *Marcus Aurelius*, the Roman Emperor, and hath written that excellent book, of the Monuments and Antiquities of *Greece*, remaining in his time; doth profess, that himself saw a Dolphin, in *Perosoline*, ( the true name was *Pordoseline* : but, for modesty sake, made *Peroseline*) a little Island by *Lesbos*; who for some kindness he had received of a boy, did wait upon him, so far as by nature possib'e, and would carry him upon his back, whither soever the boy did direct him. *Aelianus*, who lived a little before, writeth of another, that was bred and brought up ( as a Fish could be ) by a poor woman, with her son; whom afterwards he loved entirely, and rewarded both him, carrying him upon his back, whither he would, and his Nurse, the mother, plentifully, by his services, when he was bigger. He also names the same Island, but that he names it *Plerofeline* : whether he intended it of the same Dolphin, I know not. It is very possible the same thing might be acted, by more than one Dolphin, in more than one place; one Dolphin taking example of another. And I remember, in that accurate relation of *Pliny* the Second ; it is observed, that with that miraculous Dolphin, the subject of the story; always another accompanied, who certainly was pleased with the sight; but accompanied only, and did no more, durst not perchance, fearing the others jealousie. To these that offered themselves unto me, more like stories, of other ages and places, might be added, I make no question : but the two first are very sufficient, in my judgment, to ground a confidence of the truth, without seeking any further.

NOW, because it is my business here, to help such as may

may want help, in such disquisitions; it will be worth our hearing, what is objected by some, against the truth of this story. Which yet to make more probable, before I come to objections, I must not omit, besides what was before intimated, that all, or most Chronologers, both ancient and late, whom I have seen; among others, St. *Jerome*, out of *Eusebius*, take notice of it, without any opposition to the truth of it: that the memory of it, as of a true story, was preserved by a brass Statue; by a temple; and by an inscription noting the time, or *Olympiad*; and that in *Ælianus*, besides the Epigram or Inscription of the Statue, we have a fine *Hymn*, said to be composed by *Arion* himself, as a monument of his miraculous deliverance, and thankfulness to God, for it: all this besides instances of the like.

BUT what saith learned *Natalis Comes*, in his *Mythology*, to this of *Arion*? *Quæ quod fabulosa sint, nemini obscurum est*: *That all is fabulous, all men*, he thinks, *must believe*. Why so? *Nam qua de Delphinis dixerunt antiqui*, &c. that is, *For what some Ancients have written of some Dolphins, as if some men had been saved by them, I accounted it meer dreams. For the nature of animals ( or beasts ) is always the same; and from that time to this, though the number of men, that have perished in the Seas, is infinite; we do not hear of any, that have been preserved by Dolphins*. Here is first a great and gross mistake, ( it would be so in a Philosopher ) in the word *nature* or *natural*. It is *natural* to men to speak, to read, to write, to learn arts, &c. that is, Men are naturally capable of such things, if they be taught: for without some teaching, none of these things will be learned; not so much as speaking, though it be done unsensibly, as it were; yet not learned without long study. And though some other creatures, as *Parrots*, and the like, may seem capable of that, and not men only;

ly;

ly; yet their speaking, is not a true speaking, because it doth not proceed from any λόγος ἐνδιάθετος, or *inward reasoning*, which doth engender outward speech. Some things men are naturally capable of, as men; as the Sciences, which yet some men can never attain unto, though they be taught, by reason of some accidental defect. But for more clearness, because it is to our purpose, to instance in somewhat that hath more affinity: There is no man, I think, where Dogs are, but are acquainted, more or less, with their nature, and conditions. Of all creatures, generally, they love and know their masters best: this is common to them all, more or less, to be loving naturally. But what if I should tell a story of one, or more Dogs, that loved their masters so well, that they would needs die with them? Would it be a good argument, that it must be a fable, because all Dogs do it not? *Lipsius* hath one, of a Dog of his own house, that loved his mistress so well, that when she died, and he saw her dead, run into the Garden, digged himself a hole, and there ended, soon after, his life: *Hæc, tota familia nostra teste, sunt gesta.* He doth appeal to all his family, who were present, and saw it, for the truth of it. *Scaliger* hath another in his *Exercitations* against *Cardan*, every whit as strange. What if I should tell of Dogs, that have pursued the murderers of their Masters, so constantly, so vigorously, that notice being taken publickly, it came at last, by order of justice, to a duel, or combat, wherein the murderers being overcome by the Dogs, they confessed the crime? We have the story of one in *Scaliger*; and out of *Scaliger*, in *Lipsius*: the History of another, out of St. *Ambrose*, *Giraldus Cambrensis* in his *Itinerary*, doth transcribe. So he professeth. But if faithfully, then the Editions we have of St. *Ambrose*, (that which I have not at this time, I am sure) are defective. For the

R                                                                                                           latter

latter part, ( of the Duel ) is there wanting. And indeed the ſtory ſeems to me but imperfect, as it ends there : no ſenſe, I think, can be made of the words, to bring the relation to an end ; without which it is not probable that St. *Ambroſe* would have left it. But, if for, *perſecutus*, as printed in my *Ambroſe*, ſet out by *Eraſmus* at *Bazil, Anno Dom.* 1567. we read it, as I find it in an old Manuſcript I have, *perpeſſus*; ſome end may be made of it, though not ſo full, or ſo clear, as in *Giraldus*. I wiſh I were in better caſe, were it but for St. *Ambroſe*'s ſake, to look into it. For I ſhrewdly ſuſpect, becauſe I have known it done in many books, long ago ; that ſome, who were ſcandalized at the ſtory, as abſurd, or impoſſible; ( as many things, through meer ignorance, to the prejudice of truth, are often ſuſpected ) did cut off St. *Ambroſe* his relation, with thoſe words of their own deviſing, *Itaque quod erat difficilius, ultionem perſecutus eſt*, ( ſo printed, but *perpeſſus*, certainly, as in my Manuſcript, to make any ſenſe of it ) *quia defenſionem præſtare non potuit* : which words are not in *Giraldus*. I hope, ( if not already done, though unknown to me ) ſome body will take the pains, who is better able than I am, at this time, or ever like to be.

HOW many more ſtrange things, from good Authors, or certain experience, even of our times, might be added; which if a man ſhould deny, becauſe all Dogs do not ſo, or not one of a thouſand, or a million, or ſcarce one in an age; how ridiculous were it ? I remember when I lived in *Suſſex*, I heard of one Dog there ; of another, when in *Sommerſet*, but in another kind, from perſons of credit : I make no queſtion of the truth : which neverthelefs I might live fifty years longer, and not hear the like. Great pity it is, that no memory is kept of ſuch rare accidents, whereof, beſides the improvement

provement of the knowledge of nature, good use might be made upon several occasions. Did we understand the nature of *Dolphins* perfectly, we might give a reason, probably, how some come to do so, and so, sometimes; and how sutable it is to their nature; and yet how, through the defect of some one circumstance, or more, in themselves, or the party they would pitch upon; or some circumstance of time, they come to do it no oftner, though much oftner, I believe, than is generally known; or, for want of good records, remembred. But upon Boys, all stories do agree, that they commonly pitch upon such; and that they are (some of the kind at least) great lovers of musick. Which doth make well for *Arion*'s case.

THIS objection therefore, that it is not natural to Dolphins, because all Dolphins do it not, or that we read of very few, who have done, or reported to have done the like, rejected as invalid and weak; in *Arion*'s case, I should rather object, how a Boy or Man could sit a Dolphin, I will not say, playing upon an instrument: (for there is no need of that) but sit him, or ride him for a considerable time, through so many waves, and not be washed off, or drowned. To me, it doth seem very strange, to another, it may be, not so much. But if we suppose the Sea, as some Seas are known to be, ordinarily; or at some times of the year, very still and calm; then there's no further question, as to this. And indeed *Pliny* tells us of one of these *Dolphin-riders*, who being surprised by a tempest, was drowned: which the *Dolphin* (but I warrant it no further, to the Reader, than he shall like his authority) apprehending himself the cause of, did end his life upon the Land, for grief. Another question would be, how a Boy can sit a Dolphin without danger; and whether a Dolphin be naturally shaped for that use. *Pliny* indeed doth

doth exprefs, in the relation of his firſt ſtory, that the Dolphin had the providence, *pinna aculeos velut vagina condere*; and *Apion* writing of the same, τὰς ἀκάνθας μει-ςίνων: and *Ælianus* tells the ſtory of another ſuch Boy, who riding a Dolphin, did unadviſedly run his belly againſt the thorns, or prickles of his back-fin, whereof he died, and the Dolphin after him, for grief. Had I ever ſeen a Dolphin, I could judge better; or had I, at this time, either *Geſnerus*, or *Rondeletius*; or could any where, ſo far from all Libraries, that I can call Libraries, but mine own, (and that a ſorrowful one too, at this time: a remnant of a Library, rather than Library) come to the ſight of either. I have the pictures of Dolphins, in ſome books: but they do not ſatisfie me.

I FIND in the books of a very learned man, which I have, out of *Rondeletius*, that a Dolphin hath no *prickles* in his back; who thereupon doth infer, that therefore *Apion* did impoſe, and might as well, in the whole ſtory, as in that particular. But that is ſomewhat a hard judgment, by his favour. I believe *Rondeletius*, that they have none, ordinarily. But as the Camels of ſome Countries, differ from the Camels of others, by the number of their bunches, as *Pliny*, and ſome others tell us; and ſo many other creatures, of one Climat, or Country, or of different perchance, but of one kind, by ſome notable difference; ſome have horns, ſome not, and the like: why may not we believe, as poſſible, at leaſt, that there may be a kind of Dolphins, more rare, and ſeldom ſeen, who have ſuch prickles? Poſſible alſo, that thoſe, (that kind, I mean) are the Dolphins, moſt ſubject to this kind of love. Not, that I would have any body to ground any truth, upon bare conjectures: but becauſe I think ſuch objections, againſt certain experience, to be of little validity.

Neither

## *in things* CIVIL.

Neither is *Apion* the man, that we truſt too: I know what the judgment of many Ancients was of him. Yet, though *Apion* might make bold in his relations concerning *Ægypt*, and other remoter places; it is hard to believe, that *Apion*, who was well known to *Tiberius*, *Auguſtus* his immediate ſucceſſor, durſt write a ſtory of *Auguſtus* his time, for a truth, (whereof, if a truth indeed, many thouſands muſt have been witneſſes) which was fabulous, and either invented by himſelf, or lightly believed by him, upon the report of ſome idle people. Add, that *Auguſtus* his time, was not a time of ignorance, ſuch as have been ſeen before, and ſince him: but a time, *Cum humana ingenia ad ſummam ſolertiam perduƈta eſſent*, as *Seneca*, I think, doth ſome where ſpeak, of thoſe times: *When humane wit, and ratiocination was come to its height*, ſuch a height, both for *Poets*, and *Orators*, and *Artiſts*, I am ſure, as hath not been known ſince. Which is the credit of *Chriſtianiſm*, that it prevailed at ſuch a time; not as *Mahometiſm*, in times and places of greateſt darkneſs and ignorance, and is ſtill maintained with the ſame, and the power of arms. What the ignorance, and want of good learning, that theſe times do threaten, may bring, God knows. However, though *Apion* had never written concerning that Dolphin, in *Auguſtus* his time, divers others did, men of credit, whoſe books were extant in *Pliny*'s time: and had that Dolphin never been, yet that other in *Pliny*'s time, ſo atteſted by him, and by his Nephew, that other *Pliny*; a man of ſuch learning, ſuch authority, and dignity, as he was, (yea and integrity, abundantly approved to Chriſtians, by that relation he made, of the Chriſtians of his time) had been enough with me, with the conſideration of all circumſtances, which he doth relate at large, had been enough with me, I ſay, to make me believe it as certainly, as if I had ſeen it with mine eyes. No reaſon therefore, that any queſtion ſhould be made of the truth of a ſtory ſo well atteſted becauſe of that one circumſtance of the *prickles*, on Dolphins backs, in caſe it be a miſtake. Which yet perhaps, if a miſtake, may prove the miſtake of *Rondeletius*, and not of *Apian*. For *Solinus*, where he writes of Dolphins, doth atteſt, that thoſe prickles do not appear, but when they do, through anger, or ſome other extraordinary occaſion, *inhorreſcere*, and that at other times they are hid.

BUT after all this, *Lipſius* his *caveat*, who was no very ſuperſtitious man, it is well known, though being ſet upon it by others, he did write in defence of ſome ſuperſtitious miracles : ( an argument rather : but I will ſay no more, for the reſpect I bear to his memory) his *caveat*, I ſay, will not do amiſs ; who having told ſomewhat, very ſtrange, of a Mountebanks Dog, (I could ſay much more of Mountebanks Dogs, and Horſes, which I partly know to be true.) he adds, *Deſino, & vereor ad genium eum, qui profecto patuit hic miſceri :* that is, *But here I ſtop,* ( or *end*) *as fearing that from Dogs, I ſhall be forced to go* ( or *fly,* for a reaſon; that is ) *to the Devil* : ( he did not mean an *Angel,* I ſuppoſe ) *Who in this might have a hand,* or, *mix himſelf.* It is ſure enough, that as there be magical *Hares,* whereof we have ſpoken in the *Firſt Part* : ſo magical Dogs alſo, and other creatures, actuated by another Soul or Spirit, than their own, ( irrational, and ſenſitive only ) whereof none are able to judge rightly, but they that are well verſed ( no light ſtudy ) in the contemplation, or experience of *uſe and cuſtom :* as in our *Firſt Part* hath been declared. However, this *caveat* though not unſeaſonable upon ſuch an occaſion ; yet no

man,

man, I think, will have, or can have any juſt ground of ſuſpition, that it doth concern us, in this caſe of Dolphins, and their love to Boys: which, as I conceive, muſt be referred to their *nature*, or natural diſpoſition; *Natalis Comes* his reaſonings againſt it notwithſtanding. But if we take *genius*, in a more general ſenſe, for another kind of Spirits, that are neither *Devils* nor *Angels*; I cannot tell what to ſay to it. The ſame *Pliny*, but now commended, hath a ſtrange example, which we have mentioned in another place, our *Preface*, to Dr. *Dees's Revelations*, (or *Illuſions* rather) as I remember. As for their love to *Muſick*, I think it very probable, by thoſe relations that are extant: but of that, we have no like certainty, as of their love to Boys, and mankind in general. The ſame (their love to Muſick) is reported of divers other creatures beſides, but I have no certainty.

BEFORE we end this point, ſomewhat might be added, of that famous *American* Fiſh, or Monſter, called *Monati*; one whereof, a young one was bred and brought up by one of their petty Kings, in his Court, and grew to a vaſt bigneſs: very kind, and ſerviceable he was, to all that craved his help, but to Chriſtians, or *Europæans*, (whom, probably, he might diſtinguiſh by their voice, and habit, not by their faith) of whom he had received an affront. This Fiſh they write, hath carried at once upon his back, no leſs than ten men: who in the mean time, ſung and made merry, with all poſſible ſecurity. This perchance, in ſome mens judgment, may add ſomewhat of probability to *Arions* caſe, and to thoſe other relations, that have been mentioned upon it: which, in my judgment, needs no further confirmation. The Hiſtory of this *American* Fiſh (mention, at leaſt) is in all that have written of the diſcoveries of thoſe Countries: *Peter Martyr*, I am ſure, a very ſufficient witneſs, were there no other. I

I THOUGHT I had done: but I have not; I shall make some use of their relations concerning this Fish, as not doubting at all of the truth; to confirm somewhat in the relations of the Ancients concerning *Dolphins*, which hath occasioned some wonder, but more mistakes. They write that some Dolphins did seem to rejoyce at the name *Simon*. I believe it, because ordinarily then so called; and when once used to the name, what wonder, when tame and frolick, if they seemed to know their name, and to rejoyce at it? And the same thing we find attested of that *American* Fish, we now speak of, which was brought up in the King's Court. The common name of the Fish, we said before, is, *Manati*: but they had given to this, a proper name, *Matum*: that is, in their language, *noble* or *generous*: and the Fish knew his name so well, that had any (whose voice he knew, especially) but called at the River side, *Matum, Matum*: he would presently hold up his head, and offer himself. But if any write, that Dolphins generally, loved to be called by the name *Simon*, more than by any other, as *Pliny* doth intimate; this is but to say, that there is somewhat in the sound of that word, that doth better please them, than any other ordinary sound: which is not impossible. The truth is, *Pliny* doth seem to say much more, as if Dolphins loved the name *Simon*, because so agreeable to their nature: being called, *Simones, à simis naribus*, that is, *from their flat nose* : such, both in Latin and Greek, being usually called, *Simones*. This ridiculous conceit I find *Pliny* charged with, by a very learned man, who therefore well objecteth; *Sed quis credat*, &c. *But who can believe that Fishes should understand, either Greek or Latin*? Nay, they must be pretty good Grammarians too, to know the Etymology of the name, that therefore called, *Simones, à simis naribus*, from their *flat noses*.

*noses.* Can any man believe, that *Pliny* was so stupid, as to believe any such thing himself; or so careless of his credit and reputation, as wilfully to expose himself to the scorn and derision of his Readers? Yet this *Salmasius* also doth pass over, as though *Pliny* had really believed it. *Ita appellari gaudere quod simi sint, dicit.* *Pliny's* words, as ordinarily printed, are, *Dorsum iis repandum, rostrum simum. Quâ de causa, nomen simonis omnes miro modo agnoscunt, maluntque ita appellari.* It cannot be denied, that from those words, scarce any other sense can be made. But whether ever *Pliny* did write so, a thing so horrible and so prodigious, that he that believes, may as well believe all *Æsops* Fables, to be true stories; deserved, I think, before we charged him with it, to be taken into some consideration. For besides *Pliny,* if *Pliny,* I do not find any Ancient, that doth write any such thing, but only that they delight in the name *Simon*: and *Solinus,* who ordinarily doth transcribe *Pliny,* saith no such thing, but only this; *Certum habent vocabulum; quo accepto, vocantes sequntur: Nam proprie, Simones nominantur.* And *Ælian* who hath written a whole Chapter, to prove that Dolphins have some understanding, he hath no such thing. What then? I am very confident, that what *Pliny* wrote, was, or is; *Dorsum iis repandum, rostrum simum, quâ de causa, nomen Simonis: quod omnes miro modo agnoscunt, maluntque ita appellari.* So, *Pliny* saith no more, than what others say, and may very well, as before shewed, be very true. I never affected to be a *Critick*: my profession found me work enough, and would yet, had I many more years to live, and had my health. If I affected any thing besides, it is, to understand nature, to which I ever had a great inclination. Yet this I could shew, by hundreds of instances, that both *Divinity* and *Philosophy,* and all kind
of

*Of Credulity and Incredulity,*

of learning, hath suffered much, for want of true *Criticks*. But, *rara avis*: that age muſt be a happy age, that produceth two or three, that truly deſerve that name. The labour is great: but if there be not ſomewhat more of nature in it, than labour; the more labour, the more danger.

THOUGH *Cardan* with me, be of no great authority, for reaſons before expreſſed: yet he was a learned man, and I would do an enemy right, if he came in my way, as ſoon as to a friend. For in that caſe, he becomes my *neighbour*, and I bound by the laws of Chriſtianity, to look upon him, as a *friend*. The ſame learned man ( whom I did not name before, nor ſhall now; but a very learned man, and my good friend, when he lived ) I thought he did *Pliny* ſome wrong, becauſe, if he had better conſidered of it, he might have found, that that ſenſe, and therefore thoſe words, could not be his, which he did aſcribe unto him; but unto *Cardan*, he doth much more, adſcribing that ſenſe unto him, which his words will not bear. Having ſaid of *Pliny*, that he believed Dolphins underſtood humane language; a prodigious opinion: *Fidem tamen habuit Cardanus*; he addeth, *Yet Cardan did believe it*; and then produceth a paſſage of his, out of his *VII. De varietate*, cap. 37. *Delphines ſimonis quodam conſueto nomine gaudent*, &c. It is a long paſſage, but not one word in the whole paſſage to that purpoſe, for which it is alledged. *Cardan* doth give, or endeavour to give a reaſon, why Dolphins, according to the tradition of Ancients, delight in the name *Simon*, more than any other. The firſt Dolphins, or former Dolphins, having been uſed to that name, faith he, and, ( through the force of uſe and cuſtom ) delighted in it: that delight became hereditary to their poſterity. This is the ſum of *Cardans* conjecture, or opinion; if I underſtand, either

Latin

Latin or sense. And there may be more Philosophy in this, than every man will be ready to believe, or understand. For I have thought sometimes, ( I thought I had some reasons for it ) that the very thoughts of Parents, sometimes, are propagated to their posterity; how much more delights, and passions, or strong affections? If therefore any Dolphin have been long used to the name *Simon*, ( any other name, I think, would have done the same ) and taken pleasure in it; I think it is very possible, that another Dolphin, of his brood, ( and so others, after ) should naturally affect that name, more than any other. However, there's nothing in *Cardan*, in the whole passage alledged, of Dolphins understanding humane language, either Greek, or Latin, or any other: or any thing tending to that purpose. So that I must needs say, that great wrong is done him, by that learned man; who, though a very judicious man; ( I will say so of him, though he hath in my judgment said more of *Cardan* elsewhere, to his justification, than I think, if well weighed, can be made good ) yet he was too great a writer, to digest well every thing that he did write. By these instances, let the Reader consider, how much it concerneth men, younger men especially, who really seek after truth, not to take things upon trust, without sound examination; nor rashly to *believe*, or *unbelieve*, till they have good ground for either. I have now done with *Herodotus* his *Arion*.

IN the next place we shall take notice of three relations, in *Herodotus*, which he thought himself bound, as he often professeth, by the law of an Historian, to take notice of, though he did not believe them, as he doth expresly profess of some of them. We shall but mention them. The first is concerning some people in the *North*, which were reported to sleep part of the year, in Caves. This *Herodotus* doth protest against, as *incredible*:

*credible*: yet we know it is believed, at this day, by many, neither fools nor children, as very true; whereof we have given an account in our *First Part*. The second is of a people called *Neurii*, who are reported once in the year, to turn into Wolves: not into their shape, I believe, or but in part, at least; but into their conditions and qualities, absolutely, and very literally. But *Herodotus*, though affirmed by many with great asseverations, yea execration, or oaths; he faith, did not believe it. But what shall we say to some of our time, both learned and grave, who write of it, and commend it unto us, for a truth? So doth *Gasper Peucerus*, a learned Physician, I am sure, whom we have spoken of in our *First Part*: who describes the manner and the time: and a very learned man, once Prebend of this Church, (who, though dead many years, yet lives in his learned Son, one of the Prebends of this Church likewise) in a book of his, inscribed *Vates*; seems to ascribe much faith to *Peucerus*. *Delrio* the Jesuit, in his laborious *Disquisitiones Magicæ*, writing of the same thing, doth absolutely determine it, that the *Devil* cannot, really, change *substances* or forms; to whom I willingly subscribe: but that he may so qualifie the bodies, even of men, as that they shall produce the same effects, as if they were Wolves, or Lions, or the like: and *transform*, or transfigure rather, the bodies into the shapes, or appearances of such brutes. And it is St. *Augustin*'s determination also, *De Civitate Dei*, lib. 18. cap. 18. *Delrio* doth quote *Herodotus*; and with *Herodotus*, *Cambden*: *Et hodie ex vulgi opinione, quidam Hiberniti, in altera parte Hiberniæ*.

THE third relation of *Herodotus*, is, of a certain people, whom he doth call *acephali*, that is, *headless*, because their heads and eyes are in their breasts, or upper parts of their breasts. I take no notice of the other

reading

## in things CIVIL. 253

reading in *Herodotus*, αυτοκέφαλοι, becaufe not acknowledged by divers ancient Manufcripts: though both *Pliny*, and *Aulus Gellius*, and St. *Auguftin*, and fome others, mention them alfo among the ftrange Nations of the North. Whether any fuch people or no, as thefe *acephali*, *Herodotus* doth not affirm, nor deny; but delivers it upon the report of the Country, in the defcription of *Lybia*. If I be not miftaken, *Munfterus* in his Cofmography, fome where, (for I have not the book, at this time) doth deliver it for a truth. Sir *Walter Rawleigh*, I am fure, in his reports concerning *Guiana*, fet out in Latin, with Notes, at *Norimberg*, Anno Dom. 1599. by *Levinus Hulfius*, with divers Maps and brafs-Cuts; doth deliver it for a truth. St. *Auguftin* alfo, doth mention fuch, as from others; and from fome publick pictures, very artificially carved, in *Carthage*, when he lived there. And that fuch a child was born in *Mifnia*, in the year of our Lord, 1554. is recorded by *Fincelius*, *De miraculis noftri temporis*; though indeed I do not find in the picture, either nofe or mouth, but eyes only. But that might be the over-fight of the Painter, or Carver, rather.

IN all thefe three particulars, till further confirmation, as I do my felf, fo fhould I advife others, that know no more than I do, to fufpend their belief. Though truly, I muft acknowledge, this, no fmall inducement to yield affent, becaufe fuch a belief, or tradition, hath been in fo many ages; where there is no ground of fufpition, that they have taken it one from another, (a ftrong objection againft the *Phœnix*, and fome other miracles of antiquity) as, for example, that they that believed, or carved the *acephali*, to be feen in Saint *Auguftine's* time,

time, had it from *Herodotus*, who speaks of it so doubtfully; nor they that made report to *Henry* the Third, King of *France*, before spoken of, concerning the sleepers, ever had it from the said *Herodotus*, who doth protest against it, as *incredible*: or lastly, that they that pe-swaded *Penceres* of late, or St. *Augustin* long before, that there were such transmutations of Men into Wolves, before spoken of, for a certain time, did ground it, at all upon *Herodotus* his relation, or testimony; or perchance ever so much as heard of the name: and as little, I believe, upon St. *Augustins*. However, all this is not of force with me, to engage me to a belief upon grounds of reason, as I conceive. But to censure them that believe it, so they leave others, to the liberty of their own judgment; I should not do that neither, because there is so much to be said, to make it not *improbable*.

I HAD somewhat of *Oracles* before, in the relation of which, *Herodotus* may seem beyond measure curious, if not superstitious. Some reason hath been given before, yet I will not take upon me to acquit him of all superstition: by which I understand, an excess of that worship, which was in use, where, and when he lived. But besides the religion, or superstition of the place; he was also not little infected with the *Ægyptian* superstition, as by many places doth appear. But what shall we think of those strange judgments, he doth very particularly record, against those, that attempted to rob the rich Temple at *Delphi*; the chiefest seat of *Oracles* then known ( to Heathens ) in the world? This indeed *Herodotus* doth relate with more than ordinary confidence; and it were strange, if he could be ignorant of the truth of so memorable a story, which was acted, ( if true ) if not when he was a man, yet when born, and of some years. I know not of any, that doth except against it, upon any Historical, or Chronological account: but

against

against the probability of the story, in general, somewhat may be objected. Would God do such miracles, to preserve a Heathenish Temple; which he hath not done to preserve his own, at *Jerusalem*; as in the days of *Antiochus*, *&c.* nor so many Christian Churches, that have been spoiled, and robbed from time to time, in several Countries? And when more; or, more execrable profanation of holy things; when very Churches were turned into Stables; then in these late days, during the reign and rebellion of the *Fanaticks*! Another man would add perchance, and *Presbyterians*: but I would hope better things of them. They have declared against *Sacriledge* very roundly, many of them: and if the same men, should not oppose *profanation* of holy things, being things of the same nature, as vigorously; they would give men just occasion to believe, that what they have spoken, or done, against the other, was but for their own interest, or some other worldly end. But why then doth not God shew himself, at all times, as well as then, in *Herodotus* his time, and many times since? For it cannot be denied, but that every age will afford some dreadful examples, of horrible judgements against *Sacriledge and profanation of holy things*: but that it is so always, or so visible; especially, upon the actors themselves, we cannot say. But the greatest objection is, not so much, why not, always; as, why such indignation, such judgments, for the *Temples*, and *holy things* of idolaters; of *Devils*; as St. *Paul* doth call them? I would not have any man too bold, and I dread it my self; to call God to an account, of his judgments especially, which to men are most inscrutable. And I think, it is the greatest *Sacriledge* that can be committed, for any man, who perchance would scorn, that a child, or a Pesant, should aspire to penetrate into the reasons of his own counsels; to presume, that he can understand,

stand, or should understand the reason of all God doth; and not rather, when it is certain, that God hath done it, adore with humility, what God hath done. That such things hapned about the Temple of *Delphis*, as *Herodotus* doth relate, though very strange; ( so they seemed to *Herodotus* himself ) besides other reasons, I am the more apt to believe, because as strange things ( miraculous, indeed ) did happen again about the same Temple, and what did belong unto it, not long after; when the *Galli*, or *Gaules* of those times, under the command of *Brennus*, did attempt to rob it; which I know not any man, whom at this time I can call to mind, Heathen or Christian, that ever did question the truth of. Yet I should hardly say, as I find some do, that God himself was the immediate author of those *miracles*: So I hope I may speak with St. *Augustin*, and the Schoolmen, though I know, that in some sense, God is the only author of true *miracles*. *Sed quamvis execrandum idolum Delphis coleretur*, &c. *But though it was an execrable Idol, that was worshipped at* Delphi, *yet being it was worshipped by the* Gaules *for a God, no wonder, if, as sacrilegious wretches, they were chastised by the true God, with strange Thunders, and other prodigious events,* ( one was, the rending of a hill at the top, which rouled down upon divers of them, and oppressed them. See other particulars, in the late Reverend Archbishop's Chronology, *pag.* 479. ) *Which did dash some of them, and drive the rest away, so that few of them* ( the Army consisted of divers hundred thousands, whereof not a third part escaped ) *did escape the punishment, due to either attempted, or executed Sacriledge.* So a learned, and pious Chronologer of our days. But, first I make a question, whether the God, or Idol, worshipped at *Delphi*, were really acknowledged by them ( the *Gaules* I mean ) for a God. I rather believe, that they were a desperate kind of of Heathens, that scarce acknowledged any Deity. *Aristotle* writeth of them, (and upon that account, will not allow them true *fortitude*, but brutish *stupor* only) that they neither feared tempests nor earthquakes: and some body else, as I remember, that they were wont to brag, all they feared in the world, was, lest the Sky should fall, and bruise their bodies. To which, that of the *Thraces*, recorded by *Herodotus*, for boldness, and contempt of all Deity, is not unlike; that when it lightned, or did thunder, they would cast arrows up, as it were, to Heaven, to threaten God; because, saith he, they would have no other God, but their own, or a God of their own making. Now, that God should permit the Devil, who can do much more, by his own power, given him by God, when God doth permit, than cause thunder and lightning, & strange tempests; to use his power, to uphold his own Kingdom, his principal aim, we doubt it not; but withal, to confound (Gods intention) the insolency of prophane wretches, and to maintain an opinion among men, (the interest of a Deity, in the opinion of ordinary men, being most concerned, in the vindication of *Sacriledge and profanation*) that there is a God; this, I think, cannot be matter of much wonder, to any sober, intelligent man. But absolutely to say, that the true God, who in *Job's* case, life excepted, left the Devil to his own power; did it, or was the immediate author of those miracles; I do not hold so safe.

IT may further be objected, that even in those days, (for why God now doth not, commonly, shew such examples, much may be said to it, upon grounds of reason, & probability) but even, in those days, God did not punish *Sacriledge* always, though committed with the greatest contempt, and insolency, that impiety, according to the religion of those days, and profanes, could possibly devise. So *Dionysius*, the tyrant, the first of the two: who notwithstanding all his Sacriledges, and impious scoffs, died wealthy, and potent, and upon his bed; (though reported otherwise by some, but I follow the best Authors) and left a flourishing Kingdom ( if under a tyrant, it may be said of any Kingdom ) to his Son and Heir. This objection is made by Heathens, of those times, but answered by them, that it is not always the way of Providence, or Divine Justice, to punish the offenders in their own persons, or presently: but that the vengeance lighted upon his Son, who of a wealthy potent King, once guarded with a standing Army of a hundred thousand foot Souldiers, and ten thousand Horse, besides too, ( some write, five hundred ) Ships at Sea; became after many revolutions, a poor wretched School master; yea, plain begger: the scorn and contempt of all men, even the most miserable, and so died: not to mention, what hapned to his wife, and two daughters, before he died, which no man can read, without horror. A good answer, from such. For, of another world, and of a day of Judgment, the truest answer, no body could expect it from them. This wisdom, it seems, they learned from long and approved experience: except some of them had it immediately from the *Scriptures*, which we know by many testimonies, were not altogether unknown unto them. And who knows, but those horrible *Sacriledges, and profanations* lately committed, in *London*, especially; where also the rebellion, by tumults, and seditious Sermons, first began; may not, through Gods just judgment, have contributed much, to this late dreadful, and, in some respects, miraculous Fire ? But, this of *Sacriledge*, by the way only, to give some light to *Herodotus* his passage, in point of *Credulity* and *Incredulity*, which is our business. For though it might be a seasonable subject, otherwise, yet it is a subject, that hath very lately, so learnedly and so solidly been handled, by a very learned pious man; that to meddle with it otherwise, than upon such an occasion; I should think I did, ( as the Proverb goes ) *falcem, in alienam messem injicere.*

*HERODOTUS* has some strange relations of one or two notable Thieves, which may deserve to be taken into consideration. For Thieves and Robbers are men, and as men they may do actions, which deserve, if not commendation, yet *admiration*, and so objects of *Credulity* and *Incredulity*. Another use may be made, the better to escape them, or discover them, which sometimes, is hard to do, either to find them or master them. Witness that noble *Claudius*, who did so affront ( πρᾶγμα παραδοξότατον, History stiles it, *A most incredible thing* ) *Severus*, the *Roman* Emperor, ( *both for valour and wisdom*, inferior unto none, *Dio* saith ) that even then when greatest care was taken, for his apprehension, durst nevertheless, offer himself to the Emperor, kiss his hands, talk with him, and then give him the slip, and after this, keep out of his hands and reach, in despight of all means, that the Emperor, or those he employed, could use, or devise. And another in the same *Severus* his reign, named Βύλας, or Φίλιξ, ( for he had two names ) of whom some particular acts are related, how he came to *Rome* himself, delivered some of his followers, when already condemned, ( as the manner was ) to be cast unto wild beasts: how he accosted the Captain, or Centurion, that was sent against him; took him by craft, judged him, shaved his beard, and sent him back with an errand, which I shall forbear. Generally it was said of him, that Ὁρώμενος, οὐχ ἑωρᾶτο· ἐπισκόμενος, οὐχ εὑρίσκετο· ἁλισκόμενος, οὐ κατελαμβάνετο· which, I think, I may English more plainly, and not lose much of the *emphasis*; *That, when he was seen, he could not be found; when he was found, he could not be taken; when he was taken, he could not be held*. But yet he was taken, at last, not by force or policy of men, but by the treachery of a Concubine; the less to be pitied, that being so wise and wary otherwise, he would trust himself to

such

such creatures. Some years before the happy ( which made us all happy ) reſtoration of our Gracious Sovereign, ( whom God preſerve ) in a Book-ſellers ſhop; I remember I lighted upon a book, in two Volumes, intituled, *L' Hiſtoire des Larrons*, &c. that is, *The Hiſtory of Thieves*, in *France*, from what time, I know not. I am ſorry I did not buy it : it may be, I was not ſo well furniſhed : which at that time, when forced to ſell a great part of my books, could be no diſcredit. I look upon it, as a very uſeful ſubject, the better to underſtand the world; and if the ſame were done of the Thieves of *England*, ſo it were done with judgment and fidelity, which from an ordinary hand can hardly be expected, I think it would be well worth the labour. Here it may be obſerved, that there always hath been a kind of men in the world, who naturally, as I may ſay, are fitted with a marvellous kind of audacity, to attempt ſtrange things ; and by a ſtrange conſtellation, or fatality, are attended with luck, and ſucceſs ; for a long time, at leaſt, in their boldeſt attempts, beyond all. imagination. The *Greeks* have many names for ſuch kinds of men, as παλαμναι̂οι. τηχίνης. ἀλάςωρες, and the like ; ſome of which have an intimation of ſomewhat above men ; and if we ſhould ſay, beyond what is ſupernatural, ordinarily known; there is a more natural kind of *poſſeſſion*, not ſo known ; it may be there were no great error in it. When I lived (ſome years before our Reſtoration ) with Sir *John Cotton*, grandchild to famous Sir *Robert*, ( where, beſides that ineſtimable Library, known far and near ; his noble and learned company, was a daily comfort) I remember well : I could tell the day and the year, but I forbear : that, as we were together by the fire, not long before dinner ; a well ſpoken Gentleman, and though not a profeſſed Scholar, yet well acquainted with good learning ; came to him, and made relation of what had paſſed at *Weſt-minſter-*

*minſter-hall*, that day, in the cauſe of a Lady, between her, and her husband; how, among the witneſſes, that were to depoſe for the Lady, exception was taken againſt one; in the proſecution of which buſineſs, ſuch things were there publickly, without any reply, declared againſt him, that he had done in *England*, in *France*, and elſewhere; as in all my reading I could ſcarce paralel, either for the quality of the things, or for the ſucceſs, and confidence of the perſon, that he, that had done ſuch things, durſt ſhew himſelf, in a publick Court.

BUT to return to *Herodotus* his relations; The firſt of them (in his ſecond book) doth conſiſt of many parts. The firſt and ſecond part, the contriving of a ſtone in the building, that might be taken away at their pleaſure, that knew the ſecret, whereby they might have an entrance into a Treaſury-houſe: and the craft, and courage of the Son, after his Fathers death, (the Author of the contrivance) when he was fallen into the trap, without any hopes of getting out; to adviſe his Brother, and fellow-Thief, to cut off his head, leſt he might be known by it; ſo far, is credible enough. The third part alſo not altogether *incredible*; by ſuch a device, divers Towns, ſome within our memory, have been taken. But for the fourth, of the proſtitution of the Kings daughter, and the manner, how ſhe was eluded; hath too much of improbability, and ſomewhat of impoſſibility, to be believed true, as *Herodotus* well judged; which is more than I can ſay of the fifth, and laſt; it being very poſſible, in thoſe times, and in that place, when, and where, ſo many brute beaſts were worſhipped for the benefit they afforded unto men; very poſſible, I ſay, that the King ſhould apprehend ſomewhat of a Deity in that man, that could effect ſuch ſtrange things: his very curioſity, to find the truth of what he ſo much admired,

## Of Credulity and Incredulity,

admired, might provoke him to do such a thing, more probably, than that the incomprehensibleness of the *Euripus*, should be the cause of *Aristotle* his death, or the unsolubleness of the Fisher-mens riddle, should of *Homers*.

ANOTHER relation he hath in the same book, of much affinity, concerning Thieves, who by long and tedious digging under ground, did rob another Kings Treasury, which we may wonder at, that any should be so confident, or so resolute, to attempt such a thing, in so much improbability (for it was a long way, that they were to dig) of success; but have no reason, otherwise, as set out and explained by *Herodotus*, to think it incredible. This digging under ground, puts me in mind of the *Gunpowder-plot*, such a Plot, as for the horror and immanity of it, I know not whether any History can paralel. But this hath been sufficiently set out by others, both Papists and Protestants. I have somewhat to say of it, which to me seems as horrible almost, as the Plot it self; what it may do unto others, I know not. I was once in the time of the rebellion, at the table of one, that was very great then, but must not now be named. There was at the table more than one or two, whether *Priests*, or *Ministers*, rightly ordained, I cannot tell: (for, even of them, some, though not many, did basely temporize) but by their habit, and some other circumstances, of that sort of people, that were *Preachers*, in those days. How it came to be talked of, I know not; but talked of it was, I am sure, and confidently affirmed, that there never was any such thing really, as the *Gunpowder Plot*, but that it was a Plot of King *James* his contriving, to endear himself unto the people. I do not remember that my patience was ever more put to it, though I never came into such company, (which was not often, nor without great necessity) but well armed with
patience.

patience. I did not think such Bedlam talk was to be answered with words. But wanting power, indignation made me reply so much; It was strange we should doubt of it, at home, when Papists, yea Jesuits abroad, had acknowledged it. Yet I deny not, but I have heard more than once, that King *James* knew of the Plot long before it was publickly discovered; which if true, doth take away nothing of the horror and wickedness of it; or of our obligation to God Almighty, for disappointing it, sooner or later. But even so much, is more than I can find ground for, from any printed relation, or more private information, ( to me considerable ) to believe. But such was the antipathy of those men, to Monarchical Government, and their succesful rebellion for many years, had so besotted them with a conceit of being the only favourets of Heaven, that by their good will, no man, no people, must be believed to have, or to have had any share, or portion of Gods mercies, or good providence, ( which did so eminently appear in that deliverance ) but such, as were, or had been of their own crew. How well such men are like to use that liberty, which they sue for, when they have it; I submit to their judgment, or judgments, to whom it doth more properly belong.

OUR last subject, before this short digression, was of *Thieves*, occasioned by *Herodotus* his relations; who hath had the name among Historians, generally, to be the relator of *incredible* things. The subject, it may be, as either too vulgar or too vile, some may think not so worth the consideration. Though I be of another opinion, my self; yet that consideration hath made me the shorter upon it. I shall now the more willingly pass to the consideration of somewhat, that may deserve, I am sure, the attention of the most serious, if they be not too much of the humour of the times, that is, profest Atheists;

Atheists; or, which is worse, such, as would seem to acknowledge a Deity, but as *Epicurus* did, that they may not want a subject to scoff, and to blaspheam. *Herodotus* in his second book, where he treats of matters belonging unto *Ægypt*, of one of the Kings of *Ægypt*, *Sethon* by name, he hath this relation: First, that the King was a Priest; so religious, and so confident in his God, or of his God, whom he served, that he made no reckoning at all of the Souldiers, and Captains, whom his predecessors had set up, and allowed them liberal maintenance; ὡς ἐδὲν δεηθμενος αυτων *as not at all fearing, that he should ever need them.* But, how contrary to his expectation, *Sinacherib*, King of *Arabia*, and *Assyria*, comes with a great Army to invade his Kingdom; and he, forsaken by the military men of his Country, had recourse unto his God; before whose Statue (prostrate, you may be sure) he did weep, and lament, and expostulate with his God, what things (without his help) he was like to suffer. That thereupon, his God appeared unto him in a dream; bid him not fear to encounter his enemy, he would provide him assistants. In confidence whereof, that *Sethon*, without any Souldiers, accompanied only with Tradesmen, and Artifans, and Court-men, or Lawyers; did go out to meet the enemy, and came in sight of them the first day, before it was night. Who certainly (though not expressed by *Herodotus*) could not but anticipate in his thoughts with joy, the success, and the fruits of an easie victory. But that very night, saith the Historian, an host of field-Mice, did knaw their Bows and Bucklers, (their strings, I suppose) and Quivers, (or Arrows in their Quivers) so that in the morning finding themselves destitute of arms; having lost many, the rest run away. So far *Herodotus*: I think no man that hath read, in the Scriptures, both in the book of *Kings*, and in the Prophet *Esay*, the History

## *in things* CIVIL. 265

story of *Ezekias*, that pious King, not of *Ægypt*, but of the *Jews*; who being invaded by the same *Senacherib*, intended by *Herodotus*; and *Hierusalem* the royal City, hardly besieged; being in great distress, and in no capacity to make resistance; did both by himself in person, and by the Prophet *Esay*, with many tears and lamentations, address himself to God, in his *house*, (*Herodotus* saith μγαει) and there spread the threatning letter, *before the Lord*: upon which God, in a dream, or vision, ( though not expressed ) having appeared to his Prophet, sent him a gracious answer, of many words, but to this effect, that he should not fear; *Senacherib* should do him no hurt: And that very *night*, not Mice, but the Angel of the Lord, smote in the Camp of the *Assyrians*, *an hundred fourscore and five thousand*: no man, I say, that hath read all this in the Scripture, but at first hearing, will take notice of the affinity, and somewhat wonder at it. But if he observe more particularly; first, *Senacherib*, King of *Assyria*; the same in *Herodotus*, and the Scripture, invading: A King and *Priest*, in *Herodotus*; *a King and Prophet*, in the Scripture: the King, in *Herodotus*, so confident in his God, that he thought he should need no Souldiers: *Ezekias*, in the Scripture, upbraided of his confidence, by the enemy: *Let not thy God, in whom thou trustest*, &c. and publickly declaring it himself, 2 *Chron*. 32. 7,8. Their lamentation, and their application, each to his proper God, almost the same. The true God in the Scripture, and the supposed God in *Herodotus*, their answers, in effect, the same. The event, for the time, *the night*, the same, and for the main, a miraculous victory, in effect the same. And I must add, that for the time, in point of Chronology, what the Scripture doth record of *Ezekiah*, King of *Judah*; and *Herodotus*, of *Sethon*, King of *Ægypt*, is supposed by

all

all Chronologers, and Hiftorians whom I have feen, to have hapned about one time : I would ask; Can any man, that hath any knowledge of the Heathenifh ancient ftory, and hath obferved how ufual it is with them, ( as in ftories that come by obfcure tradition, it muft needs ) to detort, and adulterate, and mifapply Scripture ftories; make any queftion, but that what *Herodotus*, by tradition from the *Ægyptians*, doth relate of *Sethon*, King of *Ægypt*, is nothing elfe, but what the Scripture doth record of *Ezekiah*, in that particular, of *Senacheribs* invafion, and the event of it? Yet I muft confefs, and at the fame time profefs my wonder, that neither *Jofephus* of old, who takes notice of *Herodotus* his relation, where he hath the Bibles, concerning *Ezekiah*: nor any of our late Chronologers, not *Jofephus Scaliger*, *Calvifius*, *Helvicus*, *Capellus*, *Torniellus*, &c. nor the late learned Archbifhop, in his Chronology; nor *Hugo Grotius*, upon the place, take notice of it, as derived from the Bible. Yet *Vignier*, by many accounted the very beft and moft accurate of late Chronologers, hath fome intimation to that purpofe, that it is poffible the *Ægyptians* might have the firft ground of their ftory out of the Scripture-ftory : and that is all, which to me feemeth not poffible only, but certain. But indeed Sir *Walter Rawleigh*, who I hope ftands not in need of mine or any mans teftimony, in *England*; hath gone much further, and feems abfolutely to determine it, as I do. And it is very remarkable, that this ftory of *Ezekiah's* miraculous deliverance, is no lefs than three times related at large, in the Scripture : ( the fecond of *Kings* 18. 13. *Ifaiah* 36. 2 *Chron*. 32. ) fo careful was the Author of it, that the memory of it might be propagated to pofterity. And why fhould we not make much of this confirmation of it, from the ancienteft of prophane Hiftorians? Efpecially when fome Chriftians have made

bold,

bold, as *Torniellus* doth tell us, if not to deny it, yet to speak of it very doubtfully? Now againſt *Herodotus*, if it ſhould be objected by any, that he is a fabulous writer; though ſomewhat hath already, and much more may be ſaid, to vindicate his credit; yet in this particular, their needs no anſwer at all. For it is confirmation enough, that in thoſe days, when the thing hapned, and for a long time after, the miracle was acknowledged, and the fame of it abroad, though miſtaken, and miſrelated in ſome particulars.

*HERODOTUS* doth add, that to his days, *Sethon* his Statue was to be ſeen in the Temple of *Vulcan*, holding a Mouſe in his hand. Which Mouſe might be an ancient Hieroglyphick, ſuch as are to be ſeen in that famous *Tabula Iſiaca*, or *Ægyptiaca*, which I once had in an entire piece; but is now, I hope, to be ſeen in the publick Library of the Univerſity of *Oxford*: exhibited in parcels by *Pignorius*, with explications. In that *Table*, ſtrange figures of men, and monſters, are exhibited, holding all ſomewhat in their hands; Birds, Flowers, Cups, and I know not what; all which, to unriddle certainly, (for wild conjectures and phanſies, may be had) would require a better *Oedipus*, than any later ages have afforded. And it is very probable, which by the late Reverend and learned Archbiſhop of *Armagh*, is hinted, that thoſe *Ægyptians*, who informed *Herodotus*, as ſome before had them; took the opportunity of that Hieroglyphick, the better to countenance their ſtory of that miraculous, if true, deliverance afforded to their King, by Mice; becauſe of a tradition current in many places, in thoſe days, that Mice had done ſome ſuch thing, ſome where: mentioned by *Ariſtotle*, in his *Rhetoricks*, and by divers others, ſince him. Whence alſo they write, that *Apollo* (the Deliverer) by ſending thoſe Mice, came to be called, Σμίνθος, becauſe σμίνθος, in some Country, did signifie a *Mouse*. Another reason also, besides this, why *Mice* were sacred in some Countries, is given by *Ælian*, in his twelfth book, *De animalibus*. Were there no other considerable story, (there be many more, and some, that have reference to the Scripture) in *Herodotus*, but this; yet this one would make me to prize the book not a little: which hath made me the more willing to take notice of it. And so, of a fable, an *incredible* thing; as, of a King of *Ægypt*, if not altogether *incredible*, yet not very probable; we have brought it to a *credible*, nay certain, and sacred story.

I SHALL now proceed to the consideration of those great works of men, which were to be seen in *Herodotus* his time, and are very particularly described by him: which subject, the great work of those ancient times, in general; I have observed to ordinary men, who know little more, than the things of this age; or have looked into former times, but perfunctorily, is a principal object of *incredulity*. I remember I had a speech of *Seneca* in my *First Part*, *Homine imperito*, &c. I might English it with little alteration: *That man is a silly man, that knows no more, than the things of his own days, or age*. However, they that are well acquainted with the state and stories, past or present, of *China* or *America*, will not, perchance, have much occasion to wonder much, at any thing in the *Roman* or *Persian* story, or any other, of former times: out of which nevertheless, I make no question, but we shall produce such things, which many, when they see the evidences, though they will not know how, or will be ashamed to oppose; yet will hardly be brought to believe. So much is the world changed, in these parts at least, best known to us, from what it hath been, in former times. I remember, when I was a young Student in *Oxford*, I know not by
whose

whose recommendation, it may be, my own Father's ; for he had a great opinion of it, and publickly professed it: but so it is, that I was very busie upon *Apuleius* his *Apology, for himself* : a serious *Apology* indeed : for it was for his life, being accused of Magick, before the Governor of the place, and answered for himself in person. Happy therein : for I think scarce any, then living, for eloquence, ( wherein he is much unlike himself in all his other writings ) wit, and all manner of learning, could have performed it as he did ; so that he got off, more for his excellent parts, than for his innocency, in that particular. But whilest I was upon that book, both with delight and admiration ; I met with one passage amongst the rest, which I did much stick at. About the end, where he doth endeavour to clear himself of that, which among other particulars was laid to his charge, that he had bewitched a rich woman, to get her love, and by her love and marriage, her means ; among other things that he doth answer for himself, one is, that though her wealth was great, ( for a private woman, of no power, or dignity) yet the dowry agreed upon, was but small ; very small : and secondly, that wealth was not the thing he looked after, in marrying her, he doth argue, because soon after, he perswaded her to make over a considerable part of her estate, to her sons : among other particulars, part of her *family*, that is, ( as the word is usually taken in the Civil Law) part of her slaves and servants. Now the number that she parted with, there expressed, is, *four hundred* : and I could not but think in reason, that she would keep one half at least, to her self. So that upon that account, this woman, rich indeed, and so accounted ; yet a private woman, & such a one, as *Apuleius* doth maintain, that had no reason, being somewhat in years, to despise him, a young man, neither for his person, nor estate, nor endowments of mind, despicable: this woman, I say, must be mistress of no less than seven, or eight hundred servants.

This,

## Of Credulity and Incredulity.

This, then, to me seemed ftrange and almoft *incredible*. But afterwards, when better acquainted with the ftate of the world, at that time, and for many ages before; I thought nothing of it. The truth is, fome thoufands of fervants and flaves, in the eftate of a wealthy *Roman*, was no very extraordinary thing. But then we muft add, the multitude of fervants, or flaves, was that, which made many rich, in thofe days; which they that do not underftand, wonder many times, where there is no caufe. But to hear of thoufands kept meerly for attendance, and that by private men too, *Roman* Citizens, and the like, this may feem more ftrange and *incredible*; and yet fo well attefted, both by writers of feveral ages, and by fo many evincing circumftances, that how rationally to doubt it, I know not. I fhall content my felf with *Athenæus* his teftimony, in his fixth book of his *Deipnofophifts*, where with his *collocutors*, having fpoken of the multitude of fervants, that were kept by the Ancients, and what ufe they made of them; he makes one of them to reply: *Good friend,* Maffurius, *you cannot but know very well, that the* Romans, *moft of them, were wont to keep very many fervants;* many, *to the number of ten thoufand, fome others of twenty thoufand, and more; and thefe, not as that rich* Nicias, *the* Grecian, *for their labour, and their own profit, but for the moft part, for their attendance, in the publick.* To this, pregnant paffages of *Seneca*, and *Ammianus Marcellinus*, and fome others might be added, which I fhall forbear, becaufe done by others. Befides, *Pignorius*, a learned *Italian*, hath written a book of this argument, *De fervis*, from whom it is likely the Reader may receive what fatisfaction he will defire. It might be well worth the enquiry, perchance, of men that are States-men and Politicians, how it comes to pafs, that in former times, a very fmall portion of land, for wealth, power, and all manner of
magni-

magnificence, yea and martial exploits; hath been more confiderable, than whole Kingdoms are now, or have been thefe many years. *Sicily*, for example, but a fmall Ifland, in comparifon of *England*. It may be a rich foil, to this day: I believe it is. But to keep it felf, and to afford thofe fupplies of Corn to other Countries, to *Rome* efpecially, (wherein thofe days, the greatnefs of the City, and puloufnefs confidered, more Corn was fpent in one day, than is now, in three or four Cities, the biggeft of *Europe*, take them together: I might have faid, five or fix, I believe, and not exceed) to be reputed the *Granary* of fuch a City; (one of *Sicilie*'s titles, in thofe days) I believe is far above the prefent eftate, or ability of it. *Dionyfius* the Father, fpoken of before, who was King of but one part of it, kept a ftanding Army of 100000. foot, and 10000. horfe, befides a very confiderable Navy. *Hieron* King of *Syracufe*, the fecond of that name, who lived when *Anniball* invaded *Italy*, maintained a grandeur beyond all imagination. All Towns of *Greece*, did ring of his bounty and munificence. He did affift the *Romans*, and fupply, if not uphold them, in all their wants, plentifully: affifted others, even the *Carthaginians*, in their great need, though rather enemies otherwife, than confederates. There were in that little Ifland, in *Pliny*'s time, above feventy confiderable Towns and Cities: But whether more or fewer, for the number, there were two, I am fure, *Syracufe*, which confifted of four Cities, built at feveral times; fet out by *Tully* and fome others, eye witneffes, as the mirror of Cities, (of *Greece* efpecially, fo well ftored at that time) for all manner of fumptuoufnefs and magnificence: and *Agrigentum*, when in its flower, *not inferior to it*; which is recorded to have had eight hundred thoufand inhabitants, at one time; either of thofe, I believe, far above the prefent eftate of *Sicily*.

*Sicily*. We might obferve the fame of divers other places. But I fhall not take upon me now, to enquire into the reafons. But certain it is, that they that judge of all things, reported of former times, by what they know, or have heard, fince the world, though always the fame, in effect, yet, in many things, that refer to men, and their actions and fafhions, and the Civil government of Countries and Cities; hath put on a new face, much different from what it had in moft places; they that do, certainly, muft needs ftick at many things, as fabulous, and *incredible*; which others think they have reafon to believe, as certainly, as what they read in beft Hiftorians of this, or the former age; and which are generally believed, and pafs every where, without any contradiction. Not that I think we are bound, in reafon, to believe whatfoever is written of ancient times, though by fome approved Authors and Hiftorians. There is no queftion, but they were men, as we are: favour, and hatred, and proper intereft, might fway them too: fubject to the fame vanity, to magnifie their relations; their habitation, and Country: what the *Gracians* call properly, παραδοξολογία, and δοξοκοπία, ( a worfe vanity ) fo often obferved by *Tacitus*; that is, a defire, or pleafure to tell ftrange things, might poffefs them; and whatever elfe men are now fubject unto, they might alfo. But when men of good judgment and capacity, write of things, which, if not eye-witneffes of, yet might very well be known unto them: where, not one alone, but two or three, of feveral Countries, of whom there is no ground of reafon to believe, that they blindly followed one another; not engaged, fo far as can be found, or difcerned, by favour or otherwife, purpofely to difguife the truth; write and atteft the fame thing: when thofe things that are written, exami-ned by other circumftances, and particularities, of that

age,

age, or Country, whereof they write, are found to agree well, and to become probable enough; though, of themselves, or of another Age, or Country, not so probable, or perchance *incredible*: add unto all this, though, all not to be expected always, yet found sometimes; if the Authors lived in an age, which afforded many sober and intelligent men; when good learning, and noblest arts, did flourish, which of many *Greek* and *Roman* Historians we know to be true: in such a case, where all or most of these do concur; I shall assoon believe those things, that are written by such, though one, or more thousand of years have passed since, as those things that are written by the most approved Author or Historian of this, or the former age.

WHO would or could believe, that is not very well acquainted with the state of the world, in general; and of the *Romans* particularly, that a Citizen of *Rome*, in some office perchance, and in order to a greater; but a Citizen of *Rome*, in publick sports and fights, to last some days perchance, or some weeks, at most; should spend as much, as some great King of our time, his revenues may come to, in a whole year? And proportionably, either the same man, or some other, in buildings, in apparel, in feastings, or the like: which things singly related, no wonder, if they be not believed, they do so far exceed modern examples and abilities. Yet somewhat in that kind was seen in the days of *Henry* the Eighth, ( whose story is full of glory and magnificence, till he had taken the greatest part of the Churches goods into his hands ) when five hundred Carpenters, as I remember, for I have not the History by me, & as many Painters, & I know not how many other workmen, are recorded to have been employed, to build a Tent or Tabernacle, where he was to entertain the King of *France*, not many days, if more than one. The King of *France* his *Pavilion*, all Velvet, might be as coftly perchance, as to the fubftance; but that the materials might better be preferved for other ufes afterwards; whereas the vaft coft upon gilding and painting upon bare boards, could be of no further ufe, as I conceive. I defire the Reader not altogether to truft my relation, in this; for I truft my memory, which in fo many years, fince I read that Hiftory, may deceive me. But what fhall we fay, to the temporary Theatre of. *Mar. Scaurus* the *Roman*, who was but *Aedilis*, none of the greateft offices in *Rome*, but indeed greatly allyed; of which *Pliny*, who was well acquainted with the world; his judgment is, that it was the coftlieft, and moft magnificent piece of work, that the world ( upon record ) ever faw? His defcription is but fhort, let the Reader judge. Neither is it poffible he could miftake, I would not fay in the *valuation*; but, in the defcription of a thing, fo frefh, fo notoriously known, whereof the relicks, though they ufe to continue but for a while, did long remain. But yet I muft confefs, the next man *Curio*, who though upon another occafion, had an ambition to do fome great work, for which he might be admired, though not in matter of coft, ( for he was not of that ability ) yet in his main end, to caufe admiration, did in my opinion go beyond him. He made two great Scaffolds or Theaters, with convenient feats, which hung in the Air, as it were, having no foundation in the ground, but two fingle pins, or hinges, upon which, when they had taken their lading, ( which I cannot conceive could be lefs, than fome hundred thoufands of people: *Univerfus Pop. Romanus*; *Pliny* faith; which muft be underftood very favourably, if but of one, or two hundred thoufand men ) as either they clofed, or continued apart, they were to turn into feveral forms, or fhapes, either as two diftinct *Theaters*, or, one perfect *Amphitheater*.

As

As two distinct Theaters, in the *forenoon* : *inter sese averfa* : back to back : so, that what was done in one Theater, could be heard or seen by them of the other : different Stage-plays being exhibited in each of them. But in the *afternoon*, ( so I understand *Pliny's*, *postremo*, and, *novissimo jam die* : except we should understand it of many days ; and that he speaks this, of the last day, which is not so probable ) turning about, ( *circumacta, cornibus inter se coeuntibus* ) and closing, they made a perfect *Amphitheater*, wherein, or upon which, fencing-games ( *gladiatores* ) were exhibited; in common, now, to those, who before had been distinct, or divided spectators, of different Plays and Actors. This whole wooden frame, or structure, though it touched no ground, which was the wonder of it ; yet could not, I believe, inclose, or cover, less than a hundred, or sixscore Acres of ground. A man would think, this could not be done, without some cost : and *Pliny* faith directly, that *Curio* was no very rich man ; ( *non opibus insignis* : his wealth consisted most, in plundered and confiscated goods ) that is, for a *Roman* Citizen of those times : but however, not without cost, I believe ; but in comparison of *Scaurus* his charge, before ; or that of *Agrippas* ( but not all, in such trifles, and gambols ) after mentioned ; not great, we may say with *Pliny*; who could, and doth give an exact account. And how many thousand Carpenters, do we think, were employed about this work? But was not he a brave *Ingeneer*, that undertook such a piece of work, and acquitted himself so well, that no man in all this winding and turning, by the miscarrying of any board, plank, or pin, had any hurt ? *Pliny*, who is very elegant and witty, upon this subject, doth profess, he did not know whom to admire more, the *confidence* of the projectors, or undertakers, ( *Curio* and his prime Carpenter, or Architect ) or the *madness*

*Of Credulity and Incredulity,*

of the people, who durſt truſt their lives to ſuch a *looſe, groundleſs,* and *verſatile* a device. But, *a rare ſight,* (ſaith he ) *to ſee that people, who were the Governors of the whole Earth ; whom ſo many Nations and Kingdoms ſerved, and obeyed, to hang upon two pins, and to turn about* ( like a Weather-cock ; but *Pliny* doth not ſay ſo ; I know not whether there were any, in his time ) *upon a pageant. Pliny* in the ſame place hath divers other things to the ſame purpoſe, which it may be ſome may more wonder at, than what I have mentioned : beſides what the ſame Author hath elſewhere of the ſame argument. But they that deſire more full ſatisfaction in this point of *exceſs,* in general, to ſave themſelves the labour, of ſearching into ancient Authors ; they may, if they pleaſe, read *Lipſius, De magnitudine Romana* : or *Meurſius, De Luxu Romano* : not to name others.

I COME now to *Herodotus* again, to me, as conſiderable an Author, as any I know of all the Ancients. The firſt great work I ſhall take notice of, is the *Tower* that ſtood, as he deſcribes it, in the midſt of *Belus* his Temple, the cirumference of which Tower, being ſquare, was juſt eight *ſtadia,* that is, a mile. The height cannot be perfectly known by *Herodotus* his deſcription, but only this, that it conſiſted of eight ſeveral ſtages. St. *Jerome* certainly, was much abuſed by them, pretended eye-witneſſes, who reported it, four miles in height. This *Tower* ſtood entire, in *Herodotus* his time, and he ſpeaks of it with as much confidence, as if he had ſeen it, or rather indeed, as if he had travelled ſo far, of purpoſe to ſee it. Beſt Hiſtorians follow the deſcription both of the City *Babylon,* and of the Temple and Tower, which is made by *Herodotus.* But, which is more, very learned men do take this *Tower* deſcribed by *Herodotus,* to be the *Tower of Babel,* mentioned in the Scripture. So *Pererius,* I am ſure, that learned and judicious

ous Jesuit, and so very lately, *Samuel Bochartus*, sufficiently known ( though, to me once known very familiarly ) without my recommendation. He is very large upon it, and doth very accurately consider the words of *Scripture*, that might be objected. But I for my part, though I favour *Herodotus*, and honour the worth of them I have named; yet I must profess, I see not ground enough to move me, to be of their opinion. Why was *their language confounded*, but to *confound* that they were about, the building of a *Tower* and *City*? And the Scripture saith plainly, *they left off to build the City*: and is it likely, they were suffered to finish the *Tower*, the more daring and defying work of the two: and not more likely, that in the *City*, the *Tower* also, which it is not likely they would begin with, as less useful or necessary, must be understood? Some may, with *Pererius*, suppose, that what was extant of it in *Herodotus* his days, was but part of what was intended, by the first builders. But then a man would think, had they laid a foundation for such a height, and the work left imperfect; *Herodotus*, or some after him, had taken some notice of it: whereas the account we have of the height, then extant, and to be seen, is rather *incredible*, than gives any ground of suspition, of any *imperfection*. I should rather think, that the foundation being laid, when the work began to rise, and to make some shew, it was interrupted, and in after ages ( not many ages after I believe ) brought to that perfection, in which it was to be seen in *Herodotus* his days. Yet again, I must confess, that if the platform of the top of this Tower was so large, as to contain a large Temple, or Chappel ( ναὸς μέγας are *Herodotus* his words, which may signifie either ) it may be not unlikely, that some further or higher structure was intended, ( if not this very Temple, or Chappel ) from the beginning, if the builders had not been interrupted. So that in the conclusion, I think there may be as much said for it, as against it, that this *Tower* of *Herodotus*, was the very *Tower* of the Scripture. Should any man object, the long continuance of it, fourteen hundred years, as *Pererius* doth call it, from the first erection; a long time, for so high a structure; it will be answered, that the *Pyramids* of *Ægypt* ( as great, or greater a miracle, in my judgment, all things considered, than this *Tower* was ) have already stood twice as long, and are yet in case, according to the best account we have of them, to stand some thousand years, if the world last so long.

AND by the way, let us take notice that the account *Herodotus*, full two thousand years ago, hath given of these *Pyramids*, is yet most followed by them, in our days, that have had the curiosity to view them; and the skill withal, as able Mathematicians, and Geographers, to examine every circumstance of his description, with accurateness. We may therefore the better believe him, in the account he gives of other great works, extant in his days, which himself, not trusting the relation of others, had the curiosity to view, that he might satisfie himself, and posterity the better. As first, his account of that miraculous *Labyrinth*, which, he saith himself, though he judged the *Pyramids*, when he first saw them, far to exceed whatever was most admired in *Greece*, as the Temples of *Ephesus*, of *Samus*, or the like: yet the *Labyrinth*, he thought, went beyond even the *Pyramids*. That *Labyrinth*, where he saw twelve great Halls, with a multitude of Pillars, and stone roofs. A thousand five hundred rooms above ground, he saw; and as many, he was told, and believed, under ground, answerable to the others: but those he was not admitted to see, as *repositories* for the body of the Kings, the founders of the *Labyrinth*; and some sacred, or consecrated

Croco-

Crocodiles. Out of the *rooms*, ( *οἰκημάτων* ) he passed into ( *παστάδες* ) *chambers*, out of chambers into ( *σήκους* ) *closets*, and so into other *Halls* : so that he was ravished, he professeth, with the sight, above measure. The walls that inclosed the *Labyrinth*, were engraven with many figures; and at the end of the *Labyrinth* a *Pyramis*, adorned with variety of Animals. Truly, I make no question, but there was enough, really, to be seen, to ravish him, or any man, that had seen it. Yet we must remember, that he was in a *Labyrinth*, and might easily lose himself in his reckoning : besides, that his very admiration and astonishment, might make him less able to observe so diligently, as otherwise he might have done. And that his leaders and informers, the *Ægyptian* Priests, who knew the certainty, might of purpose, to make their miracle more miraculous, ( as they did in their years, and some other things ) add somewhat, is very possible. This may be thought, and not improbable: yet we may not conclude from bare probability, that so it is certainly. Now to say, that after this *Labyrinth*, he saw the *Lake*, called *the Lake of Mœris*, which he yet admired more, than all he had seen before, as himself doth profess, to some may sound like a fable : it doth not so to me : who am very confident, that the description he makes of it, is very exact, according to the truth of what he saw, with his own eyes. The same, I may say, of all those other strange things, which either of *Babylon*, or any other place, are recorded by *Herodotus*, as certain and true ; all, or most, attested by some others, and by later Chronologers, not questioned ; though to many, who by what they now see, or is to be seen, judge only, I doubt *incredible*.

BUT I may forget my self, and whilest I tell of strange things, that were once, pass by the miracles of our time, that are *now, to be seen*. Such is *Cœnobium*

T 4 *B. Lau-*

*B. Laurencii*, or, St. *Laurence his Hospital*, in *Spain*, according to *Bertius*, a learned Geographer, his description, and testimony. Truly, I should think so of it, by his description. And for his testimony, the words are very significant, and express; *Opus istud præstantissimis nobilissimisq;operibus, quæ vel extant usquam, vel unquam fuerunt, adnumeratur, ab iis, qui cum judicio spectare nova, iisque vetera conferre queunt.* This is more than I have heard of it, by any Travellor; yet not more, than may very well be true. For it is a true observation of *Pliny*, both of great wits, & of great works: *Alia, esse clariora; alia, majora.* If there be any other such great work of our times, which I do not mention, it is not, because I dote upon antiquity, but because I know it not; not my partiality, but my ignorance. Neither am I of that opinion, that all great, or costly works, deserve truly to be admired, but such only, as are as profitable, (publickly) as they are great: or such at least, as for their beauty and magnificence, are so ravishing, that they teach us withal, less to admire ordinary petty sights, and objects, which vulgar souls are so taken with. If *Aristotle* may be heard, (I hope he will, when men return to sobriety) that is truest *magnificence*, and deserving highest commendation, which is bestowed upon the Gods, as in the erection of magnificent Temples, and the like: not because they need it; but the better to set out their majesty, unto men: and next unto this, that magnificence, which is beneficial unto the people. So he Not to mention the Temple, consisting of one stone, the roof excepted, which *Herodotus* doth tell us of, not without some admiration of it: he tells us of a large and miraculous edifice, hewn out of a rock, consisting of one simple stone; which to transfer from *Elephanti- na*, the native place of it; to *Sai*, where *Amasis*, King of *Ægypt*, did appoint it to be placed, for a rare sight; two thousand expert mariners were employed, for the space of three years. *Herodotus*, I confess doth tell us of it, it, as much admiring: which I profefs, of all great works I have read of, I leaft admire; except it were at his prodigious vanity and prodigality, who would beftow fo much money, upon fo idle a work. As if a man abounding with wealth, would be at the charge of removing ( if it can be done ) fome great rock, fuch a rock as *Hooky*-rock in *Sommerfetſhire* is, confifting of many concamerations; wherein, when I was there, I obferved fome things, which I thought, and ftill think, might deferve confideration, as well as many things, which make much more noife: fuch a rock, I fay, to remove it, from whence it ftands, to fome place, many miles diftant. But I faid, if it can be done. *Archimedes*, I believe, or he that undertook to cut the great mountain *Athos*, into the form of a man, which fhould have born in one hand a City of 10000. inhabitants; and in the other, a river, emptying it felf into the Sea, if *Alexander* would have fet him on work; would have undertaken it, and for ought I know, brought it to pafs, if any man would, or could be at the coft. But to what end I pray? Only to fhew unto the world, that he can caft away fo much money upon nothing, and yet continue *rich*: which I fhall fooner believe, than either *wife*, or truly *magnificent*.

IT is time that I fhould have done with *Herodotus*. Yet to end in fomewhat that may be more pleafing, or more confiderable, at leaft, than this laft of *the great ſtone*; he hath one ſtory, that I neither know how to deny, being a ſtory of his own time, or little before, and which I do not find contradicted by any other; nor yet very well how to believe. It is concerning *Pythias*, the *Lydian*; neither King nor Prince, nor any thing elfe of either power, or authority, that I can find; but only a very rich

private

private man. What authority he had, was over his slaves and servants, which indeed must be very many? Is it credible, as is reported of him by *Herodotus*, that he could be so rich, as to entertain *Xerxes*, as he passed by, to invade *Greece*, and all his Army? In saying, *all his Army*, therein consists the *incredibility* of the thing; the number of which Army, according to the most contracted account that we have of it, is almost *incredible*. Though *Herodotus* say, σεπνὶν πᾶσαν, and *Xerxes* seem to acknowledge as much; yet I would not be so precise, as to press the words rigorously. We will first abate his Sea-forces, many hundred thousands: and of the Land-forces, that marched with him, we may abate many thousands, and still leave him divers hundred thousands: four or five, at the least. These, so many, *Pythias* did entertain, at his own charge, how many days I know not, because it is not expressed: but I believe, more than one. Besides this, he did offer, the story tells us, to *Xerxes*, in ready money, as a voluntary contribution towards the charges of his Army, in gold and silver ready told: so much, as comes by learned *Brerewcod* his casting, (which I shall not take upon me to examine at this time) to 3375000. *English* pounds, and this according to the less valuation of talents, as himself doth tell us. But he mistakes, when he saith, *Pythii Bithinii opes*. So much he did offer unto *Xerxes*: his wealth, as himself professed, did consist in his lands, which in that summe are not at all valued. It may be, he did offer this to *Xerxes*, as *Seneca* did his estate (not less I dare say, if not much greater) to *Nero*, to save his life, which he feared was in danger, by it. And truly, as it fared with the one, so with the other. Every body knows, out of *Tacitus*, how nobly *Nero* refused *Seneca*'s offer; and how much more, as he professed, he thought him worthy of. But at last, and it is a question,

whether

whether *Seneca* had not given some occasion, whilest he did desire to prevent it, he was commanded to die; but indulged the choice of his death. *Xerxes* answered *Pythias* as nobly, and because there wanted some thousands, to make the sum that *Pythias* had offered him, a round perfect summe, according to the calculation of those days; *Xerxes* made up, what it wanted, and bad him keep it all. But then afterwards, when *Pythias* was an humble sutor to him, that of five sons of his, that followed him, he would be pleased to discharge the eldest, to look unto his Fathers affairs; *Xerxes*, as a right tyrant, fell into a rage, and had that Son cut in two, that the Army on both sides, as they passed by, might have a sight of his body, (or one half, at least) to be a terror unto others. Yet, to speak truth, I do not find, that he took away any of his money, or goods; but for the good that he had done, spared, as he professed, his life, and his four sons, that remained, besides his estate.

I HAVE been the more willing to make use of *Herodotus* for instances, because of the respect I bear unto him for his antiquity, and because the times and Histories he doth write of, have more relation, and afford more light to the Scriptures, than any other Author, or History doth. But *Herodotus* was not my business, but this, that different times and ages of the world make many things to seem *incredible*, and not only to seem, but in very deed, *impossible*: which have been formerly very *possible*; and of such a time, such an age, if well understood, at any time *credible*: And whereas great works, great fights, have hitherto been the subject of our instances, and examples, which many other subjects might have afforded; it hath not been, without some choice, or particular end. It is far from me, to believe, that the world is grown vain, since I am grown old: which is noted by many, as a vice or reproach of old age.

Had

Had I never read any thing of the old world, but what we read in the third Chapter of the Prophet *Isaiah*; though it cannot be denied, that some ages have exceeded others, in this kind; yet I find enough there, to make me think, that to wonder at any thing, in point of wordly excess or vanity, as new and never seen before, is great folly. But this is no argument to me, not to commiserate the blindness and wretchedness of mankind, so apt to degenerate from the glory of their first creation, & the end of their making;because it hath been so always, ever since sin, by the disobedience of our first Parents, entred into the world, and made it *subject unto vanity*. Though therefore it hath been so, and will be so, generally,as long as the world doth last; yet since in the worst times, and most corrupted places, some there have been, and will always be, more or fewer,that have been, though not altogether free themselves, yet sensible, and earnestly, both for themselves, and others, striving against it: Why may not I hope, that even now, in the croud of Ladies and Gentlemen, going the broad way, as fast as they can; who have fixed their admiration hitherto, and their ambition, in their *modes* ( the invention, commonly, of some leud Taylor, or phantastick Courtier ) and *fashions*; the pomp and gaudiness of the world; that even among them, who for want of better education, in these unhappy times, are as proud of their *Patches* and *Pedlers-ware*, as some would be of Crowns and Diadems; or some noble atchievements for the publick good: when they see, or learn by such instances, how vile and vulgar, those things are, which they so much admire, and doat upon, which often fall to the share of the unworthiest of men : some may begin to think, there is, certainly, somewhat else, wherein true honour, and glory, and felicity doth consist; and that God and Nature have not made them capable of highest contemplations, to think Gold and

and Silver, Silks and Sattins, and what depends of them, the beſt of things? To this end, though ſomewhat without the trouble of long ſeeking, where there is ſo much variety, hath been brought: yet let me add, that of all I have read in any Greek or Latin Author, I do not remember any thing more effectual, to make a man that hath any thing of a man in him (a rational, I mean, and ingenuous creature,) more ſenſible of the vanity of all wordly pomp and glory, (ſuch eſpecially, as this age doth afford) than what *Polybius*, of all Hiſtorians, the moſt faithful and ſerious, in thoſe *Fragments* of his, firſt ſet out by *Fulvius Urſinus*, doth relate of *Antiochus* his pomp and magnificence, in publick fights and entertainments, at *Daphne*; a fit place for ſuch exceſs and riot. The occaſion of which, was, a frolick or vanity, to out-brave *Æmil. Paulus*, General of the *Romans*, who had exhibited ſome games in *Macedonia*, not long before conquered by them. Had *Antiochus* done it of purpoſe, by his example, to teach men contempt of worldly pomp; for whileſt his ſervants ſervants, by thouſands in a company, road in Chariots, and upon Horſes, all deckt with Gold, and Silver, and Purple, and whatſoever is moſt precious, in the account of men; himſelf rode by, meanly attired, upon an ordinary Jade, and did, at the ſame time, perform many vile offices; but, had it been, I ſay, to ſhew his contempt of worldly pomp, he might have been thought an admirable man. But the truth is, that what he did, he did it as a *mad-man*; which, with ſome other ſuch pranks, got him the name of *Antiochus* the *mad*; and in his affected perſonal vulgarneſs, had no other end, but that he might be the more admired, and lookt upon. But miſſed of his end, when the ſpectators of all this bravery, for above a month (for ſo long it laſted) notwithſtanding that their bellies, with no leſs coſt, than their eyes, had been fed;

fed; glutted and furfeited, both in their eyes and bellies; (such are the pleasures this world affordeth) began, at last, to despise, first his person, then his pomp, and forsook him. I wish my self so good an *English*man, (for there's no great difficulty in the Greek) that I were able to translate the whole narration in good and proper *English*, which without more knowledge of the world in matter of pomp, and gaudiness, than I have, can hardly be: I cannot but think, that it would do good. But, lest this might be looked upon, not so much as an argument of excessive, or *incredible* wealth, which I must not forget my primary intention; as of extraordinary *madness*, which, as before said, got him that sirname of *Antiochus* the *mad*: I would have the pomp of *Ptolemæus*, sirnamed *Philadelphus*, who was a Prince of credit, joyned with it: both to be found in one book, *Athenæus* his fifth of his *Deipnosophists*: part out of *Polybius*, and part out of *Callixenes*, an Historian of those days.

O F excess in fare and feasting, not used by Kings and Emperors, which (except we should put down the summs of the expences, as cast up by others to our hands) might seem less *incredible*; but of ordinary *Romans*, I have had no instances, because there is so much of it, in all kind of writers, that though they that are altogether illiterate, may wonder and not believe; yet they that have looked into them, but superficially, will easily believe any thing, that can be but thought possible. For certainly there is no kind of excess, in that particular, that the whole earth (then known) could afford, but hath been tried, and was, in those days, ordinary.

BUT I must do *Herodotus* some right: out of whom *Athenæus* doth relate, that one *Smindycides*, a *Sybaritan*, (noted every where, unto a Proverb, for their luxury)

luxury) did carry along with him, where he hoped to speed for a wife for his Son; Cooks for all sorts of meat, a thousand; which, by *Ælian*, is increased to three thousand; whereof a thousand *Cooks*, a thousand *Faulconers*, and a thousand *Fishermen*. Whereas in *Herodotus*, no such thing is to be found, either of *Cocks*, or any other company; but this only, that among others, who appeared suitors to *Clisthenes*, for his daughter *Agarista*; (who though no great Prince, entertained them all, in a most Princely manner) this *Smindycides* was one. Now if *Herodotus* wrote no more, I think they do him wrong, who impose that upon him, which hath too much of improbability, even of those times, to be believed. Or if he wrote so indeed, (not probable to me) yet even so, some right we do him, to perfect his Text: though I am somewhat confident, that if he did write any such thing, it was not without his ordinary *proviso*, in things so improbable; *that such a thing was reported, but by himself not believed.*

WE have spoken of many things, which to some, (I have found it so more than once) might seem *incredible*. I thought I had made an end. But I remember my self, that we live in an Island, as other Islands are, compassed with the Sea: the chief glory and security whereof, are, those wooden walls, commended unto the *Athenians*, by the Oracle, when *Xerxes* invaded the land; good Ships, and expert Mariners. And God be thanked, I think there is no Nation of the world, but will yield to the *English* the precellency of that glory, in point either of Ships, or Men: God continue it. But though, for use or service, which is the principal end of Ships; we may challenge precellency of any that are, or have been in former ages; yet in point of *credibility*, which is our business, they are greatly deceived, who think there never were greater or fairer Ships, than those that have been

been seen in these later times, since Navigation hath been so much improved by the discovery of that secret of the Loadstone, not known to former ages, of always turning to the North. If they limited it, for service of war, or long journeys, I should not be against it. But for greatness, or sumptuousness, what comparison? Let the description of two Ships, built by *Philopator*, King of *Ægypt*; made by able Authors, who were eye-witnesses, (and besides them, how many thousands) or the description of a later Ship, built by *Hieron*, King of *Syracuse*, before spoken of; concerning which, one *Moschion*, wrote a particular Volume; the truth of which descriptions made by skilful men, eye-witnesses; when so many thousands, who had seen them, were able and ready to attest, or to contradict, as they should see occasion; no man can rationally doubt of: let them be read, and I think I may be allowed, by those that have read them with any judgment, to say, that the least of those Ships, might be bigger than any ten (it might be true of twenty, for ought I know) of those *Spanish* Ships, which in Eighty Eight, appeared like so many Castles; put together; and exceed the cost of them too. I say the least of them: which, as I take it, was King *Hieron*'s Ship: which had this above the two others, that it was made for use of war also. And let me add, that I make a question, whether any Ships now, or lately, made, carry any piece of Ordnance so great, as to do that annoyance, that some Engines of that Ship, made by *Archimedes*, that noble Ingeneer, as they are there described, could do. If I have exceeded in my valuations, or proportions, I desire to be pardoned. I had no intention, I am sure: those that are better versed in such things, may soon find it, and correct my error, for which I shall thank them. And it is to be noted, that this Ship of King *Hieron*, was built only for a present,

to

to one of the Kings of *Ægypt*, whereby we may guess at the wealth, and magnificence of that petty King, if the extent of land, over which he reigned, be considered. But many such Kings there were in those days, even of single Towns, or Cities, very rich, and some, very potent. And whereas one of the Ships made by *Philopator*, is reported, or recorded rather, to have contained forty several ranks, or rows of rowers, on a side, the one above the other; which since that, Ships of 8. or 10. or 12. rowers, some have thought could hardly be made, to be serviceable, will be thought by many, not possible, and therefore *incredible*; all that I can say to it, which I am sure I can, is, that had my Father ( of Bl.M.) his *Commentaries* upon *Polybius*, upon which he bestowed a great part of his life, been finished and Printed, he would have made it clear, how it might be, and answered all objections: And it is sure enough, that the invention of many things practised by the Ancients, through ignorance of former times, now thought impossible, is lost. Though I deny not however, that I also believe, that such a vast Ship could not be much serviceable. And the rather, because *Livy* doth mention one that had been *Philip*'s, King of *Macedonia*, which was of sixteen ranks, ( *Quam sexdecim versus remorum agebant* ) so big, he saith, that it was almost unuseful. The story saith, that vast Ship before spoken of, had to the number of 400. rowers, and souldiers, to the number of 2850. All which is attested by *Plutarch* also, in his *Demetrius*. All these, in the out, or open places of the Ship. How many more, in that numerous ample buildings and edifices of the said Ship, which though neither by *Athenæus*, nor by *Plutarch* specified, or particularized; yet by that description of the two other lesser Ships, we have in *Athenæus*, we may probably guefs at : how many more thofe large buildings might contain, I fay, God knows. I believe, as many more, as all the reft put together: which will exceed the number of fome confiderable towns. But *Plutarch* doth add, that this Ship was built more for fhew, than any fervice; and that it never moved from the place, where it was built, without much danger, and difficulty. The biggeft or longeft Maft of one of thefe Ships, which was looked upon as a great providence, by the difcovery of a Shepheard, was found, ἐν τοῖς ὕμνην τῆς Βριταννίας that is, *In fome mountains of Britany*, now *England*: if that reading could be warranted. But it cannot : ἐν τοῖς ὄρεσι τῆς Βρετλίας, much more probable, if not certain. For which, good reafons are given by learned men. Not therefore for much fervice, I fay, fuch vaft Ships : yet in the account *Athenaus* doth give us, of *Philadelphus* his ftore, or provifion of Ships, he doth mention Ships of 30. 20. and 14. rows, which certainly were intended for ufe. But I have done with this : And yet now we are upon Ships, fomewhat of our times, or not long before, for the *incredibility*, befides ufefulnefs, if true and real, may deferve to be taken notice of. That a Boat, not to be funk by any tempeft, in all weathers, very nimble and ferviceable, may be made, if we may believe ~~Fiorananty~~, notwithftanding his ufual cracking and vapouring, we may believe it true. But of the two, I fhould give more credit to *Trithemius*, that learned Abbot, who doth name the man, by whom a book or difcourfe was publifhed in *Print*, wherein for a hundred thoufand Ducats, he did offer, firft the Pope, *Innocentius* the *VIII.* then the *Venetians*, and laftly the *Genuenfes*, ( fo I remember was the difcovery of the New World, for the price or charge of a very fmall Navy, offered to divers Princes, who did but laugh at it, but repented it afterwards ) to teach them the invention of a

Ship,

*in things* CIVIL. 291

Ship, unoffenfable ( if I may fo fpeak ) to all dangers of the Sea ; and by which ( or by fome other invention ) Ships ready to fink, might be preferved, and any goods out of the bottom of the Sea, eafily recovered. The lofs of this Invention, or inventions, when to be had and purchafed at fo eafie a rate, *Trithemius* doth feem very ferioufly to condole, as though he really believed it: if in it, he had not a refpect to himfelf more, who promifed fuch mighty things, which fhould have made the world happy, but never came to any thing, but to bufie diftempered brains, or to diftemper theirs, which were found before.

BUT fince *England* as an Ifland, gave me this occafion of Ships, which though true, may feem ftrange and *incredible* : I will take this occafion, to tell fomewhat that I have read of *England*, which may juftly feem as ftrange, as I am fure, it is falfe, and ridiculous ; but that the occafion of the miftake ( difference of cuftoms ) may be confiderable, to prevent the like of another Country. In *Ortelius*, or *Mercator*, I know not which, but one of the two, I am very confident, fome Greek Author, or Hiftorian, fpeaking of *England*, gives a reafonable good account of it, as I remember ; for it is many years fince I read it ; but a reafonable good account I fay, otherwife ; but this, moft falfly ; that they make their wives common to their guefts. It is fo falfe, that to go about to refute it, were ridiculous, if not fcandalous. Yet they that know the fafhions of other Countries, in the Eaft efpecially ; where to look upon a woman, that paffeth by, veiled ; or to look up, if any be at a window, or in a *Balcone*, is the caufe of death unto many : where a man may be acquainted, and in dealings, with another man ; often go to his houfe, eat and drink with him, and yet not know, not fo much as dare, to enquire, whether he have a wife or no: he may acquit the Author of that falfe report, from any intention of either lying or flandering; if he were a ftranger and bred in one of thofe Countries; only, blame his fimplicity, or want of judgment, that he would judge of other Countries, which he did not know, by thofe that he knew, and was acquainted with : who might himfelf have known, if a Scholar, or a piece of a Scholar, that fomewhat much more ftrange, than fuch ordinary falutation, ufed in *England,* and fome other Countries, had been once in ufe, even among Chriftians, when I believe chaftity, and continency was not lefs in requeft, than it is now in any place; but indeed fo unhandfom, and uncivil otherwife; in my judgment, ( worthily condemned both by the laws of fundry Heathen Princes, and by the Canons of the Church ) that I will not fo much as name it.

BUT if this man have done *England* wrong againft his will, upon a falfe fuppofition, I know not how to excufe them, *Englifh*-men born, I believe ; who have endeavoured to perfwade the world, that *Englifh* men were born with tails, fuch as brutes have naturally : or, indeed, how to excufe him, who though he would not feem to give credit to it, yet fpeaks fomewhat doubtfully of it, *Novit Deus,* &c. when he could not but know, that it was a bafe, ridiculous untruth, the device of fome Popifh Fanaticks, ( much like the calumnies of our Proteftant Fanaticks, and, of late, wicked Atheifts, againft the Church, and the Clergy ) which no fober man would give the hearing to. True it is, that *Polydore Virgil,* who long lived in *England,* in his Hiftory of *England,* ( as *Delrio* doth obferve ) did write fomething of the people of one Parifh in *Kent,* which he would have, to have hapned unto them, as a miraculous judgment, for fome affront offered by them to *Thomas* of *Becket* his Horfe, as he paffed by : and it is poffible, that

that the publick reproach of *Kentish long-tails*, raised upon another occasion, mentioned in the Histories of *England*, might be some occasion of that foolish report; or, to speak more properly, *tale*. But *Polydore* doth add, that they had been all gone long, and extinct, to whom this hapned. *Delrio* makes a doubt, whether he speaks this of a truth, or in favour to the Nation. *God knows*, saith he: and adds, *The reproach is passed upon the whole Nation, and doth yet continue among bold people, who will adventure to say any thing, whether true or false*; But, if true, ( *Delrio* goes on ) *will*. Tooker *might have done well, to ascribe to his Queen that vertue also*, &c. a base scurrilous jeer, for which the Jesuit deserved to lose his ears, to teach him, and others, to make so bold with persons so sacred, as *Kings* and *Queens* are. But the quarrel is: This Will *y Tooker*, wrote a book, it seems, ( I have it not.) *De Strumis*: whereby he doth ascribe to Kings and Queens of *England*, a power derived unto them by lawful succession, of Healing, &c. If he deny it to the Kings of *France*, as *Laurentius* doth lay it to his charge; or derive their power, from *England*; I think he was too blame. And *Laurentius*, and some others, ( *Sennertus* among others) too blame also, who writing of that subject, would appropriate it to the Kings of *France*. I remember well, that when I was in the *Isle* of *Weight*, being earnestly invited thither by some of the chiefest of the Island, ( though then, under a cloud, for their Loyalty ) I was told of some extraordinary cures done by *Charles* the First, ( since a *Martyr* ) whilest he was a Prisoner there; not only upon some that had the *Kings Evil*, ( as we call it ) but upon some others also, who laboured of other diseases. Which, if true, and certain, ( as, because told me by persons of quality, I am apt to believe ) it is pity, it should not be more known ; if not more known ; ( if, I say, because of late, since I left off going to *London*, by reason of sickness, such a stranger to new books, and so little conversant with those, that I have ) than I know it is. But I say, if *true and certain*. We need no counterfeit miracles ; his death, and his book are sufficient miracles to *canonize* him : and they that could not, cannot yet be converted from their *rebellion* and *schism*, ( I may now add, *Atheism* ) by *either* ; I think I may say of them, that though one rose from the dead, or an Angel did appear unto them from Heaven, they would not be converted, or believe.

HITHERTO, since the examination of *Epicurus* his late *Saintship*, or *Canonization*, tending to the undermining of all piety and godliness ; our chief business hath been by sundry instances, rationally discussed, to rectifie the *incredulity* of many ; all tending to the vindication of *truth*, wherein the happiness of man, and the honour of God, is so much concerned. Now though the clearing of one of the two contraries, must needs ( as before said ) imply the illustration of the other also ; yet the better to acquit our selves, let us consider of *rash belief* also, and fo what means, or cautions some instances of that also, will afford us, to prevent it. Not, that we may never be deceived, for which I know no remedy, whilest we continue men, but to believe nothing ; a remedy much worse, and more pernicious than the disease : but to prevent, as I said before, *rash belief*, which is all, that humane prudence doth pretend unto. What I observed in the First Part, upon those words of St. *Augustine*, that, *Multa credibilia, falsa*, &c. must here be remembred also. *That all men are lyars*, is the speech of one, who could not lye, or be deceived, in what he delivered absolutely, in the authority of a Prophet, or a man inspired by God. It may be answered, that

that it was *in his hafte*, ( his own confeffion ) that he faid it; in the fame *hafte*, or impatiency, that made him to utter thofe words, *I am cut off from before thine eyes*, though he lived and reigned many years after that. This might be faid, had not St. *Paul* the Apoftle, made a general application of the words, to all men. But granted that all men in fome fenfe, or other, are *lyars*; yet that fome men, accounted otherwife fober, & ferious, fhould, with much labour, devife and ftudy lyes, not for any profit they hope to reap by it, but only for the pleafure of deceiving others, and to triumph, as it were, in their error and ignorance, or rather in the common calamity of mankind; this would hardly be believed, by them efpecially, who are more ingenuous themfelves, had not all ages afforded fome pregnant examples. But though fome might do it fo, meerly, as we have faid; yet other confiderations might move others to do the fame thing, befides what we have faid, or what is moft common and ordinary, gain or profit. If a man be paffionate for a caufe, his religion, his friend, his Country, his trade, or calling; all thefe, or any of thefe, may induce him, to devife lyes, or frauds; which in that cafe, for a publick end, fome men account no lyes, or frauds, but a meritorious act. Which yet might have more colour, when it is done for a publick good, which feldom doth happen : whereas for a little vain-glory, an imaginary title, to advance the honour, and reputation of a tongue, of a town, of a family, or the like, it hath been done by fome, without any regard at all of their own fhame or confcience, or forecaft of the iffue, which probably may prove contrary to what is intended, or expected; fhame and ignominy, inftead of honour and glory, when fuch bafe means are ufed to procure it. What a world of lyes and counterfeit books, monuments and evidences, the conceit of *pia fraudes*, in for-

mer times did produce; and how many have been gulled and deceived by them, who doth not know, or hath not heard? Which kind of counterfeit books, monuments and evidences, as they are able to confound right and wrong; to overthrow whole States and Governments, Civil and Ecclesiastical, as by many instances might be proved: so is there no work, either of it self more noble, or more advantagious to mankind, than to be able to descry and discover them, and by good and satisfactory proofs, to assert what is genuine and sincere. But a work of great difficulty, which doth require perfect knowledge of the learned tongues, of times, (which, without being well acquainted with the Authors, not profest Historians only, but others also, of every age, learned and unlearned, is not attainable) of fashions and customs, and all antiquity: besides a good judgment, without which nothing can be done, in this, or any other useful work. They therefore that would reduce all learning, to natural experiments; or at least, would have all learning (not to speak of them, who account all other, altogether uselefs; who I doubt are not few) regulated by them, and those that profess the trade, whether meer Empiricks, or others; how well they provide for Religion, the peace and tranquillity of publick Estates, the maintenance of truth, whether in matters Civil or Ecclesiastical; and what will be the end of such attempts, (without any disparagement of any thing that is done, in *England*, or out of *England*, for the further discovery of Nature, which I honour, as much as any can do, be it spoken) but as some men project it, and give it out, what will be the end; though such men cannot, or will not; yet all wise men may easily foresee, and is no difficult speculation. But to go on. There is not any body I think, who deals in learning, who hath not heard of *Annius Viterbiensis* his bold and wicked attempt, by
counter-

counterfeit Historians of greatest antiquity, to confound all true Chronology, to the great prejudice of all History, and the truth of the holy Scriptures themselves. And had not this impostor lighted upon a time, which did not long precede the restoration of good learning, and that happy age, which afforded so many able men in all kind of literature; it is very possible, that those abominable forgeries and fopperies, had passed every where for Oracles, and undoubted truth. For to this day, or very lately, notwithstanding so many learned Censures, of Papists, and Protestants, of all professions, that are extant against him, and have laid the imposture as clear and visible, as the light of the Sun, when he is in his strength; there be yet, or were very lately, men of no small fame and credit in the world, who could not digest, or be perswaded, that so many fine Titles, should be cast out, as meer baubles, or forgeries. Who knows, had the times continued in that ignorance, and this impostor sped, as he did for a while; but another might have been encouraged, by some suppositious writings, and bold fictions, to advance the credit of the *Alcoran*, above the *Bible*? Much about the same time, or not long after, a learned Court-*Spaniard*, had the boldness to obtrude to the world the inventions of his own brain, for the writings of the most learned of all Emperors, ( known unto us ) that ever were; *Solomon* only, for the testimony the Scripture doth give him, excepted. And though the genuine writings of that incomparable Prince, ( but indeed so adulterated by false Copies, that little of them was to be understood ) were published not long after; yet did that forged and adulterous stuff, translated into most languages of *Europe*, Printed and re-printed, with large Comments *in Folio*; *in Quarto*: pass currently, with great

great applaufe, for a long time after; and had I never done any thing more in my life-time, than that I was the firft, that undertook that great task; to reftore that worthy Prince to himfelf, by making him intelligible; I fhould not repent that I was bred a Scholar, or that I lived where, or when, good learning was in requeft.

IT is not yet full forty years, when in a Book-fellers Shop, in St. *Paul*'s Church-yard, I lighted upon a Book intituled, *Etrufcarum Antiquitatum Fragmenta*: Printed fome where in *Italy*. A fair large book it is, of the largeft fize of books, full of Infcriptions, many cut in Brafs, and many others. I confefs that the firft fight of the book did fo ravifh me, that *I* fcarce knew where *I* was, or what *I* did. Yet, that day, with good company, *I* was to go to *Gravefend*, in a Barge or clofe Boat, which we had hired of purpofe. It was not poffible for me to fettle to any reading, (except here and there, as *I* went along, by fnatches) until *I* was got into the Boat: and then excufing my felf to the company, and alledging for my excufe, that *I* had got fuch a treafure, as if *I* had gone a hundred miles for it, *I* fhould not think it dear bought, or fought; or to that effect, *I* fell to reading. But my pride and boafting, was foon over. *I* had not read a quarter of an hour, *I* dare fay, but *I* began to fufpect, fomewhat. But in lefs than an hour, or thereabouts, my judgment was fo altered; or rather my joy, and my hopes fo confuted, and confounded; that what book a little before *I* did not think dear at forty fhillings, (that was the price fet, as *I* remember) *I* now valued, as fo much wafte paper, and no more. The truth is, when the heat or violence of my expectation (which did almoft tranfport me) was once over; *I* began to wonder at my felf with fome indignation, that *I* had had the patience to read fo much. For *I* was then verily fatisfied, that there was fcarce a line in the whole book, from which

which either by the Latin, or by the matter of it, a man not altogether a stranger to such things, might not have discovered the fraud. Yet a fraud otherwise contrived with great art & specioufness, to take them that are apt to be taken by the outward appearance. Having then a book at Press, which was almost ended, before *I* knew what any man else did; *I* could not but let the world know, what *I* thought of it. Since which time *I* have seen divers pieces, some for it, of men *I* believe, who themselves were engaged in the fraud; but more against it; by which *I* was glad to understand, that the fraud was, not only detected, but also, as it well deserved, detested in all parts of *Italy*, *Rome* especially. Among them that have contributed that way, *Leo Allatius* is one, who though he may be thought over sedulous in a thing so notoriously discernable; yet his book well deserveth the reading, because it will furnish them, who are not much versed in such things, with many arguments, (whereof some may be useful in divers things, as there proved by some instances, that have no reference to learning) how such frauds may be discovered. Yet for all this *I* know that since *I* had published my judgment, and for ought *I* know, since some of these censures, or confutations were published; divers in *England* did shew much zeal for this precious book: and *I* was told by the late most Reverend and truly learned Primate of *Ireland*, that some in *Ireland* did go to *Italy* of purpose that they might bless their eyes with the sight of those precious Monuments, or Relicks. So prone are many men, not only, inconsiderately to entertain an imposture; but also loth to forgo the opinion they have had of the worth and truth of it, when once they have entertained it. What wonder then, if *Christianism* was so soon turned into *Mahometism*, in a great part of the world; when so much force was used to bring in the one,

one, and so little learning found (such was the sad condition of those times and places) to uphold the other, and to discover the impostures of pretended *Enthusiasts*? But now I have commended *Leo Allatius* to the Reader, I must give him a caution, how he doth give credit unto those words of his, *Page* 152. *Ægyptiorum quoque cadavera bituminis beneficio post viginti aut plurium annorum myriades perpetuitatem adepta quodammodo fuisse, viderunt alii, & nos ipsi,* &c. by which he doth seem to make the world elder by many thousands of years, than it is; or ever, I think, any man, those that make it eternal excepted; made it before: which, I am very confident, was not his meaning; though, how to rectifie it, as a fault of the Printers, I know not. Had these *Antiquities* been received generally, as a true piece; besides that they contradict the Scriptures, in some places; I think half the world would have been Conjurers, and *Enthusiasts* by this time; for that is it, which they chiefly advance. Here again I may say: God preserve the Universities: without other learning, great and various learning, besides *natural experiments*, all things must necessarily come to confusion, in a short time.

IN those kind of things which pretend to antiquity, as I would not have a man peremptorily to reject any thing, upon light suspitions; for so, he may bereave himself of many rare things; and most true it is, that things almost *incredible*, (the discovery of the new world, I reserve for another place) are discovered sometimes: So on the other side, not very suddenly to believe, nor to ascribe much to his own judgment, (which all men are apt to overvalue naturally) till he have made trial of it many times; and till he perfectly understand (so far as may be, by labour and diligent inquiry) both the nature of the thing, and all circumstances of the story, which he is to judge of. There is nothing so slight almost,

*in things* CIVIL. 301

almoſt, but doth require ſome experience: and there is nothing ſo hard, almoſt, wherein long experience, where there is a natural pregnancy, may not breed perfection. I have heard of ſome men, ( but heard it only ) who by the bare handling and ſmelling, would judge better of old Coins, ( which is a great trade beyond the Seas, and concerning which many books are written ) than others, not altogether ſtrangers unto them, could by the ſight: The more precious every thing is, the more ſubject it is to impoſture; though to me, there is nothing ſo mean, but the truth of it, is precious. The worſt is, ( which ſhould teach men humility ) let a man be never ſo careful and wary, or ſo judicious and well experienced; yet either through the obſcurity of nature, in ſome things, or the cunning of men, whoſe ſtudy is to cheat, and to impoſe; he may be to ſeek ſometimes, even in thoſe things, wherein he thinks himſelf moſt perfect, and, either caught, by ſome cheat, or at a ſtand, and nonpluſt. I read in a good Author, of a ſtone ſold to *Jewiſh* Jewellers, who make a trade to deceive others, in ſuch things; for a good *Diamond*, for the price of 9000. Crowns, which proved but a Cryſtal, of little worth: and of another, ſold for a *Ruby*, for 300. Crowns, which proved ( let no man wonder; for the ſame Author doth teach, there be red *Diamonds*, as well as *white*: *Abr. Ecchel. in Hadarrhamaum, de proprietat.* &c. *Pariſ.* 1647. ) a good *Diamond*, and was ſold for 7000. Crowns. One of the beſt ( ſome will ſay, the beſt ) Anatomiſt late ages have produced, began to diſſect a *Spaniſh* Lady, of great rank, for dead, when ſhe was alive: but ſhe died, and he too, for ſhame and grief. And a skilful Chirurgeon being to open a vain in the arm ( that invincible arm ) of *Henry* the Fourth, King of *France*; cut a Nerve, or Artery, which had almoſt coſt him his life. No man therefore ſo

skilful

skilful and wary, but may erre sometimes: and in matter of impostures, which are generally the contrivance of men; it may be a question, whether somewhat, besides man, doth not concur sometimes, of purpose to illude, and to frustrate men in their most sedulous inquiries.

WHEN I read the relation of those bones found in *Daulphine*, in *France*, in a Grave made of Brick, 30. foot long, 12. broad, 8. deep. 18. foot in the ground, with some Inscriptions, and old Coins about it; the Bones, or *Sceleton*, that was found in the Grave, being 25. foot and half in length; *I* do not know what to think of it. *Riolanus* indeed, who professed both Physick and Chirurgery in *Paris*, at that time, wrote somewhat, to perswade the world, that it was a cheat. But I know *Riolanus* out of a humour, or somewhat else, would sometimes oppose, where there was no great ground: the same, I suppose, who would perswade the world, that there is no such thing in the world, as *Hermaphrodites*, of which more in our First Part. The relation of those Bones, first set out, doth import, that the Sepulcher once opened, most part of the *Sceleton*, having been in the Air from eight in the morning, to six in the night, fell into dust; some of the thicker bones, and some that were well nigh petrified, by reason of a little spring, that did run over and wash them, excepted. Those that were left, were, by the Kings order, brought to *Paris*, and by him bought, to be kept in his Cabinet of rarities, as the very bones of a Gyant. This *Riolanus* doth not deny. *Peireskius*, that great and famous Antiquary, upon accurate examination of all circumstances, did at first pass his verdict, that probably, they might be true bones of some great Gyant, of the old time: but afterwards, did rather incline, to think them the bones of an Elephant. *Riolanus*, after some conjectures,

*in things* CIVIL. 303

ctures, doth pitch upon that at the laft, to make them *foſſilia*; bred, and begot in the earth; becauſe, faith he, it is the property of ſome grounds, to produce ſome bony ſtones, or ſtony bones, which have all the properties of true bones. Or, that they might be made by art, which may be done, he faith, and in time thus metamorphoſed by the water. He hath more conjectures, but in this particular caſe, (for as to the nature of the *Foſſilia*, in general, and the marvellous works of nature, in this kind, I believe much) but in this particular caſe, in my judgment, ſo improbable, that it doth, to me, clearly appear, that he had more will to oppoſe others, than ability, to give better ſatisfaction himſelf. His exceptions, from the dimenſions, or properties of the bones, as firſt related; I ſhall not take upon me to examine, or to control, it is not my trade. Only I can ſay, there might be ſome miſtake in the relation; or ſomewhat beſides the ordinary courſe of nature, which doth happen, we know, ſometimes. I my ſelf, when I was young, did ſee a grave in *Spittle-fields*, two or three days after it was opened. The skull was broken in pieces, by him that digged the ground, and the pieces ſcattered, and ſome carried away. But by ſome pieces that were found, and put together, the whole skull, by the Kings appointment, (as I was told) being drawn out according to art, did equal a buſhel, in the compaſs of it. So I was told, and I think, by one of the Court, and a Scholar: but I am not certain. I my ſelf was then ſick of a diſeaſe, which, I think, cauſed more wonder, than the Gyants bones. It was but a pin, but a very coſtly pin, it proved, in the compaſs of ſeven years: for ſo long it was, not before it came out of my body; but, before my body was well of it; ſo that I was ſeldom out of the Chirurgeons hands. But Phyſicians, I thank God, coſt me little: Sir *Theod. Mayerne*, and Dr. *Raphael Thoris*,

*Thoris*, I had in *London*, where most of my sickness was, who were my very good friends, as they had been my Fathers. But to return: I had some of the Coins that were found in this *Spittle-field's* Grave. But, that other Grave, is my business: That that Grave, should be the Grave of *Teutobochus*, that Gyant, or Gyant-like man, mentioned by divers Ancients, (who according to *Peireskius* his casting, must have been some 10. or 12. foot high) according to an old inscription, pretended to be found in the said grave; besides other reasons that have been given, I less believe it, for that very inscription; which I am sure, cannot be of that antiquity: except we should say, that such a grave being digged up, many hundred years ago; which by a constant tradition, or by some much worn inscription, did appear to be *Teutobochus* his grave; to increase the miracle of his height and bigness, it was of purpose so re-built, and the inscription also, according the wit and *genius* of that age, so renewed. This is possible, a man may say: and somewhat of that nature, I am sure hath been done in more than one age. Witness the old Statues, which with changing of their heads, became the Statues of divers men; or perchance, of Gods and Men, successively; and many other things done in that kind: which I will not stop to call to mind, because there is no need, except I had more confidence, that it is so, indeed. I shall conclude nothing, but as I begun: when I have well considered of all particulars in the relation of these bones; what I account, certain in it, what doubtful, and perchance fabulous; and read what others have thought and written of it: and not of this only, but of many such relations of graves and bones, well attested: I am at a stand, and suspend my belief. But therefore to conclude, that all such relations are false, because we cannot absolutely resolve, or answer all doubts, and

*Queries:*

*Queres*: I hold that a very preposterous way, and very unworthy the profession of a Philosopher, or one that seeks after truth: (time may reveal many secrets, which are now hid; and diligent searching may find some) but well agreeing with the dull and sottish *Epicurean* humour, which to prevent the trouble of inquiry, and withal, fearing that we may be forced sometimes, to go to a higher cause, than the sanctuary of *Atomes*, hath found a compendious way, to reject all as fabulous; any evidence of truth to the contrary, notwithstanding, which it cannot give a reason of. We have their own words, out of *Lucian*, a great friend, if not professor of the Sect, in our *Preface* to Dr. *Dee's*. *Plato* therefore said well: Μάλα φιλοσόφε τέτο τὸ πάθ⊕, τὸ θαυμάζειν, that, *To wonder and to admire, was a quality, that well became a Philosopher*; and was indeed, *the beginning and foundation of all Philosophy*. And so *Aristotle* too; more than once, very rightly. For *to wonder and admire*, doth cause inquiry and diligence: it also sharpens the wit and brain. But to believe nothing true, that is *strange* and *admirable*; doth well become such infidels, who make their ease and their pleasure, their God. If any except, that rather *to Wonder little*, (*Nil admirari*, the Poet saith) may become a Philosopher better, as he whose work is, to dive into the causes of things, which cause wonder to the ignorant, that may be true too, rightly understood: since that, *not to Wonder, or to wonder but little, is the fruit, of having wondred much*: and that too from *Aristotle*, (that true *master of reason*, indeed; a title lately usurped by some, who have as little right to it, as any men of the world, I think) αἴτιον τὸ θαυμάζωσιν τῷ μὴ θαυμάζειν. But what if the *deceitfulness* of men, more than the *obscurity* of nature, or any other cause, be the cause of our admiration? That also must, upon such occasions, among other things,

things, be remembred; and those *Etruscæ Antiquitates*, before spoken of, may serve for a pregnant example, what pains some men, though they get nothing by it, will take to contrive a cheat; and what admiration they cannot, by true, to raise it by false miracles. What if some men, though they cannot contrive any thing, that will be ripe to work whilest they live; yet can be so base and unworthy, as to solace themselves whilest they live, with the presumption of deluded posterity, by their means ? So indeed it might happen, that four or five hundred years before that grave was opened in *Daulphine*, some such conceited man, ( if man to be called, and not Devil rather ) having lighted upon some Whales, or other fishes bones, which they write are, or have been, very frequent in that Country; might out of them contrive somewhat, towards the resemblance of a *Sceleton* of a mighty Gyant; bury them in a formal Coffin, or Grave, which might endure many ages; cast in Coins, and other convenient ware, not doubting but revolution of times, and accidents, sooner, or later, would bring them to light. What remedy, in such a case, but patience, and good circumspection, before we yield full assent, or be too confident, where such a thing may be suspected, though not easily discovered ?

I REMEMBER I have read of a monument found in *China*, the rarest thing, if true, that ever came out of the earth, in that kind. *Abrahamus Kirkerus*, in his *Prodromus*, gives a large account of it. I know what account some make of it, that it is a counterfeit thing, forged by the Jesuits of those parts. It is easily said. But upon due consideration of circumstances, ( so far as hath yet appeared unto me ) not so easie to be believed. For what was their end in it ? To promote the Christian Religion, in *China* : or to abuse us here in *Europe*, with

a

a falſe report? Truly, it is very hard to believe, that ſo much pains ſhould be taken, to ſo little purpoſe, when there was ſo little likelihood, that the impoſture could ſo long hold undiſcovered. It is a very long inſcription, and the ſtone that contained it, muſt be very large; and many hands, if not horſes, uſed to convey it too and fro. But if, which is more probable, to promote Religion in *China*; then certainly ſuch an inſcription, ſuch a ſtone was there found, digged out of the earth before many witneſſes, and afterwards ſo diſpoſed of, as the ſtory doth tell us. How could the Jeſuits prepare and convey ſuch a *ſtone* thither in a Country ſo full of people, ſo near one of the chief Cities? And if once diſcovered in their jugling, was it not more likely, to do them more hurt and their cauſe; than they could expect advantage, in caſe it had paſſed for a true ſtory? Beſides, what *Kirkerus* writeth of it, I ſuppoſe is written and atteſted by more than one; though I can name but one, *Alvarus Semedo*, the *Portugal*, (who I think was no Jeſuit) in whom I remember to have read it. I profeſs by what I have read of it, I cannot find ground of reaſon, to make me believe it an impoſture: neither hath it been my luck hitherto, to meet with any body (that I can remember) that hath gone about, upon grounds of reaſon, to refute what is written of it, but only in the way of *Seneca*'s *Sapientiſſimi*, by which any thing may be falſe or counterfeit, which we do not like, or underſtand; *fabula eſt, mendacium eſt*. In *Emanuel Dias* his Epiſtle, which *Kirkerus* doth exhibit, I find *Trigaulſius* mentioned, as being then in the Country, when, and where that hapned; who in his relations of *China*, firſt ſet out, could ſay nothing of it, becauſe they end many years before, and the book Printed, *Auguſtæ Vindelicorum*, 1615. But it ſeems, he made a ſecond Voyage, and happily a Relation of that too, which I have not ſeen.

They that have read more, may give a better account perchance; but this doth serve our purpofe, to ground fuch obfervations upon, as have reference to *credibility*, or *incredibility*. But now I have mentioned *Kirkerus* : I have not any of his books, at prefent, and therefore fhall fay lefs : but by what I have read, or feen of him, I fhould not advife any man, that loves truth, to take all for good and merchantable ware, which he doth offer. I fhall not infift in any particulars, but only this in general; as I know him a man of great parts, fo a great undertaker, and a very confident man; two fufpitious qualities, and I am fure, he hath deceived, or hath been deceived more than once.

I HAVE done with particular inftances, not becaufe the ftock of my matter, which I propofed to my felf, is fpent; but becaufe the time, which I have, or can allow my felf for this imployment, is out. I fhall now have other things to think of, if my health will give me leave to think of any thing elfe, but death. But before I end what I am now about, I think it requifite, that I add one word or two, concerning *Hiftory*, in general. Some taking the advantage of fome notable difcordance, yea manifeft *contradictions* among Hiftorians, of beft credit; have made that ufe of it themfelves, and commended it unto others, to difcredit all Hiftory; ancient efpecially, even where they agree. And truly, if upon that account, we do not think our felves bound in reafon, to believe them in things more ordinary; it is not likely we fhall, in things that may be thought very ftrange, and ( but for their authority ) *incredible*. This, to them that are not acquainted with the world, may feem fomewhat: to them that are, nothing at all. For fo are all things in the world, liable to fome defects, and irregularities: which notwithftanding, few, or none are laid afide, upon that account. That it is fo, we may

be

*in things* CIVIL.

be sorry: but *History* must not bear the blame only, since it is the general case of all things, or most, that we deal in. I must confess, it hath troubled me not a little, when I have met with such contradictions, in best Historians. For example: What *Herodotus*, and after him, *Diodor. Siculus*, and divers other Historians write of *Cyrus*, that great Monarch, ( stiled *Gods servant*, in the Scripture; of whose salvation, through faith in the promised *Messiah*, *Melancton* made no question ) his violent death by the hands of a woman, far from his own Country, or Dominions, who hath not heard? Yet *Xenophon*, a grave, and famous both Philosopher and Historian, who lived not long after, and served another *Cyrus* in his unfortunate ἀνάβασις, or *Expedition* against his brother, *Artaxerxes*, ( the History whereof, he hath written ) doth give a quite different account of his death: to wit, that he died in his bed, in his own Kingdom, ( which comprehended many kingdoms ) in much peace, with many other particulars, tending to the same purpose. Wherein nevertheless we have more reason to wonder at the thing it self, subject to so much obscurity, than at the different account of Historians. For it doth appear by *Herodotus*, and we are beholding to him, for giving us so much light, that even in his time, there were several reports, concerning this great *Cyrus* his death: so that, what he doth deliver of it, he delivers as the most probable ( in his judgment ) tradition; not as certain, and indubitable. I could instance in divers such particulars. But what is this to the body of the History of the World, for some two thousand years, ( besides the Scripture History ) to be gathered out of the generality of Historians, of all Ages and Nations: which reading, ( where men are not too far engaged into sensuality and profaneness ) by the knowledge and consideration of the many revolutions of the world, the sad chances and alterations, which publick Estates, and private persons and families are subject unto, producing commonly, ( as in *Salomon*, and *Aurelius Antoninus*, another *Salomon*, for this kind of wisdom ) a right apprehension of the vanity and contemptiblenefs of the world and all worldly things, without a *reference to God, and immortality* : they that make this good use of it, though they die young, yet may be said to have lived longer than any *Epicuræan* Sectary, though he should live two hundred years, who can give no other account of his life, but that, he hath eaten and drunk, and enjoyed bodily pleasure, with perfect ( we will suppose it so ) contentedness, so long : which things have nothing at all of a rational soul in them, but of a beast, ( of a *dog*, or a *swine* ) much more, than of a man. They therefore that despise History upon that account, might as well deprive themselves of the light of the Sun, because it is subject to some *Eclipses*.

BUT we must add, that many of these *contradictions*, which we charge upon Historians, proceed not from the Historians, but our ignorance: our ignorance, I say, either of the tongue, not perfectly known, ( wherein many are deceived, as they that think themselves very good *Grecians*, because they have read, and can understand two or three Greek Authors ) or of the times, or of the thing it self, which is spoken of; which may have reference to some of the Sciences, or some secret of Nature; or for want perchance of that light, which a diligent comparing, and consulting with good books of ancient, or later times, would afford. That it is so; so many, once thought apparent *contradictions*, both in the *Scriptures*, and other good Authors, besides Historians; now by the labour of learned men, happily cleared and reconciled, are sufficient evidences. I think there is not a book, of any age, or profession, extant; but ancient, especi-

## *in things* CIVIL.

especially; but may give some light to a judicious Reader, towards the clearing of some obscurity, either in matter of fact, or science, or work of nature. Two *Universities,* in one Kingdom, are little enough for such a work, if a man go the right way to work. But many run, where one only carrieth the prize. And if but one in a hundred, or two hundred that run, happen to speed, (as God be thanked, the Universities have always been stored with able men, in this kind, who have been a great ornament to the whole Nation) the cost is not ill bestowed upon one or two hundred, that do not, (so that it be not for want of labour, and industry) for that ones sake. Πολλοί τοι ναρθηκοφόροι, παῦροι δέ τε βάκχοι. *Er. p.* 1668. *Quàm pauci, qui capiunt magnitudinem literarum*; was a speech very frequent in the mouth of one, whom I knew very well; and I might have been the better for it, but for frequent sicknesses, and the loss of twenty years, during these late troubles and confusions.

BUT besides, many *contradictions* proceed also from a humour, in some men, or a malignity rather, to contradict others. So *Ctesias,* of old, was known to set himself to contradict *Herodotus.* To make him fabulous, and himself a considerable man, he pretended, because he had lived in *Assyria,* and served one of those great Kings; to sacred records. But it fell out much otherwise, than he expected; for *Herodotus,* in most things, wherein he dissents from him, is followed; and he, generally, accounted a fabulous foolish Historian. From what humour it proceeded, I know not. But I knew a Gentleman of great worth, who would very stifly argue, that *Constantine* the Great, never was a Christian. I do not remember, I ever heard him alledge any thing for it, which I thought of any force. But this he might, as well as *Pomponius Lætus,* a late *Italian* compiler of

*Of Credulity and Incredulity,*

History, ( suspected by some, to have had more affection for old *Heathenism*, than he had for *Christianity*) made bold to write, that *Constantius*, one of *Constantine's* Sons, died a Heathen.

OTHERS again, though they have no humour to *contradict*; yet they will hardly believe any thing, that doth contradict, or not well sute with their humour, and proper temper. So that a man had need, if possible, to know somewhat of the temper of his Historian, before he know what to think of his relations; such especially, as have somewhat of *incrediblenefs* in them. We heard a learned Physician, of our times, ( in our *First Part* ) deny, that there are *Witches*. One great argument is, because he did not believe, that any woman could be so cruel, or wicked; so that he doth not stick absolutely to profess, that should he see with his own eyes, any woman commit any of those horrible things, that are laid to their charge; he would not believe his eyes, that it is so, truly, and really; but believe it a delusion. Yet this the man, that doth tell as horrible stories of *men-Sorcerers* and *Conjurers*, without any scruple of believing, as any I have read in any books of that argument.

OF all women I have read of, ancient or late; I know not of any that stands upon the records of History, for cruelty, and all manner of wickedness, more infamous, ( or indeed comparable) than two women, that lived at one time in *France*, better than a thousand years ago: *Fredegonde*, and *Brunichild*. Queens both, but the one a Kings daughter also; the other, ascended to that height, by her baseness, first; and then, cruelty. *Medea*, of old, was nothing to either of these, as set out by some of those times. If I were to judge, I should be much put to it, which was the worse of the two. For he that reads the acts of either by themselves, will

will find so much, that he cannot but think, that either of them went to the height, of what can be thought *possible*. But however, though for their lives, never so well matched; yet in their deaths, great inequality may be observed: *Providentia, apud imperitos, laborante*: saith one, that writes of them: that is, *To the no small prejudice*, or *reproach of Gods providence*; but, *apud imperitos*, well added: that is, *with men that must know all the secrets of God, and the reasons of all his dispensations*, or else they will not believe, that there is a God, if men (such blind wretches, even the wisest that are, in comparison; acknowledged by divine *Aristotle*, but not by the *wits* and *wise* men of our time) could understand the reasons of all he doth. It is enough, that he hath been pleased to arm us against this kind of temptation, by his *Revealed Word*; so that to judge of men, by what hapneth unto them in this world, is little better, than absolute apostacy, from the right faith. But, as the story goes; *Fredegonde*, of whose wickedness we have more pregnant testimonies, than of the others; died in peace, and was happy in her Son, who made all *France* happy, as even any King did. *Brunichild* died much after the manner of *Ravailack*'s death, being tied to the tail of a wild Horse, who soon scattered her brains, and put her out of her pains; though the rest of her body was scattered afterwards, as bad as her brain, by the said wild Horse, piece after piece, in a great compass of ground, according as his wildness directed his course, over hedges, and ditches; over hills and dales? This in publick: too much, I think, for a *Queen*, and the daughter of a *King*; though some think, too little, for her *wickedness*. But this is not all. For before that, she was tortured three days in prison, with exquisite torments, the worst that could be invented, to

preserve

preserve her to publick *judgment*. And which is worst of all, this was the *judgment* upon her of a King, famous for many Princely parts; but, for none more, than for his goodness,· and clemency, which must needs aggravate her guilt very much. Yet for all that, and the judgment of so many writers since, that have passed against her; some have been found, long ago, who whether of meer compassion, or some kind of *incredulity*, began to question, whether all that had been written of her was true; and since that, that famous *French* Antiquary, *Paschier*, in his learned *Recherches*, hath taken great pains to make her a perfect *Innocent*, if not a *Martyr*. He is so long upon it, that it requires a good time, to read him; much more, should any man attempt it, to confute him. I will leave it free to them that read him, to judge as they please. But I have some reasons, to incline me rather, to *Baronius* his censure of one, that had begun to justifie her, before *Paschier*; that he did but *laterem lavare*; that is, *wash a Blackmoor, to make him white*. Besides *Baronius* his authority; *Vignier*, not inferior, I dare say, to any in knowledge of Antiquity, and a very judicious man, makes her guilty. Strange indeed, that any woman should be so wicked, and cruel; or live so long, to act so much wickedness. But again, her death, and judgment, (her person, a *Queen*, and the daughter of a *King* considered) is so full of horror, that some have attempted to make a fable of that too, as well as of her wickedness, as altogether *incredible*. But I do not find that any body takes any notice of their attempt, against such publick evidences, whilest they have nothing to say for it, but because they think it *incredible*. Her wickedness, is another thing. One particular of her indictment is, that she had been the death of ten Kings. So is the indictment: but it must be understood, of some actual Kings,

partly;

partly; and partly, of other Princes of the Royal bloud, who might have been Kings. Of ten, such; hard to believe, even of a man: much more, of a woman: whom some still look upon, as *the weaker Sex*, and upon that score will think it an *uncharitable credulity*, to harbour such cruel thoughts of them. But in very truth; If a vertuous woman, that is chast, religious, discreet; especially, if of a gracious and beautiful aspect, (for that also, is the gift of God, and doth add much) may be compared to an *Angel*: to whom can one, that hath none of those good qualities, and is set upon wickedness; more fitly be compared, than to a *Devil*? And in that case, the more *Beautiful*, the arranter Devil. *Corruptio optimi, pessima*; Philosophers and Physicians say: and our late learned King *James*, of *Glorious memory*, (whom I had the happiness, more than once, when very young, to wait upon, and can truly say, that I never parted from him, but in great admiration of his learning and piety) by the authority of his judgment, which was excellent; and by sundry pregnant instances, hath taught us, that for that very reason, women, because the *weaker Sex*, therefore the apter they are, naturally, to be *cruel* and *revengeful*.

THUS, *truth* may be tossed up, and down, sometimes; though all this, that hath been mentioned, is nothing to the master-piece of our age: *Epicurus, his Saintship, and filial fear*, or *worship*. But tossed up and down (I say) sometimes, I deny it not. But they that will take the pains, prepared first with *humility*, (which to Saint *Augustine*, is all in all, in this great business) to dig for it, may find enough of it, to comfort them, *that they shall not loath to live*. *Nihil est tanti, nisi verum*, was the speech of a Heathen, upon what occasion, I shall not inquire: but a speech, in the most obvious sense, well worthy the mouth of a Christian: *What live we for, but to learn what is truth?* Or if you will, somewhat more Paraphrastically : *What is the reward, proposed unto a rational Creature, of this, otherwise, miserable life* ; but *truth* ; or, *the knowledge of what is, truly, and really?* But should we have perfect *truth* here upon earth, we might say, What need of Heaven? For, where perfect *Truth* is, there God is.

I WOULD end in *Simplicius*, the Philosopher, his *Prayer* ; an excellent *Prayer* to this purpose; and well would become a Christian *Litany*, but that it ends in a Verse of *Homer's* ; though that, an excellent Verse also. But I will not do that Infidel, (for he lived some ages after *Christ* ) so much honour. There is enough in *the Lords Prayer*; which all true Christians, I hope, say more than once, in a day. For it comprehends all that we can, or should, at least, wish. I shall willingly end in the commendation, or recommendation of that excellent *Prayer*; which, in the late confusions, was in no small danger, ( the publick use of it ) to be banished out of the land, had not the happy Restoration of our Gracious King, *Charles, the Second*; ( whom God bless, and preserve ) and by Him of the Church; happily prevented it.

## FINIS.

## ADDITIONS.

*P*age 119. *line* 30. I should not, the wonders of thunder and lightning, as set out by *Seneca*, and others, well considered, make any great wonder of them,

Page 220. *line* 14. after these words; *Then his promiscuous mifchous company* did *from one another.* Add,

That *Epicurus* notwithſtanding that ſpecious allegation, That *true pleaſure could not, or cannot be purchaſed, without a vertuous life*; did ſtill keep to his firſt, and fundamental aſſertion, that *the happineſs of man conſiſted in bodily pleaſure*; and that as they did explain themſelves, there's no ſuch contradiction between theſe two propoſitions, as many do phanſie; any man, that ſhall but read them; or read *Cicero*, or *Seneca*, to name no others, will eaſily underſtand. Beſides, their great and chiefeſt argument uſed by them to prove, that it is ſo, that *pleaſure* is the end, becauſe even children, aſſoon as they are born, and all other creatures, without any teaching, ſeek after pleaſure, ( not *mental* certainly, but *bodily* ) will eaſily evince. Add to this, their definition of *pleaſure*, wherein they placed *happineſs*, ἰυςαϑὶς σαρκὸς κατάςημα, *a conſtant well ſetled conſtitution of the fleſh,* or *body*; what can be more plain. But becauſe they maintained, or pretended at leaſt, that *ſuch a conſtant well ſetled conſtitution of the fleſh*, or *body*, without temperance and ſobriety, ( who knows not, that from intemperance, riotouſneſs, *&c.* all, or moſt bodily diſeaſes do generally proceed ) could not be attained, or maintained; nay, they would ſay, not without *innocency*, and a *good conſcience*, ſo far, ( ſo they did explain themſelves) as may preſerve a man from fear of the laws, and publick animadverſions, and infamy, likewiſe: which things, in ordinary language, are commonly adſcribed unto vertue; therefore they alſo, to ſpeak as others did; ſometimes commended *vertue*, and a *good conſcience*; with many ſpecious words, it cannot be denied, and plauſible reaſons, but ſtill upon that account, and no otherwiſe. For they ſtill plainly maintained, that there was no difference between what was called *vertue*, and *vice*, but in conceit; and that a wiſe man would refrain

frain no manner of pleasure, or voluptuousness, but for the evil consequence to his bodily health : nor no manner of *injustice*, or *wickedness*, which his phansie did lead him unto, but for fear of the laws, and that he could never be *secure*, that it should not be known. This is acknowledged by *Diog. Laertius*, and by *Gassendus* also. By these fine devices and pretences, many were caught : so that, they that had a mind to it, or natural inclination, might live soberly, ( and some did, certainly ) and innocently, and yet profess themselves of their Sect. But others, ( the far greater number, God knows ) gladly entertaining what they were taught, and was inculcated unto them as a main principle, that, might but a man secure himself, that he should not be known, or shake off all fear of the laws, there was no difference between vertue and vice, in *nature*, but *in opinion* only ; if they did rob, and kill ; prostitute themselves to man or beast, to satisfie their lust, and the like ; ( promising themselves secrecy, as many are apt to do ) what reason had they, by this doctrine, to think the worse of themselves for it ?

There is a Letter of one of *Epicurus* his Whores, &c.

*Page* 224. *line*. 4. &c. Where I say ; That *Gassendus* himself was an Atheist, really, &c. I desire it may be read : That *Gassendus* himself, though we have too much occasion to fear, that he hath made many, was an Atheist, I will not say ; God forbid ; neither of him, nor any other particular man, who doth not openly profess it. I will say more ; I believe not. He hath commended *Piety* in others, as in that incomparable Patron of learning, noble *Peireskius*, whose life he hath learnedly set out. *Learnedly*, I am sure ; but whether so *faithfully*, always, or every where : that is, whether he do not sometimes impose his thoughts and sentiments,

or

or happily, mistakes, upon that worthy man; by what was objected to him whilest he lived, by a very learned man, in *Paris, Jean Tristan, Commentaires Historiques, Tome primier, page* 108. &c. we may very well doubt. He hath taken good pains, when many much nearer, and more concerned, (as now, God help, in these times, too many) were silent, to set out, and lay open, the horrible impieties, and blasphemies, of *Robert Flud*, a *Welch*, or *English* ( I know not which ) *Chymist* : with a shew ( if he did not afterwards fall from it ) of much zeal, for the *Catholick Faith*. Lastly, he hath written ( though still shewing too great desire, and vainly endeavouring, to extenuate grossest enormities ) against some of *Epicurus* his opinions, very well. I said therefore, I believe, not. But in discharge of my duty to God, *&c.*

*Page* 229. *line* 7. *and then content our selves with what every day doth afford.* Add, It is in the Greek, ὅπως ἀντέχεσθαι τῶν καθ' ἡμέραν: which may also be translated, *So, to take care* ( ἀντέχεσθαι, for φροντίζειν ) *of every days necessaries* : or, *What may be fit and requisite from day to day.* Which will well agree with those words of our daily Prayers, ( which have troubled many ) Τὸν ἄρτον ἡμῶν, τὸν ἐπιούσιον, δὸς ἡμῖν σήμερον. I do rather incline to this sense, because of the words that follow, διὸ φιλοσοφητέα δεῖ καὶ τούτων φροντεῖν, ᾗ ἐφ' ὅσον ἂν ἢ παρ' ἐκείνοις ὕπνος ὅτι μάλιστα παρεκδίδῳ: that is, *For these also* ( daily necessaries ) *must be taken care of, provided that the care of better things* ( or *Philosophy* ) *go along,* ( or, be not intermitted ) *and those no longer,* or *further cared for, than may stand with the vigorous pursuit of the former. Gassendus* is much mistaken in the sense of these words. And so he is, in the sense of those, Ἐλάχιστον γὰρ καὶ τὸ ὀχληρὸν, ἐκ τῆς ἐλαχίστης: which need not any correction. And yet worse, in those, Ἔτι ᾗ τὸ ἄλ-

?אית ד טּ דּ דּ׳ αδείας, πολλε ιπιόντος, &c. But besides these, there be other words in the same passage, produced by *Gassendus*, as the words of some *Epicuræan*, (which, I am sure, cannot be true of all he produceth) wherein I find my self as much grounded, as it seems he was. They that have the old translation of the book, may do well to have recourse unto it. But to return to those first words, which have given us this occasion; *Gassendus* by correcting, &c.

*ERRATA*: whether of the *Press*, or *Copy*.

Page 2. line 21. *read*, grounded upon D. 9.5. The *Cont*. 18. examples 13.31. or app. 18.26. *Galeotus* 19.3. But to return to our *spiritual* rose: the test. 22.20,21. nature, only 23.10. *Series* 32.1. *Augerius Ferr*. 37.30. writings 39.16. to have c. 40.4. those sup. 50.22. *Abstinens Consol*. 52.13,14. Sure I am, in m. 53.20. so much adm. 21. any, whon. 56.33. were comm. 57.7. Xναζ:. 58.13. goes on 59.19. particulars 60.25. *tempestatib*. 28. *Querolus* 62.33. in those d. 68.27. to the art. 30. ϟϟ͂ 69.18. *Merl*. 71.22. *Chyss*. 74.3. irrupt. 29. So he. Bes. 84.1. in the firmament 87.13. So G.16. of hair: others, (*trib*. 18. it must needs) of th. 89.29. how much m. 90.2. mistake, that it is not alw. 96.12. nor certain r. 99.6. But upon a pr. 100.3. at least 31. *feras* 102.10. otherwise: of w. 14. thing else; but 103.21. no where 104.2. hath m. aff. 110.18. after I rem. 112.7. *Cogn*. 114.2. (but not unjust) ag. 12. *leniend*. 116.29. refused 119.1. *Uella* 7. *vulgaria* 120.23. worn out 122.19. rugged. 125.3. where I.K. 129.4. *Medicam*. 5. *Archig*. 134.33. of what o. 136.33. in ext. 142,39. doth app. cease 144.23. The manner 145.26. of *Rome*, sent 146.21. y, and n.h. of more) 150. *last l*. was commendable: w. 151.15. Civ. wars 153.6. no hard thing to a. 157.30. generation only: 160.10,16, &c. *Naudæus* 161.32. ocular 165.32. Empiricks 167.15. read it 169.20. would I 170.26. dealt with 174.17. *cine tend*. 175.30. *Pipinus* 176.4. *datum* 6. *cerusc*. 18. *contrect*. 22. *dictu mir*. 25. ma cum ut. 28. ut te 178.16. Euc. 35. *Ceron*. 179.9. played 180.23. *Levinus Lemn*. 184.5. eget 185.3. that are such: f. 186.18,19. So he, the m. 188.7. it may be true 8. true, as some learned men are of opinion, of an. 192.29. nev. heard 206.32. number 215.28. chapter. 217.2. can say 221.23. to speak of *Ep*. 224.15. this, that they m. 24. The R. therefore w. 28,29. futility of D. 225. *last l*. that w. 228.2. discommended 22. doth not in P. 233.28. *The* 234.22. or discret. 235.30. *Arion* 238.18. sent 241.34, 35. I have at this t. 250.7. no great account, or auth. 25. *quond*. 254.6. *Pencerus* 256.11. *Brennus* 258.10. besides 400.250.24. besides w. 265. 22. and a *Pro*. 266. *last l* historians, now extant 268.16. works of th. 271.5. where in th. 275.9. could not be h. 279.21. *Marcus* 285.19. teach others cont. 30. *Mad* 286.16. of better cr. 34. *Smyndir*. 289.9. which, since th. 10. rowes 26,27. had four thousand rowers, besides mariners 400. and s. 31. the num. 290.25. *Fiorouanti* 293.11. Will. T. 294.23. and see w. 298. 6. and when 291.31. forgo 300.17. of *Enth*. 304.18. to the wit a.

www.ingramcontent.com/pod-product-compliance
Lightning Source LLC
Chambersburg PA
CBHW021156230426
43667CB00006B/427